Laurence Sterne, Jonathan Swift

Our Sentimental Journey through France and Italy

Laurence Sterne, Jonathan Swift

Our Sentimental Journey through France and Italy

ISBN/EAN: 9783744798167

Printed in Europe, USA, Canada, Australia, Japan

Cover: Foto ©Andreas Hilbeck / pixelio.de

More available books at **www.hansebooks.com**

Laurence Sterne

A

SENTIMENTAL JOURNEY

THROUGH

FRANCE AND ITALY

By LAURENCE STERNE

ALSO

A TALE OF A TUB

WRITTEN FOR THE

UNIVERSAL IMPROVEMENT OF MANKIND

"*Diu Multumque Desideratum*"

By JONATHAN SWIFT
DEAN OF ST. PATRICK

With Five Etchings and Portrait by Ed. Hédouin

LONDON
J. C. NIMMO AND BAIN
14, KING WILLIAM STREET, STRAND, W.C.
1882

CONTENTS.

	PAGE
PREFATORY MEMOIR TO STERNE	1
A SENTIMENTAL JOURNEY THROUGH FRANCE AND ITALY	31

A TALE OF A TUB—

The Author's Apology	181
The Bookseller's Dedication	203
The Bookseller to the Reader	209
The Dedication to Prince Posterity	211
The Author's Preface	221
Section I.—The Introduction	237
Section II.	254
Section III.—A Digression concerning Critics	273
Section IV.	287
Section V.—A Digression in the Modern Kind	305
Section VI.	315
Section VII.—A Digression in Praise of Digressions	326
Section VIII.	334
Section IX.—A Digression concerning the Origin, the Use, and Improvement of Madness in a Commonwealth	344
Section X.—A Further Digression	363
Section XI.	371
The Conclusion	389

b *

LIST OF ILLUSTRATIONS.

PORTRAIT OF STERNE . . . . . . *Frontispiece*

CALAIS . . . . . . *page* 52

THE HUSBAND 92

THE CHEVALIER DE ST. LOUIS 121

THE TEMPTATION 140

THE POSITION OF DELICACY 178

PREFATORY MEMOIR

TO

STERNE.

---o---

LAURENCE STERNE was one of those few authors who have anticipated the labours of the biographer, and left to the world what they desired should be known of their family and their life.

"Roger Sterne* (says this narrative), grandson to Archbishop Sterne, Lieutenant in Handaside's regi-

* Mr. Sterne was descended from a family of that name in Suffolk, one of which settled in Nottinghamshire. The following genealogy is extracted from Thoresby's Ducatus Leodinensis (p. 215):—

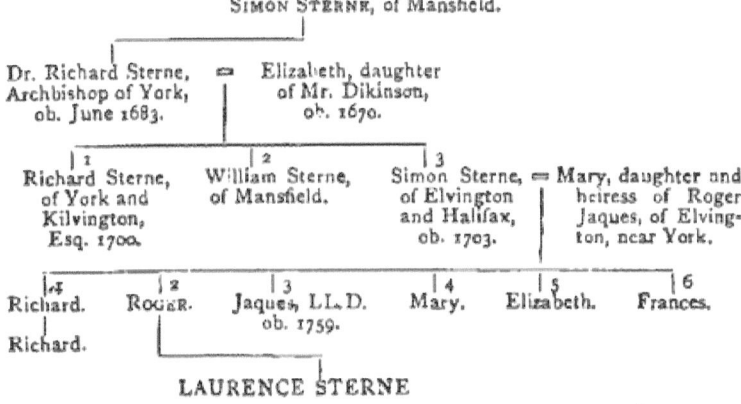

A

ment, was married to Agnes Hebert, widow of a captain of a good family. Her family name was (I believe) Nuttle;—though, upon recollection, that was the name of her father-in-law, who was a noted sutler in Flanders, in Queen Anne's wars, where my father married his wife's daughter (*N.B.* he was in debt to him), which was in September 25, 1711, old style.—This Nuttle had a son by my grandmother,—a fine person of a man, but a graceless whelp!—what became of him I know not.—The family (if any left) live now at Clonmel, in the south of Ireland; at which town I was born, November 24, 1713, a few days after my mother arrived from Dunkirk.—My birthday was ominous to my poor father, who was, the day of our arrival, with many other brave officers, broke, and sent adrift into the wide world, with a wife and two children;—the elder of which was Mary. She was born at Lisle, in French Flanders, July 10, 1712, new style.—This child was the most unfortunate:—She married one Weemans, in Dublin, who used her most unmercifully;—spent his substance, became a bankrupt, and left my poor sister to shift for herself; which she was able to do but for a few months, for she went to a friend's house in the country, and died of a broken heart. She was a most beautiful woman, of a fine figure, and deserved a better fate.—The regiment in which my father served being broke, he left Ireland as soon as I was able to be carried, with the rest of his family, and came to the family seat at Elvington, near York, where his mother lived. She was daughter to Sir Roger Jacques, and an heiress. There we sojourned for about ten months, when the regiment was established, and our household decamped with bag and baggage for Dublin. —Within a month of our arrival, my father left us, being ordered to Exeter; where, in a sad winter, my mother and her two children followed him, travelling from Liverpool, by land, to Plymouth.—(Melancholy description of this journey, not necessary to be transmitted here.)—In twelve months we were all sent back to Dublin.—My mother, with three of us (for she lay-in at Plymouth of a boy, Joram), took ship at Bristol, for Ireland, and had a narrow escape from being cast away, by a leak springing up in the vessel.—At length, after many perils and struggles, we got to Dublin.— There my father took a large house, furnished it, and in a year and a half's time spent a great deal of money. In the year one thousand seven hundred and nineteen, all unhinged again; the regiment was ordered, with many others, to the Isle of Wight, in order to embark for Spain, in the Vigo expedition. We accompanied the regiment, and were driven into Milford Haven, but landed at Bristol; from thence, by land, to Plymouth again, and to the Isle of Wight; —where, I remember, we stayed encamped some time before the embarkation of the troops—(in this expedition, from Bristol to Hampshire, we lost poor Joram, a pretty boy, four years old, of the small-pox)—my mother, sister, and myself remained at the Isle of Wight during the Vigo expedition, and until the regiment had got back to Wicklow, in Ireland; from whence my father sent for us.—We had poor Joram's loss supplied, during our stay in the Isle of Wight, by the birth of a girl, Anne, born September the twenty-third, one thousand seven hundred and nineteen.—This pretty blossom fell at the age of three years, in the barracks of Dublin. She was, as I well remember, of a fine delicate frame, not made to last long,—as were most of my father's babes. We embarked for Dublin, and had all been cast away by a most violent storm; but through the intercessions of my mother, the captain was prevailed upon to turn back into Wales, where we stayed a month, and at length got into Dublin, and travelled by land to Wicklow; where my father had for some weeks given us over for lost. We lived in the barracks at Wicklow one year—(one thousand seven hundred and twenty) when Devijeher (so called after Colonel Devijeher) was born; from thence we decamped to stay half a year with Mr. Featherston, a clergyman, about seven miles from Wicklow; who, being a relation of my mother's, invited us to his parsonage at Animo. It was in this parish, during our stay, that I had that wonderful escape in falling through a mill-race whilst the mill was going, and of being taken up unhurt: the story is incredible, but known for truth in all that part of Ireland, where hundreds of the common people flocked to see me. From hence we followed the regiment to Dublin, where we lay in the barracks a year. In this year (one thousand seven hundred and twenty-one) I learnt to write, &c. The regiment ordered in twenty-two to Carrickfergus, in the north of Ireland. We all decamped; but got no further than Drogheda;—thence ordered to Mullengar, forty miles west, where, by Providence, we stumbled upon a kind relation, a collateral descendant from Archbishop Sterne, who took us all to his castle, and kindly entertained us for a year, and sent us to the regiment to Carrickfergus, loaded with kindnesses, &c. A most rueful and tedious journey had we all (in March) to Carrickfergus, where we arrived in six or seven days.—Little Devijeher here died; he was three years old; he had been left behind at nurse at a farmhouse near Wicklow, but was fetched to us by my father the summer after:—another child sent to fill his place, Susan. This babe, too, left us behind in this weary journey. The autumn of that year, or the spring afterwards (I forget which), my father got leave of his colonel to fix me at school,—which he did near Halifax, with an able master; with whom I stayed some time, till, by God's care of me, my cousin Sterne, of Elvington, became a father to me, and sent me to the university, &c. &c. To pursue the thread of our story, my father's regiment was, the year after, ordered to Londonderry, where another sister was brought forth, Catherine, still living; but most unhappily estranged from me by my uncle's wickedness and her own folly. From this station the regiment was sent to defend Gibraltar, at the siege, where my father was run through the body by Captain Phillips, in a duel (the quarrel began about a goose!); with much difficulty he survived, though with an impaired constitution, which was not able to withstand the hardships it was put to; for he was sent to Jamaica, where he soon fell by the country fever, which took away his senses first, and made a child of him; and then, in a month or two, walking about continually without complaining, till the moment he sat down in an arm-chair, and breathed his last, which was at Port Antonio, on the north of the island. My father was a little smart man, active to the last degree in all exercises, most patient of fatigue and disappointments, of which it pleased God to give him full measure. He was, in his temper, somewhat rapid and hasty, but of a kindly sweet disposition, void of all design; and so innocent in his own intentions, that he suspected no one; so that you might have cheated him ten times in a day, if nine had not been sufficient for your purpose. My poor father died in March 1731. I remained at Halifax till about the latter end of that year, and cannot omit mentioning this anecdote of myself and schoolmaster:—He had the ceiling of the schoolroom new white-washed; the ladder remained there. I, one unlucky day, mounted it, and wrote with a brush, in large capital letters, LAU. STERNE, for which the usher severely whipped me. My master was very much hurt at this, and said, before me, that never should that name be effaced, for I was a boy of genius, and he was sure I should come to preferment. This expression made me forget the stripes I had received. In the year thirty-two* my cousin sent me

---

* He was admitted of Jesus' College, in the University of Cambridge, 6th July 1733, under the tuition of Mr. Cannon.
Matriculated 29th March 1735.
Admitted to the degree of B.A. in January 1736.
Admitted M.A. at the commencement of 1740.

to the university, where I stayed some time. 'Twas there that I commenced a friendship with Mr. H——, which has been lasting on both sides. I then came to York, and my uncle got me the living of Sutton; and at York I became acquainted with your mother, and courted her for two years:—she owned she liked me, but thought herself not rich enough, or me too poor, to be joined together. She went to her sister's in S——; and I wrote to her often. I believe then she was partly determined to have me, but would not say so. At her return she fell into a consumption;— and one evening that I was sitting by her, with an almost broken heart to see her so ill, she said, 'My dear Laurey, I never can be yours, for I verily believe I have not long to live! but I have left you every shilling of my fortune.' Upon that she showed me her will. This generosity overpowered me. It pleased God that she recovered, and I married her in the year 1741. My uncle* and myself were then upon very good terms; for he soon got me the Prebendary of York;—but he quarrelled with me afterwards, because I would not write paragraphs in the newspapers;— though he was a party man, I was not, and detested such dirty work, thinking it beneath me. From that period he became my bitterest enemy.† By my wife's

* Jaques Sterne, LL.D. He was Prebendary of Durham, Canon Residentiary, Precentor, and Prebendary of York, Rector of Rise, and Rector of Hornsey cum Riston, both in the East Riding of the county of York. He died June 9th, 1759.

† It hath, however, been insinuated that he for some time wrote a periodical electioneering paper at York, in defence of the Whig interest. —*Monthly Review*, vol. liii., p. 344.

means I got the living of Stillington; a friend of hers in the south had promised her that if she married a clergyman in Yorkshire, when the living became vacant, he would make her a compliment of it. I remained near twenty years at Sutton, doing duty at both places. I had then very good health. Books, painting,* fiddling, and shooting were my amusements. As to the squire of the parish, I cannot say we were upon a very friendly footing; but at Stillington, the family of the C——s showed us every kindness: 'twas most truly agreeable to be within a mile and a half of an amiable family, who were ever cordial friends. In the year 1760 I took a house at York for your mother and yourself, and went up to London to publish† my two first volumes of Shandy.‡ In that year Lord Falconbridge presented me with the curacy of Coxwould; a sweet retirement in comparison of Sutton. In sixty-two I went to France before the peace was concluded; and you both followed me. I left you both in France, and in two years after, I went

---

* A specimen of Mr. Sterne's abilities in the art of designing may be seen in Mr. Wodhul's Poems, 8vo, 1772.

† The first edition was printed in the preceding year at York.

‡ The following is the order in which Mr. Sterne's publications appeared:—

1747. The Case of Elijah and the Widow of Zerephath considered. A Charity Sermon preached on Good Friday, April 17, 1747, for the support of two charity schools in York.

1750. The Abuses of Conscience. Set forth in a Sermon preached in the Cathedral Church of St. Peter, York, at the Summer Assizes, before the Hon. Mr. Baron Clive, and the Hon. Mr. Baron Smythe, on Sunday, July 29, 1750.

1759. Vol. I. and II. of Tristram Shandy.

1760. Vol. I. and II. of Sermons.

to Italy for the recovery of my health; and when I called upon you, I tried to engage your mother to return to England with me:* she and yourself are at length come, and I have had the inexpressible joy of seeing my girl everything I wished for.

"*I have set down these particulars relating to my family and self for my Lydia, in case hereafter she might have a curiosity, or a kinder motive, to know them.*"

To these notices, the following brief account of his death has been added by another writer:—

As Mr. Sterne, in the foregoing narrative, hath brought down the account of himself until within a few months of his death, it remains only to mention that he left York about the end of the year 1767, and came to London, in order to publish *The Sentimental Journey*, which he had written during the preceding summer at his favourite living of Coxwould. His health had been for some time declining; but he continued to visit his friends, and retained his usual flow of spirits. In February 1768 he began to perceive the approaches of death; and with the concern of a good man, and the solicitude of an affectionate parent,

---

1761. Vols. III. and IV. of Tristram Shandy.
1762. Vols. V. and VI. of Tristram Shandy.
1765. Vols. VII. and VIII. of Tristram Shandy.
1766. Vols. III., IV., V., and VI. of Sermons.
1767. Vol. IX. of Tristram Shandy.
1768. The Sentimental Journey.
The remainder of his works were published after his death.

* From this passage, it appears that the present account of Mr. Sterne's Life and Family was written about six months only before his death.

devoted his attention to the future welfare of his daughter. His letters, at this period, reflect so much credit on his character, that it is to be lamented some others in the collection were permitted to see the light. After a short struggle with his disorder, his debilitated and worn-out frame submitted to fate on the 18th day of March 1768, at his lodgings in Bond Street. He was buried at the new burying-ground belonging to the parish of St. George, Hanover Square, on the 22d of the same month, in the most private manner; and hath since been indebted to strangers for a monument very unworthy of his memory, on which the following lines are inscribed:—

<blockquote>
Near to this Place
Lies the Body of
The Reverend LAURENCE STERNE, A.M.
Died September 13th, 1768,*
Aged 53 Years.
</blockquote>

To these Memoirs we can only add a few circumstances. The Archbishop of York, referred to as great-grandfather of the author, was Dr. Richard Sterne, who died in June 1683. The family came from Suffolk to Nottinghamshire, and are described by Guillam as bearing Or a cheveron, between three crosses flory sable. The crest is that Starling proper, which the pen of Yorick has rendered immortal.

Sterne was educated at Jesus College, Cambridge, and took the degree of Master of Arts there in 1740.

---

* It is scarcely necessary to observe that this date is erroneous.

His protector and patron, in the outset of life, was his uncle, Jaques Sterne, D.D., who was Prebendary of Durham, Canon Residentiary, Precentor, and Prebendary of York, with other good preferments. Dr. Sterne was a keen Whig, and zealous supporter of the Hanoverian succession. The politics of the times being particularly violent, he was engaged in many controversies, particularly with Dr. Richard Burton (the original of Dr. Slop), whom he had arrested upon a charge of high treason, during the affair of 1745. Laurence Sterne, in the Memoir which precedes these notices, represents himself as having quarrelled with his uncle, because he would not assist him with his pen in controversies of this description.

When settled in Yorkshire, Sterne had represented his time as much engaged with books, fiddling, and painting. The former seem to have been in a great measure supplied by the library of Skelton Castle, the abode of his intimate friend and relation, John Hall Stevenson, author of the witty and indecent collection entitled *Crazy Tales*, where there is a very humorous description of his ancient residence, under the name of Crazy Castle. This library had the same cast of antiquity which belonged to the castle itself, and doubtless contained much of that rubbish of ancient literature, in which the labour and ingenuity of Sterne contrived to find a mine. Until 1759, Sterne had only printed two Sermons; but in that year he surprised the world, by publishing the two first volumes of *Tristram Shandy*. Sterne states himself, in a letter to a friend, as being "tired of employing his brains for other people's advantage—a foolish sacrifice I have made for some years to an ungrateful person."—This passage probably alludes to his quarrel with his uncle; and as he mentions having taken a small house in York for the education of his daughter, it is probable that he looked to his pen for some assistance, though, in a letter to a nameless doctor, who had accused him of writing in order to have *nummum in loculo*, he declares he wrote not to be fed, but to be famous. *Tristram*, however, procured the author both fame and profit. The brilliant genius which mingled with so much real or affected eccentricity,—the gaping astonishment of the readers who could not conceive the drift or object of the publication, with the ingenuity of those who attempted to discover the meaning of passages which really had none, gave the book a most extraordinary degree of eclat. But the applause of the public was not unmingled with censure. Sterne was not on good terms with his professional brethren: he had too much wit, and too little forbearance in the use of it; too much vivacity, and too little respect for his cloth and character, to maintain the formalities, not to say the decencies, of the clerical station; and he had, in the full career of his humour, assigned to some of his grave compeers ridiculous epithets and characters, which they did not resent the less that they were certainly witty, and probably applicable. Indeed, to require a man to pardon an insult on account of the wit which accompanies the infliction, although it is what jesters often seem to expect, is desiring him to admire the painted feathers which wing the dart by which he is wounded. The tumult was therefore loud on all sides; but amid shouts of applause and cries of censure, the notoriety of *Tristram* spread still wider and wider, and the fame of Sterne rose in proportion. The author therefore triumphed, and bid the critics defiance. "I shall be attacked and pelted," he says, in one of his letters, "either from cellar or garret, write what I will; and besides, must expect to have a party against me of many hundreds, who either do not, or will not, laugh—'tis enough that I divide the world—at least I will rest contented with it." On another occasion he says, "If my enemies knew that, by this rage of abuse and ill-will, they were effectually serving the interests both of myself and works, they would be more quiet; but it has been the fate of my betters, who have found that the way to fame is like the way to heaven, through much tribulation; and till I shall have the honour to be as much maltreated as Rabelais and Swift were, I must continue humble, for I have not filled up the measure of half their persecutions."

The author went to London to enjoy his fame, and met with all that attention which the public gives to men of notoriety. He boasts of being engaged fourteen dinners deep, and received this hospitality as a tribute; while his contemporaries saw the festivity in a very different light. "Any man who has a name, or who has the power of pleasing," said Johnson, "will be very generally invited in London. The *man Sterne*, I am told, has had engagements for three months."

Johnson's feelings of morality and respect for the priesthood led him to speak of Sterne with contempt; but when Goldsmith added, "And a very dull fellow," he replied with his emphatic, "Why, no, sir."

The two first volumes of *Tristram* proved introductors—singular in their character, certainly—to two volumes of Sermons which the simple name of the Reverend Laurence Sterne (ere yet he became known as the author of a fine novel) would never have recommended to notice, but which were sought for and read eagerly under that of Yorick. They maintained the character of the author for wit, genius, and eccentricity.

The third and fourth volumes of *Tristram* appeared in 1761, and the fifth and sixth in 1762. Both these publications were as popular as the two first volumes. The seventh and eighth, which came forth in 1765, did not attract so much attention. The novelty was in a great measure over; and although they contain some of the most beautiful passages which ever fell from the author's pen, yet neither Uncle Toby nor his faithful attendant were sufficient to attract the public attention in the same degree as before. Thus the popularity of this singular work was for a time impeded by that singular and affected style, which had at first attracted by its novelty, but which ceased to please when it was no longer new. Four additional volumes of Sermons appeared in 1766; and in 1767 the ninth and last volume of *Tristram Shandy*. "I shall publish," he says, "but one this year; and the next I shall begin a new work of four volumes, which, when finished, I shall continue *Tristram* with fresh spirit."

The new work was unquestionably his *Sentimental Journey*; for which, according to the evidence of La Fleur, Sterne had made much larger collections than were ever destined to see the light. The author's health was now become extremely feeble; and his Italian travels were designed, if possible, to relieve his consumptive complaints. The remedy proved unsuccessful; yet he lived to arrive in England, and to prepare for the press the first part of the *Sentimental Journey*, which was published in 1768.

In this place we may insert with propriety those notices of Sterne and his valet La Fleur, which appear in Mr. Davis's interesting selection of anecdotes, which he has entitled an *Olio*.

"La Fleur was born in Burgundy: when a mere child he conceived a strong passion to see the world, and at eight years of age ran away from his parents. His prevenancy was always his passport, and his wants were easily supplied—milk, bread, and a straw bed amongst the peasantry, were all he wanted for the night, and in the morning he wished to be on his way again. This rambling life he continued till he attained his tenth year, when being one day on the Pont Neuf at Paris, surveying with wonder the objects that surrounded him, he was accosted by a drummer, who easily enlisted him in the service. For six years La Fleur beat his drum in the French army; two years more would have entitled him to his discharge, but he preferred anticipation, and, exchanging dress with a peasant, easily made his escape. By having recourse to his old expedients, he made his way to Montreuil, where he introduced himself to Varenne, who fortunately took a fancy to him. The little accommodations he needed were given him with cheerfulness; and as what we sow we wish to see flourish, this worthy landlord promised to get him a master; and as he deemed the best not better than La Fleur merited, he promised to recommend him to *un Milord Anglois*. He fortunately could perform as well as promise, and he introduced him to Sterne, ragged as a colt, but full of health and hilarity. The little picture which Sterne has drawn of La Fleur's Amours is so far true:—He was fond of a very pretty girl at Montreuil, the elder of two sisters who, if living, he said, resembled the Maria of Moulines; her he afterwards married, and, whatever proof it might be of his affection, was none of his prudence, for it made him not a jot richer or happier than he was before. She was a mantua-maker, and her closest application could produce no more than *six sous* a day; finding that her assistance could go little towards their support, and after having had a daughter by her, they separated, and he went to service. At length, with what money he had got together by his servitude, he returned to his wife, and they took a public-house in Royal Street, Calais.—There ill luck attended him,—war broke out; and the loss of the English sailors, who navigated the packets, and who were his principal customers, so reduced his little business, that he was obliged again to quit his wife, and confide to her guidance the little trade which was insufficient to support them both. He returned in March 1783, but his wife had fled. A strolling company of comedians passing through the town, had seduced her from her home, and no tale or tidings of her have ever since reached him. From the period he lost his wife, says our informant, he has frequently visited England, to whose natives he is extremely partial, sometimes as a sergeant, at others as an express. Where zeal and diligence were required, La Fleur was never yet wanting."

In addition to La Fleur's account of himself (continues Mr. Davis), the writer of the preceding obtained from him several little circumstances relative to his master, as well as the characters depicted by him, a few of which, as they would lose by abridgment, I shall give *verbatim*.

"There were moments," said La Fleur, "in which my master appeared sunk into the deepest dejection—when his calls upon me for my services were so seldom, that I sometimes apprehensively pressed in upon his privacy, to suggest what I thought might divert his melancholy. He used to smile at my well-meant zeal, and I could see was happy to be relieved. At others, he seemed to have received a new soul—he launched into the levity natural *à mon pays*," said La Fleur, "and cried gaily enough, '*Vive la Bagatelle!*' It was in one of those moments that he became acquainted with the Grisette at the glove shop—she afterwards visited him at his lodgings, upon which La Fleur made not a single remark; but on naming the *fille de chambre*, his other visitant, he exclaimed, 'It was certainly a pity she was so pretty and *petite.*'"

The lady mentioned under the initial L. was the Marquise Lamberti; to the interest of this lady he was indebted for the passport, which began to make him seriously uneasy. Count de B. (Bretuil), notwithstanding the Shakespeare, La Fleur thinks, would have troubled himself little about him. Choiseul was Minister at the time.

" Poor Maria

Was, alas! no fiction.—When we came up to her, she was grovelling in the road like an infant, and throwing the dust upon her head—and yet few were more lovely. Upon Sterne's accosting her with tenderness, and raising her in his arms, she collected herself, and resumed some composure—told him her tale of misery, and wept upon his breast—my master sobbed aloud. I saw her gently disengage herself from his arms, and she sung him the service to the Virgin; my poor master covered his face with his hands, and walked by her side to the cottage where she lived; there he talked earnestly to the old woman."

"Every day," said La Fleur, "while we stayed there, I carried them meat and drink from the hotel, and when we departed from Moulines, my master left his blessings and some money with the mother."—"How much," added he, "I know not—he always gave more than he could afford."

Sterne was frequently at a loss upon his travels for

ready money. Remittances were become interrupted by war, and he had wrongly estimated his expenses; he had reckoned along the post-roads, without adverting to the wretchedness that was to call upon him in his way.

At many of our stages my master has turned to me with tears in his eyes—"These poor people oppress me, La Fleur; how shall I relieve me?" He wrote much, and to a late hour. I told La Fleur of the inconsiderable quantity he had published; he expressed extreme surprise. "I know," said he, "upon our return from this tour, there was a large trunk completely filled with papers." "Do you know anything of their tendency, La Fleur?" "Yes; they were miscellaneous remarks upon the manners of the different nations he visited; and in Italy he was deeply engaged in making the most elaborate inquiries into the differing governments of the towns, and the characteristic peculiarities of the Italians of the various states."

To effect this, he read much; for the collections of the Patrons of Literature were open to him: he observed more. Singular as it may seem, Sterne endeavoured in vain to speak Italian. His valet acquired it on their journey; but his master, though he applied now and then, gave it up at length as unattainable.—"I the more wondered at this," said La Fleur, "as he must have understood Latin."

The assertion, sanctioned by Johnson, that Sterne was licentious and dissolute in conversation, stands thus far contradicted by the testimony of La Fleur.

"His conversation with women," he said, "was of the most interesting kind; he usually left them serious, if he did not find them so."

The Dead Ass

Was no invention. The mourner was as simple and affecting as Sterne has related. La Fleur recollected the circumstance perfectly.

To Monks

Sterne never exhibited any particular sympathy. La Fleur remembered several pressing in upon him, to all of whom his answer was the same—*Mon père, je suis occupé. Je suis pauvre comme vous.*

In February 1768, Laurence Sterne, his frame exhausted by long debilitating illness, expired at his lodgings in Bond Street, London. There was something in the manner of his death singularly resembling the particulars detailed by Mrs. Quickly, as attending that of Falstaff, the compeer of Yorick for infinite jest, however unlike in other particulars. As he lay on his bed totally exhausted, he complained that his feet were cold, and requested the female attendant to chafe them. She did so, and it seemed to relieve him. He complained that the cold came up higher; and whilst the assistant was in the act of chafing his ankles and legs, he expired without a groan. It was also remarkable that his death took place much in the manner which he himself had wished; and that the last offices were rendered him, not in his own house, or by the hand of kindred affection, but in an inn, and by strangers.

We are well acquainted with Sterne's features and personal appearance, to which he himself frequently alludes. He was tall and thin, with a hectic and consumptive appearance. His features, though capable of expressing with peculiar effect the sentimental emotions by which he was often affected, had also a shrewd, humorous, and sarcastic expression, proper to the wit and the satirist. His conversation was animated and witty; but Johnson complained that it was marked by license, better suiting the company of the lord of Crazy Castle than of the great moralist. It has been said, and probably with truth, that his temper was variable and unequal, the natural consequence of irritable temperament, and continued bad health. But we will not readily believe that the parent of Uncle Toby could be a harsh, or habitually a bad-humoured man. Sterne's letters to his friends, and especially to his daughter, breathe all the fondness of affection; and his resources, such as they were, seem to have been always at the command of those whom he loved.

If we consider Sterne's reputation as chiefly founded on *Tristram Shandy*, he must be considered as liable to two severe charges;—those, namely, of indecency, and of affectation. Upon the first accusation Sterne was himself peculiarly sore, and used to justify the licentiousness of his humour by representing it as a mere breach of decorum, which had no perilous consequence to morals. The following anecdote we have from a sure source. Soon after *Tristram* had appeared, Sterne asked a Yorkshire lady of fortune and condition whether she had read his book. "I have not, Mr. Sterne," was the answer; "and, to be plain with you, I am informed it is not proper for female perusal."—"My dear good lady," replied the author, "do not be gulled by such stories: the book is like your young heir there (pointing to a child of three years old, who was rolling on the carpet in his white tunics); he shows at times a good deal that is usually concealed, but it is all in perfect innocence!" This witty excuse may be so far admitted; for it cannot be said that the licentious humour of *Tristram Shandy* is of the kind which applies itself to the passions, or is calculated to corrupt society. But it is a sin against taste, if allowed to be harmless as to morals. A handful of mud is neither a firebrand nor a stone; but to fling it about in sport, argues coarseness of taste, and want of common manners.

Sterne, however, began and ended by braving the censure of the world in this particular. A remarkable passage in one of his letters shows how lightly he was disposed to esteem the charge; and what is singular enough, his plan for turning it into ridicule seems to have been serious. "Crebillon (*le fils*) has made a convention with me, which, if he is not too lazy, will be no bad *persiflage*. As soon as I get to Toulouse, he has agreed to write me an expostulatory letter on the indecencies of T. Shandy— which is to be answered by recrimination upon the liberties in his own works. These are to be printed together—Crebillon against Sterne—Sterne against Crebillon—the copy to be sold, and the money equally divided: this is good Swiss policy."

In like manner, the greatest admirers of Sterne must own, that his style is affected, eminently, and in a degree which even his wit and pathos are inadequate to support. The style of Rabelais, which he assumed for his model, is to the highest excess rambling, excursive, and intermingled with the greatest absurdities. But Rabelais was in some measure compelled to adopt this Harlequin's habit, in order that, like licensed jesters, he might, under the cover of his folly, have permission to vent his satire against church and state. Sterne assumed the manner of his master, only as a mode of attracting attention, and of making the public stare; and, therefore, his extravagancies, like those of a feigned madman, are cold and forced, even in the midst of his most irregular flights. A man may, in the present day, be, with perfect impunity, as wise or as witty as he can, without assuming the cap and bells of the ancient jester as an apology; and that Sterne chose voluntarily to appear under such a disguise, must be set down as mere affectation, and ranked with the tricks of black or marbled pages, as used merely *ad captandum vulgus*. All popularity thus founded, carries in it the seeds of decay; for eccentricity in composition, like fantastic modes of dress, however attractive when first introduced, is sure to be caricatured by stupid imitators, to become soon unfashionable, and of course to be neglected.

If we proceed to look more closely into the manner of composition which Sterne thought proper to adopt, we find a sure guide in the ingenious Dr. Ferriar of Manchester, who, with most singular patience, has traced our author through the hidden sources whence he borrowed most of his learning, and many of his more striking and peculiar expressions. Rabelais (much less read than spoken of), the lively but licentious miscellany called *Moyen de Parvenir*, and D'Aubigné's *Baron de Fœneste*, with many other forgotten authors of the sixteenth century, were successively laid under contribution. Burton's celebrated work on Melancholy (which Dr. Ferriar's Essay instantly raised to double price in the book-market) afforded Sterne an endless mass of quotations, with which he unscrupulously garnished his pages, as if they had been collected in the course of his own extensive reading. The style of the same author, together with that of Bishop Hall, furnished the author of *Tristram* with many of those whimsical expressions, similes, and illustrations, which were long believed the genuine effusions of his own eccentric wit. For proofs of this sweeping charge we must refer the readers to Dr. Ferriar's well-known Essay and Illustrations, as he delicately terms them, of Sterne's Writings, in which it is clearly shown that he, whose manner and style were so long thought original, was, in fact, the most unhesitating plagiarist who ever cribbed from his predecessors in order to garnish his own pages.

It must be owned, at the same time, that Sterne selects the materials of his mosaic work with so much art, places them so well, and polishes them so highly, that in most cases we are disposed to pardon the want of originality, in consideration of the exquisite talent with which the borrowed materials are wrought up into the new form.

One of Sterne's most singular thefts, considering the tenor of the passage stolen, is his declamation against literary depredators of his own class: "Shall we," says Sterne, "for ever make new books, as apothecaries make new medicines, by pouring only out of one vessel into another? Are we for ever to be twisting and untwisting the same rope—for ever in the same track? for ever at the same pace?" The words of Burton are, "As apothecaries, we make new mixtures, every day pour out of one vessel into another; and as the Romans robbed all the cities in the world to set out their bad-sited Rome, we skim the cream of other men's wits, pick the choice flowers of their tilled gardens, to set out our own sterile plots. We weave the same web, still twist the same rope again and again." We cannot help wondering at the coolness with which Sterne could transfer to his own work so eloquent a tirade against the very arts which he was practising.

Much has been said about the right of an author to avail himself of his predecessors' labours; and certainly, in a general sense, he that revives the wit and learning of a former age, and puts it into the form likely to captivate his own, confers a benefit on his contemporaries. But to plume himself with the very language and phrases of former writers, and to pass their wit and learning for his own, was the more unworthy in Sterne, as he had enough of original talent, had he chosen to exert it, to have dispensed with all such acts of literary petty larceny.

Tristram Shandy is no narrative, but a collection of scenes, dialogues, and portraits, humorous or affecting, intermixed with much wit, and with much learning, original or borrowed. It resembles the irregularities of a Gothic room, built by some fanciful collector, to contain the miscellaneous remnants of antiquity which his pains have accumulated, and bearing as little proportion in its parts as the pieces of rusty armour with which it is decorated. Viewing it in this light, the principal figure is Mr. Shandy the elder, whose character is formed in many respects upon that of Martinus Scriblerus. The history of Martin was designed by the celebrated club of wits, by whom it was commenced, as a satire upon the ordinary pursuits of learning and science. Sterne, on the contrary, had no particular object of ridicule; his business was only to create a person, to whom he could attach the great quantity of extraordinary reading, and antiquated learning, which he had collected. He, therefore, supposed in Mr. Shandy a man of an active and metaphysical, but at the same time a whimsical, cast of mind, whom too much and too miscellaneous learning had brought within a step or two of madness, and who acts in the ordinary affairs of life upon the absurd theories adopted by the pedants of past ages.

He is most admirably contrasted with his wife, well described as a good lady of the true poco-curante school, who neither obstructed the progress of her husband's hobbyhorse, to use a phrase which Sterne has rendered classical, nor could be prevailed upon to spare him the least admiration for the grace and dexterity with which he managed it.

Yorick, the lively, witty, sensitive, and heedless Parson, is the well-known personification of Sterne himself, and undoubtedly, like every portrait of himself drawn by a master of the art, bore a strong resemblance to the original. Still, however, there are shades of simplicity thrown into the character of Yorick, which did not exist in that of Sterne. We cannot believe that the jests of the latter were so void of malice prepense, or that his satire entirely flowed out of honesty of mind and mere jocundity of humour. It must be owned, moreover, that Sterne was more like to have stolen a passage out of Stevinus if he could have found one to his purpose, than to have left one of his manuscripts in the volume, with the careless indifference of Yorick. Still, however, we gladly recognise the general likeness between the author and the child of his fancy, and willingly pardon the pencil, which, in the delicate task of self-delineation, has softened some traits and improved others.

Uncle Toby, with his faithful Squire, the most delightful characters in the work, or perhaps in any other, are drawn with such a pleasing force and discrimination, that they more than entitle the author to a free pardon for his literary peculations, his indecorum, and his affectation; nay, authorise him to leave the court of criticism not forgiven only, but applauded and rewarded, as one who has exalted and honoured humanity, and impressed upon his readers such a lively picture of kindness and benevolence, blended with courage, gallantry, and simplicity, that their hearts must be warmed by, whenever it is recalled to memory. Sterne, indeed, might boldly plead in his own behalf, that the passages which he borrowed from others, were of little value, in comparison to those which are exclusively original; and that the former might have been written by many persons, while in his own proper line he stands alone and inimitable. Something of extravagance may, perhaps, attach to Uncle Toby's favourite amusements. Yet in England, where men think and act with little regard to the ridicule or censure of their neighbours, there is no impossibility, perhaps no great improbability in supposing, that a humorist might employ such a mechanical aid as my Uncle's bowling-green, in order to encourage and assist his imagination in the pleasing but delusive task of castle-building. Men have been called children of a larger growth, and among the antic toys and devices with which they are amused, the device of my Uncle, with whose pleasures we are so much disposed to sympathise, does not seem so unnatural upon reflection as it may appear at first sight.

It is well known (through Dr. Ferriar's labours) that Dr. Slop with all his obstetrical engines, may be identified with Dr. Burton of York, who published a treatise of Midwifery in 1751. This person, as we have elsewhere noticed, was on bad terms with Sterne's uncle; and though there had come strife and unkindness between the uncle and the nephew, yet the latter seems to have retained aversion against the enemy of the former. But Sterne, being no politician, had forgiven the Jacobite, and only persecutes the Doctor with his raillery, as a quack and a Catholic.

It is needless to dwell longer on a work so generally known. The style employed by Sterne is fancifully ornamented, but at the same time vigorous and masculine, and full of that animation and force which can only be derived by an intimate acquaintance with the early English prose-writers. In the power of approaching and touching the finer feelings of the heart, he has never been excelled, if indeed he has ever been equalled; and may be at once recorded as one of the most affected, and one of the most simple writers,—as one of the greatest plagiarists, and one of the most original geniuses whom England has produced. Dr. Ferriar, who seemed born to trace and detect the various mazes through which Sterne carried on his depredations upon ancient and dusty authors, apologises for the rigour of his inquest, by doing justice to those merits which were peculiarly our author's own. We cannot better close this article than with the sonnet in which his ingenious inquisitor makes the amende honourable to the shade of Yorick.

> "Sterne, for whose sake I plod through miry ways,
> Of antique wit and quibbling mazes drear,

"Let not thy shade malignant censure fear,
Though aught of borrowed mirth my search betrays.
Long slept that mirth in dust of ancient days;
(Erewhile to Guise or wanton Valois dear)
Till waked by thee in Skelton's joyous pile,
She flung on Tristram her capricious rays;
But the quick tear that checks our wondering smile,
In sudden pause or unexpected story,
Owns thy true mastery—and Le Fevre's woes,
Maria's wanderings, and the Prisoner's throes,
Fix thee conspicuous on the throne of glory."

A SENTIMENTAL JOURNEY

THROUGH

FRANCE AND ITALY.

———*o*———

———They order, said I, this matter better in France.

———You have been in France? said my gentleman, turning quick upon me, with the most civil triumph in the world.———Strange! quoth I, debating the matter with myself, That one-and-twenty miles sailing, for 'tis absolutely no further from Dover to Calais, should give a man these rights;—I'll look into them. So, giving up the argument,—I went straight to my lodgings, put up half a dozen shirts and a black pair of silk breeches;—"the coat I have on," said I, looking at the sleeve, "will do,"—took a place in the Dover stage; and, the packet sailing at nine the next morning, —by three I had got sat down to my dinner upon a fricaseed chicken, so incontestibly in France, that, had I died that night of an indigestion, the whole world could not have suspended the effects of the *droits d'aubaine;**—my shirts, and black pair of silk breeches, —portmanteau and all, must have gone to the King of France;—even the little picture which I have so long worn, and so often told thee, Eliza, I would carry with me into my grave, would have been torn from my neck!—Ungenerous! to seize upon the wreck of an unwary passenger, whom your subjects had beckoned to their coast!—by Heaven! Sire, it is not well done; and much does it grieve me 'tis the monarch of a people so civilised and courteous, and so renowned for sentiment and fine feelings, that I have to reason with!——

But I have scarce set foot in your dominions.

CALAIS.

When I had finished my dinner, and drank the King of France's health, to satisfy my mind that I bore him no spleen, but, on the contrary, high honour for the humanity of his temper,—I rose up an inch taller for the accommodation.

—No, said I, the Bourbon is by no means a cruel race: they may be misled, like other people; but there is a mildness in their blood. As I acknowledged this, I felt a suffusion of a finer kind upon my cheek, more warm and friendly to man than what Burgundy (at least of two livres a bottle, which was such as I had been drinking) could have produced.

---

* All the effects of strangers (Swiss and Scots excepted) dying in France, are seized, by virtue of this law, though the heir be upon the spot;—the profit of these contingencies being farmed, there is no redress.

—Just God! said I, kicking my portmanteau aside, what is there in this world's goods which should sharpen our spirits, and make so many kind-hearted brethren of us fall out so cruelly as we do by the way?

When man is at peace with man, how much lighter than a feather is the heaviest of metals in his hand! he pulls out his purse, and holding it airily and uncompressed, looks round him, as if he sought for an object to share it with.—In doing this, I felt every vessel in my frame dilate,—the arteries beat all cheerily together, and every power which sustained life performed it with so little friction, that 'twould have confounded the most *physical precieuse* in France: with all her materialism, she could scarce have called me a machine.

I'm confident, said I to myself, I should have overset her creed.

The accession of that idea carried Nature, at that time, as high as she could go;—I was at peace with the world before, and this finished the treaty with myself.

—Now, was I a king of France, cried I, what a moment for an orphan to have begged his father's portmanteau of me!

THE MONK.

CALAIS.

I HAD scarce uttered the words, when a poor monk, of the order of St. Francis, came into the room, to beg something for his convent. No man cares to have his virtues the sport of contingencies,—or one man may be generous, as another man is puissant,—*sed non quoad hanc :*—or be it as it may,—for there is no regular reasoning upon the ebbs and flows of our humours, they may depend upon the same causes, for aught I know, which influence the tides themselves;—'twould oft be no discredit to us to suppose it was so: I'm sure, at least for myself, that in many a case I should be more highly satisfied to have it said by the world—" I had had an affair with the moon, in which there was neither sin nor shame," than have it pass altogether as my own act and deed, wherein there was so much of both.

—But be this as it may,—the moment I cast my eyes upon him I was predetermined not to give him a single sous: and, accordingly, I put my purse into my pocket, buttoned it up, set myself a little more upon my centre, and advanced up gravely to him. There was something, I fear, forbidding in my look: I have his figure this moment before my eyes, and think there was that in it which deserved better.

The monk, as I judged from the break in his tonsure, a few scattered white hairs upon his temples being all that remained of it, might be about seventy; but from his eyes, and that sort of fire which was in them, which seemed more tempered by courtesy than years, could be no more than sixty:—truth might lie between,—he was certainly sixty-five; and the general air of his countenance, notwithstanding something seemed to have been planting wrinkles in it before their time, agreed to the account.

It was one of those heads which Guido has often

painted,—mild, pale, penetrating, free from all commonplace ideas of fat contented ignorance looking downwards upon the earth;—it looked forwards, but looked as if it looked at something beyond this world. How one of his order came by it, Heaven above, who let it fall upon a monk's shoulders, best knows; but it would have suited a Brahmin, and, had I met it upon the plains of Indostan, I had reverenced it.

The rest of his outline may be given in a few strokes; one might put it into the hands of any one to design, for 'twas neither elegant nor otherwise, but as character and expression made it so: it was a thin, spare form, something above the common size, if it lost not the distinction by a bend forward in the figure,—but it was the attitude of entreaty; and, as it now stands presented to my imagination, it gained more than it lost by it.

When he had entered the room three paces, he stood still; and laying his left hand upon his breast (a slender white staff with which he journeyed being in his right)—when I had got close up to him, he introduced himself with the little story of the wants of his convent, and the poverty of his order;—and did it with so simple a grace,—and such an air of deprecation was there in the whole cast of his look and figure,—I was bewitched not to have been struck with it.

—A better reason was, I had predetermined not to give him a single sous.

THE MONK.

CALAIS.

——'Tis very true, said I, replying to a cast upwards with his eyes, with which he had concluded his address;—'tis very true,—and Heaven be their resource who have no other but the charity of the world! the stock of which, I fear, is no way sufficient for the many *great claims* which are hourly made upon it.

As I pronounced the words *great claims,* he gave a slight glance with his eye downwards upon the sleeve of his tunic :—I felt the full force of the appeal;—I acknowledge it, said I :—a coarse habit, and that but once in three years, with meagre diet,—are no great matters; and the true point of pity is, as they can be earned in the world with so little industry, that your order should wish to procure them by pressing upon a fund which is the property of the lame, the blind, the aged, and the infirm!—the captive, who lies down counting over and over again the days of his afflictions, languishes also for his share of it; and had you been of the *order of Mercy,* instead of the order of St. Francis, poor as I am, continued I, pointing at my portmanteau, full cheerfully should it have been opened to you, for the ransom of the unfortunate.——The monk made me a bow.——But of all others, resumed I, the unfortunate of our own country, surely, have the first rights; and I have left thousands in distress upon our own shore.——The monk gave a cordial wave with his head,—as much as to say, No doubt, there is misery enough in every corner of the world, as well as within our convent.——But we distinguish, said I, laying my hand upon the sleeve of his tunic, in return for his appeal,—we distinguish, my good father, betwixt those who wish only to eat the bread of their own labour, and those who eat the bread of other people's, and have no other plan in life but to get through it in sloth and ignorance, *for the love of God.*

The poor Franciscan made no reply: a hectic of a moment passed across his cheek, but could not tarry:—Nature seemed to have had done with her resentments in him; he showed none:—but letting his staff fall within his arm, he pressed both his hands with resignation upon his breast, and retired.

THE MONK.

CALAIS.

My heart smote me the moment he shut the door. —Psha! said I, with an air of carelessness, three several times,—but it would not do; every ungracious syllable I had uttered crowded back into my imagination; I reflected I had no right over the poor Franciscan but to deny him; and that the punishment of that was enough to the disappointed, without the addition of unkind language. I considered his grey hairs:—his courteous figure seemed to re-enter, and gently ask me what injury he had done me?—and why I could use him thus?—I would have given twenty livres for an advocate.—I have behaved very ill, said I, within myself; but I have only just set out upon my travels, and shall learn better manners as I get along.

THE DESOBLIGEANT.

CALAIS.

When a man is discontented with himself, it has one advantage, however, that it puts him into an excellent frame of mind for making a bargain. Now, there being no travelling through France and Italy without a chaise,—and Nature generally prompting us to the thing we are fittest for, I walked out into the coach-yard to buy or hire something of that kind to my purpose: an old *disobligeant*,* in the furthest corner of the court, hit my fancy at first sight; so I instantly got into it, and finding it in tolerable harmony with my feelings, I ordered the waiter to call Monsieur Dessein, the master of the hotel,—but Monsieur Dessein being gone to vespers, and not caring to face the Franciscan, whom I saw on the opposite side of the court, in conference with a lady just arrived at the inn,—I drew the taffeta curtain betwixt us, and, being determined to write my journey, I took out my pen and ink, and wrote the preface to it in the *desobligeant*.

PREFACE.

IN THE DESOBLIGEANT.

It must have been observed, by many a peripatetic philosopher, That Nature has set up, by her own unquestionable authority, certain boundaries and fences

---

* A chaise so called in France, from its holding but one person.

to circumscribe the discontent of man; she has effected her purpose in the quietest and easiest manner, by laying him under almost insuperable obligation to work out his ease, and to sustain his sufferings at home. It is there only that she has provided him with the most suitable objects to partake of his happiness, and bear a part of that burden which, in all countries and ages, has ever been too heavy for one pair of shoulders. 'Tis true, we are endued with an imperfect power of spreading our happiness sometimes beyond *her* limits; but 'tis so ordered, that, from the want of languages, connections, and dependencies, and from the difference in educations, customs, and habits, we lie under so many impediments in communicating our sensations out of our own sphere, as often amount to a total impossibility.

It will always follow from hence, that the balance of sentimental commerce is always against the expatriated adventurer: he must buy, what he has little occasion for, at their own price;—his conversation will seldom be taken in exchange for theirs without a large discount,—and this, by the by, eternally driving him into the hands of more equitable brokers, for such conversation as he can find, it requires no great spirit of divination to guess at his party.

This brings me to my point, and naturally leads me (if the see-saw of this *desobligeant* will but let me get on) into the efficient as well as final causes of travelling.

Your idle people that leave their native country, and go abroad for some reason or reasons which may be derived from one of these general causes:—

> Infirmity of body,
> Imbecility of mind, or
> Inevitable necessity.

The two first include all those who travel by land or by water, labouring with pride, curiosity, vanity, or spleen, subdivided and combined *in infinitum.*

The third class includes the whole army of peregrine martyrs; more especially those travellers who set out upon their travels with the benefit of the clergy, either as delinquents, travelling under the direction of governors recommended by the magistrate;—or young gentlemen, transported by the cruelty of parents and guardians, and travelling under the direction of governors recommended by Oxford, Aberdeen, and Glasgow.

There is a fourth class, but their number is so small, that they would not deserve a distinction were it not necessary, in a work of this nature, to observe the greatest precision and nicety, to avoid a confusion of character: and these men I speak of are such as cross the seas, and sojourn in a land of strangers, with a view of saving money for various reasons, and upon various pretences; but, as they might also save themselves and others a great deal of unnecessary trouble by saving their money at home, and, as their reasons for travelling are the least complex of any other species of emigrants, I shall distinguish these gentlemen by the name of

> Simple Travellers.

Thus the whole circle of travellers may be reduced to the following heads:—

> Idle Travellers,
> Inquisitive Travellers,

>   Lying Travellers,
>   Proud Travellers,
>   Vain Travellers,
>   Splenetic Travellers.

Then follow

>   The Travellers of Necessity,
>   The Delinquent and Felonious Traveller,
>   The Unfortunate and Innocent Traveller,
>   The Simple Traveller.

And last of all (if you please) The Sentimental Traveller (meaning thereby myself), who have travelled, and of which I am now sitting down to give an account,—as much out of *Necessity,* and the *besoin de voyager,* as any one in the class.

I am well aware, at the same time, as both my travels and observations will be altogether of a different cast from any of my forerunners, that I might have insisted upon a whole niche entirely to myself;—but I should break in upon the confines of the *Vain* Traveller, in wishing to draw attention towards me, till I have some better grounds for it than the mere *Novelty of my Vehicle.* It is sufficient for my reader, if he has been a Traveller himself, that with study and reflection hereupon, he may be able to determine his own place and rank in the catalogue;—it will be one step towards knowing himself, as it is great odds but he retains some tincture and resemblance of what he imbibed or carried out to the present hour.

The man who first transplanted the grape of Burgundy to the Cape of Good Hope (observe he was a

Dutchman) never dreamt of drinking the same wine at the Cape that the same grape produced upon the French mountains,—he was too phlegmatic for that;—but, undoubtedly, he expected to drink some sort of vinous liquor; but whether good, bad, or indifferent,—he knew enough of this world to know that it did not depend upon his choice, but that what is generally called *chance* was to decide his success: however, he hoped for the best; and in these hopes, by an intemperate confidence in the fortitude of his head, and the depth of his discretion, *Mynheer* might possibly overset both in his new vineyard; and, by discovering his nakedness, become a laughing-stock to his people.

Even so it fares with the poor Traveller, sailing and posting through the politer kingdoms of the globe, in pursuit of knowledge and improvements.

Knowledge and improvements are to be got by sailing and posting for that purpose; but whether useful knowledge and real improvements, is all a lottery;—and, even where the adventurer is successful, the acquired stock must be used with caution and sobriety, to turn to any profit:—but, as the chances run prodigiously the other way, both as to the acquisition and application, I am of opinion, That a man would act as wisely, if he could prevail upon himself to live contented without foreign knowledge or foreign improvements, especially if he lives in a country that has no absolute want of either;—and, indeed, much grief of heart has it oft and many a time cost me, when I have observed how many a foul step the Inquisitive Traveller has measured, to see sights and look into discoveries, all which, as Sancho Pança said to Don Quixote, they might have seen dry-shod at home. It is an age so full of light, that there is scarce a country or corner of Europe, whose beams are not crossed and interchanged with others.—Knowledge, in most of its branches, and in most affairs, is like music in an Italian street, whereof those may partake who pay nothing.—But there is no nation under Heaven,—and God is my record (before whose tribunal I must one day come and give an account of this work)—that I do not speak it vauntingly,—But there is no nation under Heaven abounding with more variety of learning, —where the sciences may be more fitly wooed, or more surely won, than here,—where Art is encouraged, and will soon rise high,—where Nature (take her altogether) has so little to answer for,—and, to close all, where there is more wit and variety of character to feed the mind with:—Where, then, my dear countrymen, are you going?

—We are only looking at this chaise, said they. ——Your most obedient servant, said I, skipping out of it, and pulling off my hat.——We were wondering, said one of them, who, I found, was an *Inquisitive Traveller*,—what could occasion its motion.——'Twas the agitation, said I, coolly, of writing a preface.—— I never heard, said the other, who was a *Simple Traveller*, of a preface wrote in a *desobligeant*.——It would have been better, said I, in a *vis-a-vis*.

As an Englishman does not travel to see Englishmen, I retired to my room.

CALAIS.

I PERCEIVED that something darkened the passage more than myself, as I stepped along it to my room; it was effectually Mons. Dessein, the master of the hotel, who had just returned from vespers, and, with his hat under his arm, was most complaisantly following me, to put me in mind of my wants. I had wrote myself pretty well out of conceit with the *desobligeant*; and Mons. Dessein speaking of it with a shrug, as if it would no way suit me, it immediately struck my fancy that it belonged to some *Innocent Traveller*, who, on his return home, had left it to Mons. Dessein's honour to make the most of. Four months had elapsed since it had finished its career of Europe, in the corner of Mons. Dessein's coach-yard: and having sallied out from thence but a vampt-up business at the first, though it had been twice taken to pieces on Mount Sennis, it had not profited much by its adventures,— but by none so little as the standing so many months unpitied in the corner of Mons. Dessein's coach-yard. Much, indeed, was not to be said for it,—but something might,—and, when a few words will rescue Misery out of her distress, I hate the man who can be a churl of them.

—Now, was I the master of this hotel, said I, laying the point of my forefinger on Mons. Dessein's breast, I would inevitably make a point of getting rid of this unfortunate *desobligeant;* it stands swinging reproaches at you every time you pass by it.

Mon Dieu! said Mons. Dessein,—I have no interest

——Except the interest, said I, which men of a certain turn of mind take, Mons. Dessein, in their own sensations.—I'm persuaded, to a man who feels for others as well as for himself, every rainy night, disguise it as you will, must cast a damp upon your spirits. You suffer, Mons. Dessein, as much as the machine.

I have always observed, when there is as much *sour* as *sweet* in a compliment, that an Englishman is eternally at a loss within himself whether to take it or let it alone; a Frenchman never is; Mons. Dessein made me a bow.

C'est bien vrai, said he. But, in this case, I should only exchange one disquietude for another, and with loss. Figure to yourself, my dear sir, that in giving you a chaise which would fall to pieces before you had got half way to Paris,—figure to yourself how much I should suffer, in giving an ill impression of myself to a man of honour, and lying at the mercy, as I must do, *d'un homme d'esprit*.

The dose was made up exactly after my own prescription; so I could not help taking it,—and returning Mons. Dessein his bow, without more casuistry we walked together towards his remise, to take a view of his magazine of chaises.

IN THE STREET.

CALAIS.

It must needs be a hostile kind of a world, when the buyer (if it be but of a sorry post-chaise) cannot go forth with the seller thereof into the street, to terminate the difference betwixt them, but he instantly falls into the same frame of mind, and views his conventionist with the same sort of eye, as if he was going along with him to Hyde Park Corner to fight a duel. For my own part, being but a poor swordsman, and no way a match for Mons. Dessein, I felt the rotation of all the movements within me, to which the situation is incident;—I looked at Monsieur Dessein through and through,—eyed him as he walked along in profile, then *en face;*—thought he looked like a Jew,—then a Turk,—disliked his wig,—cursed him by my gods,—wished him at the Devil!

—And is all this to be lighted up in the heart for a beggarly account of three or four Louis d'ors, which is the most I can be overreached in?—Base passion! said I, turning myself about, as a man naturally does upon a sudden reverse of sentiment,—base, ungentle passion! thy hand is against every man, and every man's hand against thee.——Heaven forbid! said she, raising her hand up to her forehead, for I had turned full in front upon the lady whom I had seen in conference with the monk:—she had followed us unperceived.——Heaven forbid, indeed! said I, offering her my own;—she had a black pair of silk gloves, open only at the thumb and two forefingers, so accepted it without reserve,—and I led her up to the door of the remise.

Monsieur Dessein had *diabled* the key above fifty times, before he found out he had come with a wrong one in his hand. We were as impatient as himself to have it opened; and so attentive to the obstacle, that

I continued holding her hand almost without knowing it: so that Mons. Dessein left us together, with her hand in mine, and with our faces turned towards the door of the remise, and said he would be back in five minutes.

Now, a colloquy of five minutes, in such a situation, is worth one of as many ages, with your faces turned towards the street. In the latter case, 'tis drawn from the objects and occurrences without;—when your eyes are fixed upon a dead blank,—you draw purely from yourselves. A silence of a single moment, upon Mons. Dessein's leaving us, had been fatal to the situation,— she had infallibly turned about; so I began the conversation instantly.

—But what were the temptations (as I write not to apologise for the weaknesses of my heart in this tour, but to give an account of them)—shall be described with the same simplicity with which I felt them.

THE REMISE DOOR.

CALAIS.

When I told the reader, that I did not care to get out of the *desobligeant*, because I saw the monk in close conference with the lady just arrived at the inn, I told him the truth; but I did not tell him the whole truth; for I was full as much restrained by the appearance and figure of the lady he was talking to. Suspicion crossed my brain, and said, he was telling her what had passed: something jarred upon it within me,—I wished him at his convent.

When the heart flies out before the understanding, it saves the judgment a world of pains.—I was certain she was of a better order of beings:—however I thought no more of her, but went on and wrote my preface.

The impression returned upon my encounter with her in the street; a guarded frankness with which she gave me her hand, showed, I thought, her good education and her good sense; and, as I led her on, I felt a pleasurable ductility about her, which spread a calmness over all my spirits.

—Good God! how a man might lead such a creature as this round the world with him!

I had not yet seen her face,—'twas not material; for the drawing was instantly set about, and, long before we had got to the door of the remise, Fancy had finished the whole head, and pleased herself as much with its fitting her goddess, as if she had dived into the Tiber for it;—but thou art seduced, and a seducing slut; and albeit thou cheatest us seven times a-day with thy pictures and images, yet with so many charms dost thou do it, and thou deckest out thy pictures in the shapes of so many angels of light, 'tis a shame to break with thee.

When we had got to the door of the remise, she withdrew her hand from across her forehead, and let me see the original:—it was a face of about six-and-twenty,—of a clear transparent brown, simply set off without rouge or powder;—it was not critically handsome, but there was that in it which, in the frame of mind I was in, attached me much more to it,—it was interesting; I fancied it wore the characters of a widowed look, and in that state of its declension which had passed the two first paroxysms of sorrow, and was quietly beginning to reconcile itself to its loss;—but a thousand other distresses might have traced the same lines; I wished to know what they had been,—and was ready to inquire (had the same *bon ton* of conversation permitted as in the days of Esdras),—" *What aileth thee? and why art thou disquieted? and why is thy understanding troubled?*"—In a word, I felt benevolence for her, and resolved, some way or other, to throw in my mite of courtesy,—if not of service.

Such were my temptations;—and in this disposition to give way to them, was I left alone with the lady, with her hand in mine, and with our faces both turned closer to the door of the remise than what was absolutely necessary.

THE REMISE DOOR.

CALAIS.

THIS certainly, fair lady, said I, raising her hand up a little lightly as I began, must be one of Fortune's whimsical doings; to take two utter strangers by their hands,—of different sexes, and, perhaps, from different corners of the globe, and in one moment place them together in such a cordial situation as Friendship herself could scarce have achieved for them, had she projected it for a month.

—And your reflection upon it shows how much, Monsieur, she has embarrassed you by the adventure.

When the situation is what we would wish, nothing

D

is so ill-timed as to hint at the circumstances which make it so.——You thank Fortune, continued she;—you had reason,—the heart knew it, and was satisfied; and who but an English philosopher would have sent notice of it to the brain to reverse the judgment?

In saying this, she disengaged her hand, with a look which I thought a sufficient commentary upon the text.

It is a miserable picture which I am going to give of the weakness of my heart, by owning that it suffered a pain, which worthier occasions could not have inflicted.—I was mortified with the loss of her hand; and the manner in which I had lost it carried neither oil nor wine to the wound: I never felt the pain of a peevish inferiority so miserably in my life.

The triumphs of a true feminine heart are short upon these discomfitures. In a very few seconds she laid her hand upon the cuff of my coat, in order to finish her reply; so, some way or other, God knows how, I regained my situation.

——She had nothing to add.

I forthwith began to model a different conversation for the lady, thinking, from the spirit as well as moral of this, that I had been mistaken in her character; but, upon turning her face towards me, the spirit which had animated the reply was fled,—the muscles relaxed, and I saw the same unprotected look of distress which first won me to her interest:—melancholy! to see such sprightliness the prey of sorrow,—I pitied her from my soul; and though it may seem ridiculous enough to a torpid heart,—I could have taken her into my arms, and cherished her, though it was in the open street, without blushing.

The pulsations of the arteries along my fingers pressing across hers, told her what was passing within me. She looked down:—a silence of some moments followed.

I fear, in this interval, I must have made some slight efforts towards a closer compression of her hand, from a subtle sensation I felt in the palm of my own,—not as if she was going to withdraw hers,—but as if she thought about it;—and I had infallibly lost it a second time, had not instinct, more than reason, directed me to the last resource in these dangers,—to hold it loosely, and in a manner as if I was every moment going to release it of myself: so she let it continue till Mons. Dessein returned with the key; and, in the meantime, I set myself to consider how I should undo the ill impressions which the poor monk's story, in case he had told it her, must have planted in her breast against me.

THE SNUFF-BOX.

CALAIS.

THE good old monk was within six paces of us as the idea of him crossed my mind; and was advancing towards us a little out of the line, as if uncertain whether he should break in upon us or no.—He stopped, however, as soon as he came up to us, with a world of frankness, and, having a horn snuff-box in his hand, he presented it open to me.——You shall taste mine, said I, pulling out my box (which was a small tortoise one), and putting it into his hand.———'Tis most excellent, said the monk.———Then do me the favour, I replied, to accept of the box and all; and when you take a pinch out of it, sometimes recollect it was the peace-offering of a man who once used you unkindly, but not from his heart.

The poor monk blushed as red as scarlet. *Mon Dieu!* said he, pressing his hands together, you never used me unkindly.———I should think, said the lady, he is not likely.———I blushed in my turn; but from what movements, I leave to the few who feel, to analyse.——— Excuse me, madam, replied I,—I treated him most unkindly; and from no provocations.———'Tis impossible, said the lady.———My God! cried the monk, with a warmth of asseveration which seemed not to belong to him,—the fault was in me, and in the indiscretion of my zeal.———The lady opposed it; and I joined with her,—in maintaining it was impossible that a spirit so regulated as his could give offence to any.

I knew not that contention could be rendered so sweet and pleasurable a thing to the nerves as I then felt it. We remained silent, without any sensation of that foolish pain which takes place, when, in such a circle, you look for ten minutes in one another's faces without saying a word. Whilst this lasted, the monk rubbed his horn box upon the sleeve of his tunic; and as soon as it had acquired a little air of brightness by the friction, he made a low bow, and said, 'Twas too late to say whether it was the weakness or goodness of our tempers which had involved us in this contest;—

CALAIS

but, be it as it would,—he begged we might exchange boxes.—In saying this, he presented his to me with one hand, as he took mine from me in the other; and having kissed it,—with a stream of good nature in his eyes, he put it into his bosom,—and took his leave.

I guard this box as I would the instrumental parts of my religion, to help my mind on to something better. In truth, I seldom go abroad without it; and oft and many a time have I called up by it the courteous spirit of its owner to regulate my own, in the jostlings of the world; they had found full employment for his, as I learnt from his story, till about the forty-fifth year of his age, when upon some military services ill requited, and meeting at the same time with a disappointment in the tenderest of passions, he abandoned the sword and the sex together, and took sanctuary, not so much in his convent as in himself.

I feel a damp upon my spirits as I am going to add, that in my last return through Calais, upon inquiring after Father Lorenzo, I heard he had been dead near three months; and was buried, not in his convent, but, according to his desire, in a little cemetery belonging to it, about two leagues off. I had a strong desire to see where they had laid him,—when, upon pulling out his little horn box, as I sat by his grave, and plucking up a nettle or two at the head of it, which had no business to grow there, they all struck together so forcibly upon my affections, that I burst into a flood of tears;—but I am as weak as a woman; and I beg the world not to smile, but pity me.

THE REMISE DOOR.

CALAIS.

I HAD never quitted the lady's hand all this time; and had held it so long, that it would have been indecent to have let it go, without first pressing it to my lips: the blood and spirits, which had suffered a revulsion from her, crowded back to her as I did it.

Now the two travellers, who had spoke to me in the coach-yard, happened at that crisis to be passing by, and observing our communications, naturally took it into their heads that we must be *man and wife* at least; so stopping as soon as they came up to the door of the remise, the one of them, who was the Inquisitive Traveller, asked us, if we set out for Paris the next morning?——I could only answer for myself, I said; —and the lady added she was for Amiens.——We dined there yesterday, said the Simple Traveller.—— You go directly through the town, added the other, in your road to Paris.——I was going to return a thousand thanks for the intelligence, *that Amiens was in the road to Paris*; but, upon pulling out my poor monk's little horn box to take a pinch of snuff, I made them a quiet bow, and wished them a good passage to Dover.—They left us alone.

—Now where would be the harm, said I to myself, if I was to beg of this distressed lady to accept of half of my chaise?—and what mighty mischief could ensue?

Every dirty passion and bad propensity in my nature took the alarm as I stated the proposition:—It will oblige you to have a third horse, said *Avarice*, which will put twenty livres out of your pocket.—You know not what she is, said *Caution;* or what scrapes the affair may draw you into, whispered *Cowardice.*

—Depend upon it, Yorick, said *Discretion,* 'twill be said you went off with a mistress; and came, by assignation, to Calais for that purpose.

—You can never after, cried *Hypocrisy,* aloud, show your face in the world;—nor rise, quoth *Meanness,* in the church;—nor be anything in it, said *Pride,* but a lousy prebendary.

But 'tis a civil thing, said I;—and as I generally act from the first impulse, and therefore seldom listen to these cabals, which serve no purpose that I know of, but to encompass the heart with adamant,—I turned instantly about to the lady.

But she had glided off unperceived, as the cause was pleading, and had made ten or a dozen paces down the street by the time I had made the determination; so I set off after her with a long stride, to make her the proposal with the best address I was master of; but observing she walked with her cheek half resting upon the palm of her hand,—with the slow, short-measured step of thoughtfulness, and with her eyes, as she went step by step, fixed upon the ground, it struck me she was trying the same cause herself.—God help her! said I, she has some mother-in-law, or tartufish aunt, or nonsensical old woman, to consult upon the occasion, as well as myself: so not caring to interrupt the process, and deeming it more gallant to take her at discretion than surprise, I faced about, and took a short turn or two before the door of the remise, whilst she walked musing on one side.

IN THE STREET.

CALAIS.

Having, on first sight of the lady, settled the affair in my fancy, "that she was of the better order of beings;"—and then laid it down as a second axiom, as indisputable as the first, That she was a widow, and wore a character of distress,—I went no further; I got ground enough for the situation which pleased me;—and had she remained close beside my elbow till midnight, I should have held true to my system, and considered her only under the general idea.

She had scarce got twenty paces distant from me, ere something within me called out for a more particular inquiry; it brought on the idea of a further separation:—I might possibly never see her more:—the heart is for saving what it can; and I wanted the traces through which my wishes might find their way to her, in case I should never rejoin her myself. In a word, I wished to know her name,—her family,—her condition;—and as I knew the place to which she was going, I wanted to know from whence she came; but there was no coming at all this intelligence: a hundred little delicacies stood in the way. I formed a score different plans.—There was no such thing as a man's asking her directly;—the thing was impossible.

A little French *debonnaire* captain, who came dancing down the street, showed me it was the easiest thing in the world;—for, popping in betwixt us, just as the lady was returning back to the door of the remise, he introduced himself to my acquaintance, and before he had well got announced, begged I would do him the honour to present him to the lady.—I had not been presented myself;—so turning about to her, he did it just as well, by asking her if she had come from Paris?——No; she was going that route, she said.——*Vous n'êtes pas de Londres?*——She was not, she replied.——Then Madame must have come through Flanders. *Apparemment vous êtes Flammande?* said the French captain.——The lady answered, she was.——*Peut-être de Lisle?* added he.——She answered, she was not of Lisle.——Nor Arras?—nor Cambray?—nor Ghent? —nor Brussels?——She answered she was of Brussels. ——He had had the honour, he said, to be at the bombardment of it last war;—that it was finely situated, *pour cela*,—and full of noblesse when the Imperialists were driven out by the French (the lady made a slight curtsey);—so giving her an account of the affair, and of the share he had had in it,—he begged the honour to know her name,—so made his bow.

—*Et Madame a son Mari?* said he, looking back when he had made two steps,—and without staying for an answer,—danced down the street.

Had I served seven years apprenticeship to good-breeding, I could not have done as much.

THE REMISE.

CALAIS.

As the little French captain left us, Mons. Dessein came up with the key of the remise in his hand, and forthwith let us into his magazine of chaises.

The first object which caught my eye, as Mons. Dessein opened the door of the remise, was another old tattered *desobligeant*; and, notwithstanding it was the exact picture of that which had hit my fancy so much in the coach-yard but an hour before,—the very sight of it stirred up a disagreeable sensation within me now; and I thought 'twas a churlish beast into whose heart the idea could first enter to construct such a machine; nor had I much more charity for the man who could think of using it.

I observed the lady was as little taken with it as myself: so Mons. Dessein led us on to a couple of chaises which stood abreast, telling us, as he recommended them, that they had been purchased by my Lord A. and B. to go the *grand tour*, but had gone no further than Paris; so were, in all respects, as good as new. They were too good;—so I passed on to the third, which stood behind, and forthwith began to chaffer for the price.——But 'twill scarce hold two, said I, opening the door and getting in.——Have the goodness, madam, said Mons. Dessein, offering his arm, to step in.——The lady hesitated half a second, and stepped in; and the waiter that moment beckoning to speak to Mons. Dessein, he shut the door of the chaise upon us, and left us.

THE REMISE DOOR.

CALAIS.

C'EST *bien comique*, 'tis very droll, said the lady, smiling, from the reflection that this was the second time we had been left together by a parcel of nonsensical contingencies,—*c'est bien comique,* said she.

———There wants nothing, said I, to make it so, but the comic use which the gallantry of a Frenchman would put it to,—to make love the first moment,—and an offer of his person the second.

———'Tis their *fort,* replied the lady.

———It is supposed so at least;—and how it has come to pass, continued I, I know not; but they have certainly got the credit of understanding more of love, and making it better than any other nation upon earth; but, for my own part, I think them arrant bunglers; and, in truth, the worst set of marksmen that ever tried Cupid's patience.

—To think of making love by *sentiments!*

I should as soon think of making a genteel suit of clothes out of remnants;—and to do it,—pop,—at first sight by declaration,—is submitting the offer and themselves with it, to be sifted with all their *pours* and *contres,* by an unheated mind.

The lady attended as if she expected I should go on.

—Consider then, madam, continued I, laying my hand upon hers,—

That grave people hate Love for the name's sake,—

That selfish people hate it for their own,—

Hypocrites for Heaven's,—

And that all of us, both old and young, being ten times worse frightened than hurt by the very *report,*———

What a want of knowledge in this branch of commerce a man betrays, whoever lets the word come out of his lips till an hour or two at least after the time that his silence upon it becomes tormenting! A course of small, quiet attentions, not so pointed as to alarm, nor so vague as to be misunderstood,—with now and then a look of kindness, and little or nothing said upon it,—leaves Nature for your mistress, and she fashions it to her mind.

—Then I solemnly declare, said the lady, blushing, you have been making love to me all this while.

THE REMISE.

CALAIS.

Monsieur Dessein came back to let us out of the chaise, and acquaint the lady that Count de L——, her brother, was just arrived at the hotel. Though I had infinite good-will for the lady, I cannot say that I rejoiced in my heart at the event,—and could not help telling her so;—for it is fatal to a proposal, madam, said I, that I was going to make you.

——You need not tell me what the proposal was, said she, laying her hand upon both mine, as she interrupted me.—A man, my good sir, has seldom an offer of kindness to make to a woman, but she has a presentiment of it some moments before.

——Nature arms her with it, said I, for immediate preservation.——But I think, said she, looking in my face, I had no evil to apprehend;—and to deal frankly with you, had determined to accept it.——If I had—(she stopped a moment)—I believe your good-will would have drawn a story from me, which would have made pity the only dangerous thing in the journey.

In saying this, she suffered me to kiss her hand twice; and, with a look of sensibility mixed with concern, she got out of the chaise,—and bid adieu.

IN THE STREET.

CALAIS.

I NEVER finished a twelve-guinea bargain so expeditiously in my life. My time seemed heavy upon the loss of the lady; and knowing every moment of it would be as two, till I put myself into motion,—I ordered post-horses directly, and walked towards the hotel.

Lord! said I, hearing the town-clock strike four, and recollecting that I had been little more than a single hour in Calais,—

What a large volume of adventures may be grasped within this little span of life, by him who interests his heart in everything, and who, having eyes to see what time and chance are perpetually holding out to him as he journeyeth on his way, misses nothing he can *fairly* lay his hands on!

—If this won't turn out something,—another will; —no matter,—'tis an essay upon human nature;—I get my labour for my pains,—'tis enough;—the pleasure of the experiment has kept my senses and the best part of my blood awake, and laid the gross to sleep.

I pity the man who can travel from Dan to Beersheba, and cry, 'Tis all barren;—and so it is: and so is all the world to him who will not cultivate the fruits it offers. I declare, said I, clapping my hands cheerily together, that was I in a desert, I would find out wherewith in it to call forth my affections:—if I could not do better, I would fasten them upon some sweet myrtle, or seek some melancholy cypress to connect myself to;—I would court their shade, and greet them kindly for their protection;—I would cut my name upon them, and swear they were the loveliest trees throughout the desert; if their leaves withered, I would teach myself to mourn:—and when they rejoiced, I would rejoice along with them.

The learned Smelfungus travelled from Boulogne to Paris,—from Paris to Rome,—and so on;—but he set out with the spleen and jaundice; and every object he passed by was discoloured or distorted.—He wrote an account of them; but 'twas nothing but the account of his miserable feelings.

I met Smelfungus in the grand portico of the Pantheon:—he was just coming out of it.——*'Tis nothing but a huge cock-pit,** said he.——I wish you had said nothing worse of the Venus of Medicis, replied I;—for in passing through Florence, I had heard he had fallen foul upon the goddess, and used her worse than a common strumpet, without the least provocation in nature.

I popped upon Smelfungus again at Turin, in his return home; and a sad tale of sorrowful adventures he had to tell, wherein he spoke of " moving accidents by flood and field, and of the cannibals who each other

---

* Vide S——'s Travels.

eat: the Anthropophagi."—He had been flayed alive, and bedeviled, and used worse than St. Bartholomew, at every stage he had come at.

I'll tell it, cried Smelfungus, to the world.——You had better tell it, said I, to your physician.

Mundungus, with an immense fortune, made the whole tour; going on from Rome to Naples,—from Naples to Venice,—from Venice to Vienna,—to Dresden, to Berlin, without one generous connection or pleasurable anecdote to tell of; but he had travelled straight on, looking neither to his right hand nor his left, lest Love or Pity should seduce him out of his road.

Peace be to them, if it is to be found; but Heaven itself, was it possible to get there with such tempers, would want objects to give it;—every gentle spirit would come flying upon the wings of Love to hail their arrival.—Nothing would the souls of Smelfungus and Mundungus hear of, but fresh anthems of joy, fresh raptures of love, fresh congratulations of their common felicity.—I heartily pity them: they have brought up no faculties for this work; and was the happiest mansion in Heaven to be allotted to Smelfungus and Mundungus, they would be so far from being happy, that the souls of Smelfungus and Mundungus would do penance there to all eternity.

MONTREUIL.

I HAD once lost my portmanteau from behind my chaise, and twice got out in the rain, and one of the times up to the knees in dirt, to help the postilion to tie it on, without being able to find out what was wanting.—Nor was it till I got to Montreuil, upon the landlord's asking me if I wanted not a servant, that it occurred to me that *that* was the very thing.

A servant! that I do, most sadly, quoth I.—— Because, Monsieur, said the landlord, there is a clever young fellow, who would be very proud of the honour to serve an Englishman.——But why an English one more than any other?——They are so generous, said the landlord.——I'll be shot if this is not a livre out of my pocket, quoth I to myself, this very night.—— But they have wherewithal to be so, Monsieur, added he.——Set down one livre more for that, quoth I.—— It was but last night, said the landlord, *qu'un my Lord Anglois presentoit un ecu à la fille de chambre.*—— *Tant pis, pour Mademoiselle Janatone*, said I.

Now Janatone being the landlord's daughter, and the landlord supposing I was young in French, took the liberty to inform me, I should not have said *tant pis*—but *tant mieux*. *Tant mieux, toujours, Monsieur*, said he, when there is anything to be got;—*tant pis*, when there is nothing.——It comes to the same thing, said I.——*Pardonnez moi*, said the landlord.

I cannot take a fitter opportunity to observe, once for all, that *tant pis* and *tant mieux* being two of the great hinges in French conversation, a stranger would do well to set himself right in the use of them, before he gets to Paris.

A prompt French marquis at our ambassador's table, demanded of Mr. H—— if he was H—— the poet.

——No, said Mr. H——, mildly.——*Tant pis*, replied the marquis.

—It is H—— the historian, said another.——*Tant mieux*, said the marquis.——And Mr. H——, who is a man of an excellent heart, returned thanks for both.

When the landlord had set me right in this matter, he called in La Fleur, which was the name of the young man he had spoke of,—saying only first, That as for his talents he would presume to say nothing—Monsieur was the best judge what would suit him; but for the fidelity of La Fleur, he would stand responsible in all he was worth.

The landlord delivered this in a manner which instantly set my mind to the business I was upon;—and La Fleur, who stood waiting without, in that breathless expectation which every son of Nature of us have felt in our turns, came in.

MONTREUIL.

I AM apt to be taken with all kinds of people at first sight; but never more so than when a poor devil comes to offer his service to so poor a devil as myself; and as I know this weakness, I always suffer my judgment to draw back something on that very account,—and this more or less, according to the mood I am in, and the case;—and, I may add, the gender too of the person I am to govern.

When La Fleur entered the room, after every discount I could make for my soul, the genuine look and air of the fellow determined the matter at once in his favour; so I hired him first,—and then began to inquire what he could do.—But I shall find out his talents, quoth I, as I want them;—besides, a Frenchman can do everything.

Now poor La Fleur could do nothing in the world but beat a drum, and play a march or two upon the fife. I was determined to make his talents do: and can't say my weakness was ever so insulted by my wisdom, as in the attempt.

La Fleur had set out early in life, as gallantly as most Frenchmen do, with *serving* for a few years: at the end of which, having satisfied the sentiment, and found, moreover, that the honour of beating a drum was likely to be its own reward, as it opened no further track of glory to him,—he retired *à ses terres*, and lived *comme il plaisoit à Dieu;*—that is to say, upon nothing.

———And so, quoth Wisdom, you have hired a drummer to attend you in this tour of yours through France and Italy!———Psha! said I, and do not one half of our gentry go with a humdrum *compagnon du voyage* the same round, and have the piper and the Devil and all to pay besides? When man can extricate himself with an *equivoque* in such an unequal match,—he is not ill off.———But you can do something else, La Fleur? said I.———*O qu'oui!* he could make spatterdashes and play a little on the fiddle.———Bravo! said Wisdom.———Why I play a bass myself, said I;—we shall do very well. You can shave and dress a wig a little, La Fleur?———He had all the dispositions in the world.———It is enough for Heaven, said I, interrupting him,—and ought to be enough for me.—So supper coming in, and having a frisky English spaniel on one side of my chair, and a

French valet, with as much hilarity in his countenance as ever Nature painted in one, on the other,—I was satisfied to my heart's content with my empire; and if monarchs knew what they would be at, they might be as satisfied as I was.

MONTREUIL.

As La Fleur went the whole tour of France and Italy with me, and will be often upon the stage, I must interest the reader a little further in his behalf, by saying that I had never less reason to repent of the impulses which generally do determine me, than in regard to this fellow;—he was a faithful, affectionate, simple soul as ever trudged after the heels of a philosopher; and notwithstanding his talents of drum-beating and spatterdash-making, which, though very good in themselves, happened to be of no great service to me, yet was I hourly recompensed by the festivity of his temper;—it supplied all defects:—I had a constant resource in his looks in all difficulties and distresses of my own—(I was going to have added, of his too); but La Fleur was out of the reach of everything; for whether it was hunger or thirst, or cold or nakedness, or watchings, or whatever stripes of ill luck La Fleur met with in our journeyings, there was no index in his physiognomy to point them out by,—he was eternally the same; so that if I am a piece of a philosopher, which Satan now and then puts it into my head I am,—it always mortifies the pride of the conceit, by reflecting how much I owe to the complexional philosophy of this poor fellow, for shaming me into one of a better kind. With all this, La Fleur had a small cast of the coxcomb;—but he seemed at first sight to be more a coxcomb of nature than of art; and before I had been three days in Paris with him,—he seemed to be no coxcomb at all.

MONTREUIL.

THE next morning, La Fleur entering upon his employment, I delivered to him the key of my portmanteau, with an inventory of my half a dozen shirts and a silk pair of breeches: and bid him fasten all upon the chaise,—get the horses put to,—and desire the landlord to come in with his bill.

——*C'est un garçon de bonne fortune*, said the landlord, pointing through the window to half a dozen wenches who had got round about La Fleur, and were most kindly taking their leave of him, as the postilion was leading out the horses. La Fleur kissed all their hands round and round again, and thrice he wiped his eyes, and thrice he promised he would bring them all pardons from Rome.

—The young fellow, said the landlord, is beloved by all the town; and there is scarce a corner in Montreuil where the want of him will not be felt. He has but one misfortune in the world, continued he, " He is always in love."——I am heartily glad of it, said I; 'twill save me the trouble every night of putting my breeches under my head.—In saying this, I was making not so much La Fleur's eloge as my own, having been in love with one princess or other almost all my life, and I hope I shall go on so till I die, being firmly persuaded, that if ever I do a mean action, it must be in some interval betwixt one passion and another: whilst this interregnum lasts, I always perceive my heart locked up,—I can scarce find in it to give misery a sixpence: and therefore I always get out of it as fast as I can; and the moment I am rekindled, I am all generosity and good-will again, and would do anything in the world, either for or with any one, if they will but satisfy me there is no sin in it.

—But in saying this,—surely I am commending the passion,—not myself.

A FRAGMENT.

———The town of Abdera, notwithstanding Democritus lived there, trying all the powers of irony and laughter to reclaim it, was the vilest and most profligate town in all Thrace. What for poisons, conspiracies, and assassinations,—libels, pasquinades, and tumults, there was no going there by day;—'twas worse by night.

Now, when things were at the worst, it came to pass, that the Andromeda of Euripides, being represented at Abdera, the whole orchestra was delighted with it; but of all the passages which delighted them, nothing operated more upon their imaginations than the tender strokes of nature which the poet had wrought up in that pathetic speech of Perseus, *O Cupid, prince of Gods and men,* &c. Every man almost spoke pure iambics the next day, and talked of nothing but Perseus his pathetic address,—" O Cupid, prince of Gods and men!" in every street of Abdera, in every house,—"O Cupid! Cupid!"—In every mouth, like the natural notes of some sweet melody which drop from it, whether it will or no,—nothing but "Cupid! Cupid! prince of Gods and men!"—The fire caught, —and the whole city, like the heart of one man, opened itself to Love.

No pharmacopolist could sell one grain of hellebore, —not a single armourer had a heart to forge one instrument of death;—Friendship and Virtue met together, and kissed each other in the street;—the golden age returned, and hung over the town of Abdera;—every Abderite took his oaten pipe; and every Abderitish woman left her purple web, and chastely sat her down, and listened to the song.

——'Twas only in the power, says the Fragment, of the God whose empire extendeth from heaven to earth, and even to the depths of the sea, to have done this.

MONTREUIL.

WHEN all is ready, and every article is disputed and paid for at the inn, unless you are a little soured by the adventure, there is always a matter to compound at the door, before you can get into your chaise, and that is, with the sons and daughters of poverty, who surround you. Let no man say, "Let them go to the Devil!"—'tis a cruel journey to send a few miserables; and they have had sufferings enow without it. I always think it better to take a few sous out in my hand; and I would counsel every gentle traveller to do so likewise; he need not be so exact in setting down his motives for giving them—they will be registered elsewhere.

For my own part, there is no man gives so little as I do; for few, that I know, have so little to give: but as this was the first public act of my charity in France, I took the more notice of it.

——A well-a-way! said I;—I have but eight sous in the world, showing them in my hand, and there are eight poor men and eight poor women for 'em.

A poor tattered soul, without a shirt on, instantly withdrew his claim, by retiring two steps out of the circle, and making a disqualifying bow on his part. Had the whole *parterre* cried out, *Place aux dames*, with one voice, it would not have conveyed the sentiment of a deference for the sex with half the effect.

Just Heaven! for what wise reasons hast thou ordered it, that beggary and urbanity, which are at such variance in other countries, should find a way to be at unity in this?

I insisted upon presenting him with a single sous, merely for his *politesse*.

A poor little dwarfish, brisk fellow, who stood over against me in the circle, putting something first under his arm, which had once been a hat, took his snuff-box out of his pocket, and generously offered a pinch on both sides of him: it was a gift of consequence, and modestly declined.—The poor little fellow pressed it upon them with a nod of welcomeness.——*Prenez-en,* —*prenez*, said he, looking another way; so they each took a pinch.——Pity thy box should ever want one, said I to myself; so I put a couple of sous into it,—

taking a small pinch out of his box to enhance their value, as I did it.——He felt the weight of the second obligation more than of the first,—'twas doing him an honour,—the other was only doing him a charity;—and he made me a bow to the ground for it.

——Here! said I to an old soldier with one hand, who had been campaigned and worn out to death in the service,—here's a couple of sous for thee.——*Vive le Roi!* said the old soldier.

I had then but three sous left: so I gave one, simply *pour l'amour de Dieu*, which was the footing on which it was begged.——The poor woman had a dislocated hip; so it could not be well upon any other motive.

Mon cher et très-charitable Monsieur.—— There's no opposing this, said I.

My Lord Anglois;—the very sound was worth the money—so I gave *my last sous for it.*—But, in the eagerness of giving, I had overlooked a *pauvre honteux*, who had no one to ask a sous for him, and who, I believe, would have perished, ere he could have asked one for himself; he stood by the chaise, a little without the circle, and wiped a tear from a face which I thought had seen better days.——Good God! said I, and I have not one single sous left to give him.—— But you have a thousand! cried all the powers of Nature, stirring within me;—so I gave him——no matter what,—I am ashamed to say *how much* now,— and was ashamed to think how little then; so if the reader can form any conjecture of my disposition, as these two fixed points are given him, he may judge within a livre or two what was the precise sum.

I could afford nothing for the rest, but *Dieu vous benisse.*——*Et le bon vous Dieu benisse encore*, said the old soldier, the dwarf, &c. The *pauvre honteux* could say nothing,—he pulled out a little handkerchief, and wiped his face as he turned away;—and I thought he thanked me more than them all.

THE BIDET.

HAVING settled all these little matters, I got into my post-chaise with more ease than ever I got into a post-chaise in my life; and La Fleur having got one large jack-boot on the far side of a little *bidet*,* and another on this (for I count nothing of his legs) he cantered away before me as happy and as perpendicular as a prince.

—But what is happiness! what is grandeur in this painted scene of life!—A dead ass, before we had got a league, put a sudden stop to La Fleur's career;—his bidet would not pass by it,—a contention arose betwixt them, and the poor fellow was kicked out of his jack-boots the very first kick.

La Fleur bore his fall like a French Christian, saying neither more nor less upon it than *Diable!* so presently got up, and came to the charge again astride his bidet, beating him up to it as he would have beat his drum.

The bidet flew from one side of the road to the other, then back again, then this way—then that way, and, in short, every way but by the dead ass:—La Fleur insisted upon the thing,—and the bidet threw him.

* Post-horse.

——What's the matter, La Fleur, said I, with this bidet of thine?——*Monsieur*, said he, *c'est un cheval le plus opiniatre du monde.*——Nay, if he is a conceited beast, he must go his own way, replied I.——So La Fleur got off him, and giving him a good sound lash, the bidet took me at my word, and away he scampered back to Montreuil.——*Peste!* said La Fleur.

It is not *mal-à-propos* to take notice here, that though La Fleur availed himself but of two different terms of exclamation in this encounter,—namely, *Diable!* and *Peste!* that there are, nevertheless, three in the French language, like the positive, comparative, and superlative, one or the other of which serve for every unexpected throw of the dice in life.

Le Diable! which is the first and positive degree, is generally used in ordinary emotions of the mind, where small things only fall out contrary to your expectations,—such as, the throwing one's doublets,—La Fleur's being kicked off his horse, and so forth.—Cuckoldom, for the same reason, is always—*Le Diable!*

But, in cases where the cast has something provoking in it, as in that of the bidet's running away after, and leaving La Fleur aground in jack-boots,—'tis the second degree;

'Tis then *Peste!*

And for the third——

——But here my heart is wrung with pity and fellow-feeling, when I reflect what miseries must have been their lot, and how bitterly so refined a people must have smarted to have forced them upon the use of it.

—Grant me, O ye powers which touch the tongue with eloquence in distress!—whatever is my *cast*, grant me but decent words to exclaim in, and I will give my nature way.

—But as these were not to be had in France, I resolved to take every evil just as it befell me, without any exclamation at all.

La Fleur, who had made no such covenant with himself, followed the bidet with his eyes till it was got out of sight,—and then, you may imagine, if you please, with what word he closed the whole affair.

As there was no hunting down a frightened horse in jack-boots, there remained no alternative but taking La Fleur either behind the chaise or into it.

I preferred the latter, and, in half an hour, we got to the post-house at Nampont.

THE DEAD ASS.

NAMPONT.

——And this, said he, putting the remains of a crust into his wallet,—and this should have been thy portion, said he, hadst thou been alive to have shared it with me.——I thought by the accent, it had been an apostrophe to his child; but 'twas to his ass, and to the very ass we had seen dead in the road, which had occasioned La Fleur's misadventure. The man seemed to lament it much; and it instantly brought into my mind Sancho's lamentation for his; but he did it with more true touches of nature.

The mourner was sitting upon a stone bench at the

door, with the ass's pannel and its bridle on one side, which he took up from time to time,—then laid them down,—looked at them, and shook his head. He then took his crust of bread out of his wallet again, as if to eat it, held it some time in his hand,—then laid it upon the bit of his ass's bridle,—looked wistfully at the little arrangement he had made,—and then gave a sigh.

The simplicity of his grief drew numbers about him, and La Fleur among the rest, whilst the horses were getting ready; as I continued sitting in the post-chaise, I could see and hear over their heads.

——He said he had come last from Spain, where he had been from the furthest borders of Franconia; and had got so far on his return home when his ass died. Every one seemed desirous to know what business could have taken so old and poor a man so far a journey from his own home.

——It had pleased Heaven, he said, to bless him with three sons, the finest lads in all Germany; but having, in one week, lost two of the eldest of them by the small-pox, and the youngest falling ill of the same distemper, he was afraid of being bereft of them all; and made a vow, if Heaven would not take him from him also, he would go, in gratitude, to St. Iago in Spain.

When the mourner got thus far on his story, he stopped to pay Nature her tribute,—and wept bitterly.

He said, Heaven had accepted the conditions, and that he had set out from his cottage with this poor creature, who had been a patient partner of his journey;

—that it had eat the same bread with him all the way, and was unto him as a friend.

Everybody who stood about heard the poor fellow with concern.—La Fleur offered him money.—The mourner said he did not want it; it was not the value of the ass, but the loss of him. The ass, he said, he was assured, loved him;—and, upon this, told them a long story of a mischance upon their passage over the Pyrenean Mountains, which had separated them from each other three days; during which time the ass had sought him as much as he had sought the ass; and that they had scarce either eat or drank till they met.

——Thou hast one comfort, friend, said I, at least, in the loss of thy poor beast,—I am sure thou hast been a merciful master to him.——Alas! said the mourner, I thought so when he was alive;—but now that he is dead, I think otherwise. I fear the weight of myself and my afflictions together, have been too much for him,—they have shortened the poor creature's days, and I fear I have them to answer for.——Shame on the world! said I to myself. Did we but love each other as this poor soul loved his ass,—'twould be something.

THE POSTILION.

NAMPONT.

THE concern which the poor fellow's story threw me into required some attention; the postilion paid not the least to it, but set off upon the *pavé* in a full gallop.

The thirstiest soul in the most sandy desert of Arabia could not have wished more for a cup of cold water than mine did for grave and quiet movements; and I should have had an high opinion of the postilion, had he but stolen off with me in something like a pensive pace.—On the contrary, as the mourner finished his lamentation, the fellow gave an unfeeling lash to each of his beasts, and set off clattering like a thousand devils.

I called to him as loud as I could, for Heaven's sake to go slower:—and the louder I called, the more unmercifully he galloped.——The deuce take him and his galloping too, said I, he'll go on tearing my nerves to pieces till he has worked me into a foolish passion, and then he'll go slow, that I may enjoy the sweets of it.

The postilion managed the point to a miracle: by the time he had got to the foot of a steep hill, about half a league from Nampont,—he had put me out of temper with him,—and then with myself for being so.

My case then required a different treatment; and a good rattling gallop would have been of real service to me.

——Then, prithee, get on,—get on, my good lad, said I.

——The postilion pointed to the hill.——I then tried to return back to the story of the poor German and his ass;—but I had broke the clue,—and could no more get into it again than the postilion could into a trot.

——The deuce go, said I, with it all! Here am I,

sitting as candidly disposed to make the best of the worst, as ever wight was, and all runs counter.

There is one sweet lenitive at least for evils which Nature holds out to us: so I took it kindly at her hands, and fell asleep, and the first word which roused me was Amiens.

―――Bless me! said I, rubbing my eyes,―this is the very town where my poor lady is to come.

AMIENS.

THE words were scarce out of my mouth, when the Count de L――'s post-chaise, with his sister in it, drove hastily by: she had just time to make me a bow of recognition,―and of that particular kind of it which told me she had not yet done with me. She was as good as her look; for, before I quite finished my supper, her brother's servant came into the room with a billet, in which she said she had taken the liberty to charge me with a letter, which I was to present myself to Madame R―― the first morning I had nothing to do at Paris. There was only added, she was sorry, but from what *penchant* she had not considered, that she had been prevented telling me her story,―that she still owed it me; and if my route should ever lay through Brussels, and I had not by then forgot the name of Madame de L――, that Madame de L―― would be glad to discharge her obligation.

―――Then I will meet thee, said I, fair spirit! at Brussels;―'tis only returning from Italy, through Germany to Holland, by the route of Flanders, home; ―'twill scarce be ten posts out of my way; but were it ten thousand! with what a moral delight will it crown my journey, in sharing in the sickening incidents of a tale of misery told to me by such a sufferer! To see her weep, and, though I cannot dry up the fountain of her tears, what an exquisite sensation is there still left, in wiping them away from off the cheeks of the first and fairest of women, as I'm sitting with my handkerchief in my hand in silence the whole night beside her!

There was nothing wrong in the sentiment; and yet I instantly reproached my heart with it in the bitterest and most reprobate of expressions.

It had ever, as I told the reader, been one of the singular blessings of my life, to be almost every hour of it miserably in love with some one: and my last flame happening to be blown out by a whiff of jealousy on the sudden turn of a corner, I had lighted it up afresh at the pure taper of Eliza but about three months before,—swearing, as I did it, that it should last me through the whole journey.—Why should I dissemble the matter? I had sworn to her eternal fidelity;—she had a right to my whole heart;—to divide my affections was to lessen them;—to expose them, was to risk them; where there is risk, there may be loss:—and what wilt thou have, Yorick, to answer to a heart so full of trust and confidence,—so good, so gentle, and unreproaching?

——I will not go to Brussels, replied I, interrupting myself;—but my imagination went on,—I recalled her looks at that crisis of our separation, when neither of us had power to say Adieu! I looked at the picture she had tied in a black riband about my neck,—and blushed as I looked at it.—I would have given the world to have kissed it,—but was ashamed. And shall this tender flower, said I, pressing it between my hands,—shall it be smitten to its very root, and smitten, Yorick! by thee, who hast promised to shelter it in thy breast?

Eternal Fountain of Happiness! said I, kneeling down upon the ground,—be thou my witness,—and every pure spirit which tastes it, be my witness also, that I would not travel to Brussels, unless Eliza went along with me, did the road lead me towards Heaven!

In transports of this kind, the heart, in spite of the understanding, will always say too much.

THE LETTER.

AMIENS.

Fortune had not smiled upon La Fleur; for he had been unsuccessful in his feats of chivalry,—and not one thing had offered to signalize his zeal for my service from the time he had entered into it, which was almost four-and-twenty hours. The poor soul burned with impatience; and the Count de L——'s servant coming with the letter, being the first practicable occasion which offered, La Fleur had laid hold of it, and, in order to do honour to his master, had taken him into a back-parlour in the *auberge*, and treated him with a cup or two of the best wine in Picardy; and the Count de L——'s servant, in return, and not to be behindhand in politeness with La Fleur, had taken him back with him to the Count's hotel. La Fleur's *prevenancy* (for there was a passport in his very looks) soon set every servant in the kitchen at ease with him; and as a Frenchman, whatever be his talents, has no sort of prudery in showing them, La Fleur, in less than five minutes, had pulled out his fife, and, leading off the dance himself with the first note, set the *fille de chambre*, the *maitre d'hotel*, the cook, the scullion, and all the household, dogs and cats, besides an old monkey, a-dancing! I suppose there never was a merrier kitchen since the flood.

Madame de L——, in passing from her brother's apartments to her own, hearing so much jollity below stairs, rung up her *fille de chambre* to ask about it; and hearing it was the English gentleman's servant who had set the whole house merry with his pipe, she ordered him up.

As the poor fellow could not present himself empty, he had loaded himself in going upstairs with a thousand compliments to Madame de L——, on the part of his master,—added a long apocrypha of inquiries after Madame de L——'s health, told her that Monsieur his master was *au desespoire* for her re-establishment from the fatigues of her journey,—and, to close all, that Monsieur had received the letter which Madame had done him the honour——And he has done me the honour, said Madame de L——, interrupting La Fleur, to send a billet in return?

Madame de L—— had said this with such a tone of reliance upon the fact, that La Fleur had not power to disappoint her expectations;—he trembled for my honour,—and, possibly, might not altogether be unconcerned for his own, as a man capable of being attached to a master who could be wanting *en égards vis-à-vis d'une femme;* so that, when Madame de L—— asked La Fleur if he had brought a letter,—— *O qu'oui,* said La Fleur; so laying down his hat upon the ground, and taking hold of the flap of his right side-pocket with his left hand, he began to search for the letter with his right;—then contrariwise;—*Diable!* —then sought every pocket, pocket by pocket, round, not forgetting his fob;—*Peste!*—then La Fleur emptied them upon the floor,—pulled out a dirty cravat,—a handkerchief,—a comb,—a whip-lash,—a night-cap,— then gave a peep into his hat,—*Quelle étourderie!* He had left the letter upon the table in the *auberge;*—he would run for it, and be back with it in three minutes.

I had just finished my supper when La Fleur came in to give me an account of his adventure: he told the whole story simply as it was; and only added, that if Monsieur had forgot (*par hazard*) to answer Madame's letter, the arrangement gave him an opportunity to recover the *faux pas;*—and if not, that things were only as they were.

Now I was not altogether sure of my *etiquette,* whether I ought to have wrote or no; but if I had,— a devil himself could not have been angry; 'twas but the officious zeal of a well-meaning creature for my honour; and however he might have mistook the road, or embarrassed me in so doing,—his heart was in no fault,—I was under no necessity to write;—and, what weighed more than all,—he did not look as if he had done amiss.

—'Tis all very well, La Fleur, said I.——'Twas sufficient. La Fleur flew out of the room like lightning, and returned with pen, ink, and paper, in his hand; and coming up to the table, laid them close before me, with such a delight in his countenance, that I could not help taking up the pen.

I began, and began again; and though I had nothing to say, and that nothing might have been expressed in half a dozen lines, I made half a dozen different beginnings, and could no way please myself.

In short, I was in no mood to write.

La Fleur stepped out and brought a little water in a glass to dilute my ink,—then fetched sand and sealing wax.—It was all one; I wrote, and blotted, and tore off, and burnt, and wrote again.—*Le Diable l'emporte*, said I half to myself,—I cannot write this self-same letter, throwing the pen down despairingly as I said it.

As soon as I had cast down my pen, La Fleur advanced with the most respectful carriage up to the table, and making a thousand apologies for the liberty he was going to take, told me he had a letter in his pocket, wrote by a drummer in his regiment to a corporal's wife, which, he durst say, would suit the occasion.

I had a mind to let the poor fellow have his humour. ——Then prithee, said I, let me see it.

La Fleur instantly pulled out a little dirty pocketbook, crammed full of small letters and billets-doux in a sad condition, and laying it upon the table, and then untying the string which held them all together, run them over, one by one, till he came to the letter in question.—*La voila!* said he, clapping his hands; so unfolding it first, he laid it before me, and retired three steps from the table whilst I read it.

THE LETTER.

MADAME,—Je suis pénétré de la douleur la plus vive, et réduit en même temps au desespoir par ce retour imprevû du Corporal, qui rend notre entrevue de ce soir la chose du monde la plus impossible.

Mais vive la joie! et toute la mienne sera de penser à vous.

L'amour n'est *rien* sans sentiment.

Et le sentiment est encore *moins* sans amour.

On dit qu'on ne doit jamais sa desesperer.

On dit aussi que Monsieur le Corporal monte le garde Mercredi: alors ce sera mon tour.

Chacun à son tour.

En attendant—Vive l'amour! et vive la bagatelle! Je suis, Madame, Avec toutes les sentiments les plus respectueux et les plus tendres, tout à vous,

JAQUES ROQUE.

It was but changing the Corporal into the Count— and saying nothing about mounting guard on Wednesday,—and the letter was neither right nor wrong;—so to gratify the poor fellow, who stood trembling for my honour, his own, and the honour of his letter,—I took the cream gently off it,—and, whipping it up in my own way,—sealed it up, and sent it to Madame de L——; and the next morning we pursued our journey to Paris.

PARIS.

When a man can contest the point by dint of equipage, and carry on all floundering before him with half a dozen lackies and a couple of cooks,—'tis very well in such a place as Paris,—he may drive in at which end of a street he will.

A poor prince, who is weak in cavalry, and whose whole infantry does not exceed a single man, had best quit the field, and signalize himself in the cabinet, if he can get up into it.—I say *up into it*,—for there is no descending perpendicularly amongst 'em with a " *Me voici, mes enfans*,"—here I am,—whatever many may think.

I own, my first sensations, as soon as I was left solitary and alone in my own chamber in the hotel, were far from being so flattering as I had prefigured them. I walked up gravely to the window in my dusty black coat, and looking through the glass, saw all the world in yellow, blue, and green, running at the ring of pleasure.—The old with broken lances, and in helmets which had lost their vizards;—the young, in armour bright, which shone like gold, beplumed with each gay feather of the east,—all—all tilting at it like fascinated knights in tournaments of yore for fame and love.

——Alas, poor Yorick! cried I, what art thou doing here? On the very first onset of all this glittering clatter, thou art reduced to an atom;—seek—seek some winding alley, with a tourniquet at the end of it, where chariot never rolled, nor flambeau shot its rays;—there thou mayest solace thy soul in converse sweet with some kind *grisette* of a barber's wife, and get into such coteries!

——May I perish! if I do, said I, pulling out a letter which I had to present to Madame de R——. —I'll wait upon this lady the very first thing I do. So I called La Fleur to go seek me a barber directly, —and come back and brush my coat.

THE WIG.

PARIS.

WHEN the barber came, he absolutely refused to have anything to do with my wig: 'twas either above or below his art: I had nothing to do but to take one ready made of his own recommendation.

——But I fear, friend, said I, this buckle won't stand.——You may immerge it, replied he, into the ocean, and it will stand——

What a great scale is everything upon in this city! thought I.—The utmost stretch of an English periwig-maker's ideas could have gone no further than to have "dipped it into a pail of water."—What difference! 'tis like time to eternity!

I confess I do hate all cold conceptions as I do the puny ideas which engender them; and am generally so struck with the great works of Nature, that, for my own part, if I could help it, I never would make a comparison less than a mountain at least. All that can be said against the French sublime in this instance of it is this:—That the grandeur is *more* in the *word*, and *less* in the *thing*. No doubt the ocean fills the mind with vast ideas; but Paris being so far inland, it was not likely I should run post a hundred miles out of it to try the experiment:—the Parisian barber meant nothing.

The pail of water standing beside the great deep, makes certainly but a sorry figure in speech;—but 'twill be said,—it has one advantage—'tis in the next room, and the truth of the buckle may be tried in it, without more ado, in a single moment.

In honest truth, and upon a more candid revision of the matter, *The French expression professes more than it performs.*

I think I can see the precise and distinguishing marks of national characters more in these nonsensical *minutiæ*, than in the most important matters of state; where great men of all nations talk and talk so much alike, that I would not give ninepence to choose among them.

I was so long in getting from under my barber's hands, that it was too late to think of going with my letter to Madame R—— that night: but, when a man is once dressed at all points for going out, his reflections turn to little account; so taking down the name of the Hotel de Modene, where I lodged, I walked forth, without any determination where to go;—I shall consider of that, said I, as I walk along.

THE PULSE.

PARIS.

HAIL, ye small sweet courtesies of life, for smooth do ye make the road of it! like grace and beauty, which beget inclinations to love at first sight: 'tis ye who open this door, and let the stranger in.

——Pray, Madame, said I, have the goodness to tell me which way I must turn to go to the *Opera Comique*.

——Most willingly, Monsieur, said she, laying aside her work.

I had given a cast with my eye into half a dozen shops as I came along, in search of a face not likely to be disordered by such an interruption; till, at last, this hitting my fancy, I had walked in.

She was working a pair of ruffles as she sat in a low chair on the far side of the shop facing the door.

——*Très volontiers;* most willingly, said she, laying her work down upon a chair next her, and rising up from the low chair she was sitting in, with so cheerful a movement and so cheerful a look, that, had I been laying out fifty Louis d'ors with her, I should have said—" This woman is grateful."

You must turn, Monsieur, said she, going with me to the door of the shop, and pointing the way down the street I was to take,—you must turn first to your left hand,—*mais prenez garde,*—there are two turns; and be so good as to take the second,—then go down a little way, and you'll see a church, and when you are past it, give yourself the trouble to turn directly to the right, and that will lead you to the foot of the *Pont Neuf*, which you must cross—and there any one will do himself the pleasure to show you.

She repeated her instructions three times over to me, with the same good-natured patience the third time as the first;—and if *tones and manners* have a meaning, which certainly they have, unless to hearts which shut them out,—she seemed really interested that I should not lose myself.

I will not suppose it was the woman's beauty, notwithstanding she was the handsomest *grisette*, I think, I ever saw, which had much to do with the sense I had of her courtesy; only I remember, when I told her how much I was obliged to her, that I looked very full in her eyes,—and that I repeated my thanks as often as she had done her instructions.

I had not got ten paces from the door, before I found I had forgot every tittle of what she had said:—so looking back, and seeing her still standing in the door of the shop, as if to look whether I went right or not, —I returned back, to ask her whether the first turn was to my right or left, for that I had absolutely forgot. ——Is it possible? said she, half laughing. 'Tis very possible, replied I, when a man is thinking more of a woman than of her good advice.

As this was the real truth, she took it, as every woman takes a matter of right, with a slight curtesy.

——*Attendez*, said she, laying her hand upon my arm to detain me, whilst she called a lad out of the back shop to get ready a parcel of gloves. I am just going to send him, said she, with a packet into that quarter; and if you will have the complaisance to step in, it will be ready in a moment, and he shall attend you to the place. So I walked in with her to the far side of the shop; and taking up the ruffle in my hand which she laid upon the chair, as if I had a mind to sit, she sat down herself in her low chair, and I instantly sat myself down beside her.

He will be ready, Monsieur, said she, in a moment. ——And in that moment, replied I, most willingly would I say something very civil to you for all these courtesies. Any one may do a casual act of good nature, but a continuation of them shows it is a part of the temperature; and, certainly, added I, if it is the same blood which comes from the heart, which descends to the extremes (touching her wrist) I am sure you must have one of the best pulses of any woman in the world. Feel it, said she, holding out her arm. So laying down my hat, I took hold of her fingers in one hand, and applied the two forefingers of my other to the artery.

Would to Heaven! my dear Eugenius, thou hadst passed by, and beheld me sitting in my black coat, and in my lackadaisical manner, counting the throbs of it, one by one, with as much true devotion as if I had been watching the critical ebb or flow of her fever! How wouldst thou have laughed and moralized upon my new profession!—and thou shouldst have laughed and moralized on.—Trust me, my dear Eugenius, I should have said, "there are worse occupations in this world *than feeling a woman's pulse.*"—But a *grisette's!*

thou wouldst have said,—and in an open shop, Yorick!

—So much the better: for when my views are direct, Eugenius, I care not if all the world saw me feel it.

THE HUSBAND.

PARIS.

I HAD counted twenty pulsations, and was going on fast towards the fortieth, when her husband coming unexpected from a back-parlour into the shop, put me a little out in my reckoning.——'Twas nobody but her husband, she said—so I began a fresh score.— Monsieur is so good, quoth she, as he passed by us, as to give himself the trouble of feeling my pulse.—— The husband took off his hat, and making me a bow, said, I did him too much honour; and having said that, he put on his hat and walked out.

Good God! said I to myself, as he went out,—and can this man be the husband of this woman?

Let it not torment the few who know what must have been the grounds of this exclamation, if I explain it to those who do not.

In London, a shopkeeper and a shopkeeper's wife seem to be one bone and one flesh. In the several endowments of mind and body, sometimes the one, sometimes the other has it, so as in general to be upon a par, and to tally with each other as nearly as man and wife need to do.

In Paris, there are scarce two orders of beings more different; for the legislative and executive powers of

THE HUSBAND

the shop not resting in the husband, he seldom comes there:—in some dark and dismal room behind he sits commerceless in his thrum night-cap, the same rough son of Nature that Nature left him.

The genius of a people, where nothing but the monarchy is salique, having ceded this department, with sundry others, totally to the women—by a continual higgling with customers of all ranks and sizes from morning to night, like so many rough pebbles shook long together in a bag, by amicable collisions, they have worn down their asperities and sharp angles, and not only become round and smooth, but will receive, some of them, a polish like a brilliant—Monsieur *le Mari* is little better than the stone under your foot——

—Surely,—surely, man! it is not good for thee to sit alone; thou wast made for social intercourse and gentle greetings; and this improvement of our natures from it, I appeal to, as my evidence.

—And how does it beat, Monsieur? said she.—— With all the benignity, said I, looking quietly in her eyes, that I expected.——She was going to say something civil in return, but the lad came into the shop with the gloves.—*Apropos*, said I, I want a couple of pairs myself.

THE GLOVES.

PARIS.

THE beautiful *grisette* rose up when I said this, and, going behind the counter, reached down a parcel, and untied it: I advanced to the side over-against her:

they were all too large. The beautiful *grisette* measured them one by one across my hand.—It would not alter the dimensions.—She begged I would try a single pair, which seemed to be the least.—She held it open; —my hand slipped into it at once.—It will not do, said I, shaking my head a little.—No, said she, doing the same thing.

There are certain combined looks of simple subtlety, —where whim, and sense, and seriousness, and nonsense, are so blended, that all the languages of Babel set loose together, could not express them:—they are communicated and caught so instantaneously, that you can scarce say which party is the infector. I leave it to your men of words to swell pages about it, —it is enough in the present to say again, the gloves would not do; so folding our hands within our arms, we both lolled upon the counter;—it was narrow, and there was just room for the parcel to lay between us.

The beautiful *grisette* looked sometimes at the gloves, then sideways to the window, then at the gloves,—and then at me. I was not disposed to break silence;—I followed her example: so I looked at the gloves, then to the window, then at the gloves, and then at her— and so on alternately.

I found I lost considerably in every attack:—she had a quick black eye, and shot through two such long and silken eyelashes with such penetration, that she looked into my very heart and veins.—It may seem strange; but I could actually feel she did.

It is no matter, said I, taking up a couple of the pairs next me, and putting them into my pocket.

I was sensible the beautiful *grisette* had not asked a single livre above the price. I wished she had asked a livre more; and was puzzling my brains how to bring the matter about.—Do you think, my dear sir, said she, mistaking my embarrassment, that I could ask a sous too much of a stranger—and of a stranger whose politeness, more than his want of gloves, has done me the honour to lay himself at my mercy?—*M'encroyez capable?*—Faith! not I, said I; and if you were, you are welcome. So counting the money into her hand, and with a lower bow than one generally makes to a shopkeeper's wife, I went out; and her lad with his parcel followed me.

THE TRANSLATION.

PARIS.

THERE was nobody in the box I was let into, but a kindly old French officer. I love the character, not only because I honour the man whose manners are softened by a profession which makes bad men worse, but that I once knew one,—for he is no more,—and why should I not rescue one page from violation by writing his name in it, and telling the world it was Captain Tobias Shandy, the dearest of my flock and friends, whose philanthropy I never think of at this long distance from his death, but my eyes gush out with tears. For his sake, I have a predilection for the whole corps of veterans; and so I strode over the two back rows of benches, and placed myself beside him.

The old officer was reading attentively a small pamphlet (it might be the book of the opera) with a large pair of spectacles. As soon as I sat down, he took his spectacles off, and putting them into a shagreen case, returned them and the book into his pocket together. I half rose up, and made him a bow.

Translate this into any civilized language in the world, the sense is this:—

"Here's a poor stranger come into the box; he seems as if he knew nobody; and is never likely, was he to be seven years in Paris if every man he comes near keeps his spectacles upon his nose:—'tis shutting the door of conversation absolutely in his face, and using him worse than a German."

The French officer might as well have said it all aloud: and if he had, I should in course have put the bow I made him into French too, and told him, "I was sensible of his attention, and returned him a thousand thanks for it."

There is not a secret so aiding to the progress of sociality, as to get master of this *short hand*, and to be quick in rendering the several turns of looks and limbs, with all their inflections and delineations, into plain words. For my own part, by long habitude, I do it so mechanically, that when I walk the streets of London, I go translating all the way; and have more than once stood behind the circle, where not three words have been said, and have brought off twenty different dialogues with me, which I could have fairly wrote down and sworn to.

I was going one evening to Martini's concert at Milan, and was just entering the door of the hall, when the Marquisina de F—— was coming out, in a sort of hurry;—she was almost upon me before I saw her: so I gave a spring to one side, to let her pass. She had done the same, and on the same side too: so we ran our heads together: she instantly got to the other side to get out: I was just as unfortunate as she had been; for I had sprung to that side, and opposed her passage again. We both flew together to the other side, and then back,—and so on:—it was ridiculous; we both blushed intolerably; so I did at last the thing I should have done at first;—I stood stock still, and the Marquisina had no more difficulty. I had no power to go into the room till I had made her so much reparation as to wait and follow her with my eye to the end of the passage. She looked back twice, and walked along it rather sideways, as if she would make room for any one coming upstairs to pass her.—No, said I, that's a vile translation: the Marquisina has a right to the best apology I can make her; and that opening is left for me to do it in:—so I ran and begged pardon for the embarrassment I had given her, saying it was my intention to have made her way. She answered she was guided by the same intention towards me;—so we reciprocally thanked each other. She was at the top of the stairs; and seeing no *cicisbeo* near her, I begged to hand her to her coach; so we went down the stairs, stopping at every third step to talk of the concert and the adventure.—Upon my word, madam, said I, when I had handed her in, I made six different efforts to let you go out.—And I made six efforts, replied she, to let you enter.—I wish to Heaven you would make a seventh, said I.—With all my heart, said she, making room—Life is too short to be long about the forms of it;—so I instantly stepped in, and she carried me home with her.——And what became of the concert, St. Cecilia, who, I suppose, was at it, knows more than I.

I will only add, that the connection which arose out of the translation, gave me more pleasure than any one I had the honour to make in Italy.

THE DWARF.

PARIS.

I HAD never heard the remark made by any one in my life, except by one; and who that was, will probably come out in this chapter; so that being pretty much unprepossessed, there must have been grounds for what struck me the moment I cast my eyes over the *parterre*,—and that was, the unaccountable sport of Nature in forming such numbers of dwarfs. No doubt, she sports at certain times in almost every corner of the world; but in Paris, there is no end to her amusements—The goddess seems almost as merry as she is wise.

As I carried my idea out of the *Opera Comique* with me, I measured everybody I saw walking in the streets by it.—Melancholy application! especially where the size was extremely little,—the face extremely dark,—the eyes quick,—the nose long,—the teeth white,—the jaw prominent,—to see so many miserables, by force of accidents, driven out of their own proper class into the very verge of another, which it gives me pain to write down:—every third man a pigmy!—some by ricketty heads and humpbacks;—others by bandy-legs;—a third set arrested by the hand of Nature in the sixth and seventh years of their growth;—a fourth, in their perfect and natural state, like dwarf apple-trees; from the first rudiments and stamina of their existence, never meant to grow higher.

A Medical Traveller might say, 'tis owing to undue bandages;—a Splenetic one, to want of air;—and an Inquisitive Traveller, to fortify the system, may measure the height of their houses,—the narrowness of their streets, and in how few feet square in the sixth and seventh stories such numbers of the *Bourgeoisie* eat and sleep together. But I remember, Mr. Shandy the Elder, who accounted for nothing like anybody else, in speaking one evening of these matters, averred, That children, like other animals, might be increased almost to any size, provided they came right into the world; but the misery was, the citizens of Paris were so cooped up, that they had not actually room enough to get them.—I do not call it getting anything, said he—'tis getting nothing——Nay, continued he, rising in his argument, 'tis getting worse than nothing, when all you have got, after twenty or five-and-twenty years of the tenderest care and most nutritious aliment bestowed upon it, shall not at last be as high as my leg. Now, Mr. Shandy being very short, there could be nothing more said of it.

As this is not a work of reasoning, I leave the solution as I found it, and content myself with the truth only of the remark, which is verified in every lane and bye-lane of Paris. I was walking down that which leads from the Carousal to the Palais Royal, and observing a little boy in some distress at the side of the gutter which ran down the middle of it, I took hold of his hand, and helped him over. Upon turning up his face to look at him after, I perceived he was about forty.——Never mind, said I, some good body will do as much for me when I am ninety.

I feel some little principles within me, which incline me to be merciful towards this poor blighted part of my species, who have neither size nor strength to get on in the world.—I cannot bear to see one of them trod upon; and had scarce got seated beside my old French officer ere the disgust was exercised, by seeing the very thing happen under the box we sat in.

At the end of the orchestra, and betwixt that and the first side-box, there is a small esplanade left, where, when the house is full, numbers of all ranks take sanctuary. Though you stand, as in the *parterre*, you pay the same price as in the orchestra. A poor defenceless being of this order had got thrust, somehow or other, into this luckless place;—the night was hot, and he was surrounded by beings two feet and a half higher than himself. The dwarf suffered inexpressibly on all sides; but the thing which incommoded him most, was a tall, corpulent German, near seven feet high, who stood directly betwixt him and all possibility of his seeing either the stage or the actors. The poor dwarf did all he could to get a peep at what was going forwards, by seeking for some little opening betwixt the German's arm and his body, trying first on one side, then on the other; but the German stood square in the most unaccommodating posture that can be imagined:—the dwarf might as well have been placed at the bottom of the deepest draw-well in Paris; so he civilly reached up his hand to the German's sleeve, and told him his distress.—The German turned his head back, looked down upon him as Goliah did upon David,—and unfeelingly resumed his posture.

I was just then taking a pinch of snuff out of my monk's little horn box.—And how would thy meek and courteous spirit, my dear monk! so tempered to *bear and forbear!*—how sweetly would it have lent an ear to this poor soul's complaint!

The old French officer seeing me lift up my eyes with an emotion, as I made the apostrophe, took the liberty to ask me what was the matter——I told him the story in three words, and added, how inhuman it was.

By this time the dwarf was driven to extremes, and in his first transports, which are generally unreasonable, had told the German he would cut off his long queue with his knife.——The German looked back coolly, and told him he was welcome, if he could reach it.

An injury sharpened by an insult, be it to whom it will, makes every man of sentiment a party: I could have leaped out of the box to have redressed it.—The old French officer did it with much less confusion; for leaning a little over, and nodding to a sentinel, and pointing at the same time with his finger at the distress,—the sentinel made his way to it.—There was no occasion to tell the grievance—the thing told itself;

so thrusting back the German instantly with his musket,—he took the poor dwarf by the hand, and placed him before him.——This is noble! said I, clapping my hands together.——And yet you would not permit this, said the old officer, in England.

——In England, dear sir, said I, *we sit all at our ease.*

The old French officer would have set me at unity with myself, in case I had been at variance,—by saying it was a *bon mot ;*—and as a *bon mot* is always worth something in Paris, he offered me a pinch of snuff.

THE ROSE.

PARIS.

It was now my turn to ask the old French officer, "What was the matter?" for a cry of "*Haussez les mains, Monsieur l'Abbé,*" re-echoed from a dozen different parts of the *parterre,* was as unintelligible to me as my apostrophe to the monk had been to him.

He told me it was some poor Abbé in one of the upper *loges,* who he supposed had got planted *perdu* behind a couple of *grisettes,* in order to see the opera, and that the *parterre* espying him, were insisting upon his holding up both his hands during the representation.——And can it be supposed, said I, that an ecclesiastic would pick the *grisettes'* pockets?—The old French officer smiled, and whispering in my ear, opened a door of knowledge which I had no idea of.

——Good God! said I, turning pale with astonishment,—is it possible, that a people so smit with sentiment should at the same time be so unclean, and so unlike themselves.—*Quelle grossierté!* added I.

——The French officer told me it was an illiberal sarcasm at the church, which had begun in the theatre about the time the Tartuffe was given in it, by Molière: —but, like other remains of Gothic manners, was declining.—Every nation, continued he, have their refinements and *grossiertés*, in which they take the lead, and lose it of one another by turns;—that he had been in most countries, but never in one where he found not some delicacies, which others seemed to want. *Le pour et le contre se trouvant en chaque nation;* there is a balance, said he, of good and bad everywhere; and nothing but the knowing it is so, can emancipate one-half of the world from the prepossession which it holds against the other:—that the advantage of travel, as it regarded the *sçavoir vivre,* was by seeing a great deal both of men and manners; it taught us mutual toleration; and mutual toleration, concluded he, making me a bow, taught us mutual love.

The old French officer delivered this with an air of such candour and good sense, as coincided with my first favourable impressions of his character:—I thought I loved the man; but I fear I mistook the object:—'twas my own way of thinking,—the difference was, I could not have expressed it half so well.

It is alike troublesome to both the rider and his beast,—if the latter goes pricking up his ears, and starting all the way at every object which he never saw before.—I have as little torment of this kind as any creature alive; and yet I honestly confess, that many a thing gave me pain, and that I blushed at many a word the first month,—which I found inconsequent and perfectly innocent the second.

Madame de Rambouliet, after an acquaintance of about six weeks with her, had done me the honour to take me in her coach about two leagues out of town. —Of all women, Madame de Rambouliet is the most correct:—and I never wish to see one of more virtues and purity of heart.—In our return back, Madame de Rambouliet desired me to pull the cord.——I asked her if she wanted anything——*Rien que pour pisser,* said Madame de Rambouliet.

Grieve not, gentle traveller, to let Madame de Rambouliet p—ss on.—And, ye fair mystic nymphs, go each one *pluck your rose,* and scatter them in your path,— for Madame de Rambouliet did no more.—I handed Madame de Rambouliet out of the coach; and had I been the priest of the chaste *Castalia,* I could not have served at her fountain with a more respectful decorum.

THE FILLE DE CHAMBRE.

PARIS.

WHAT the old French officer had delivered upon travelling, bringing Polonius's advice to his son, upon the same subject, into my head,—and that bringing in Hamlet,—and Hamlet the rest of Shakespeare's Works, I stopped at the Quai de Conti, in my return home, to purchase the whole set.

The bookseller said he had not a set in the world. ——*Comment!* said I, taking one up out of a set which lay on the counter betwixt us.———He said, they were sent him only to be got bound; and were to be sent back to Versailles in the morning to the Count de B———.

———And does the Count de B———, said I, read Shakespeare?——— *C'est un Esprit fort*, replied the bookseller.—He loves English books; and what is more to his honour, Monsieur, he loves the English too.———You speak this so civilly, said I, that it is enough to oblige an Englishman to lay out a louis d'or or two at your shop.———The bookseller made a bow, and was going to say something, when a young decent girl, about twenty, who by her air and dress seemed to be *fille de chambre* to some devout woman of fashion, came into the shop and asked for *Les Egarements du Cœur et de l'Esprit*. The bookseller gave her the book directly; she pulled out a little green satin purse, run round with a riband of the same colour, and putting her finger and thumb into it, she took out the money and paid for it. As I had nothing more to stay me in the shop, we both walked out of the door together.

———And what have you to do, my dear, said I, with *The Wanderings of the Heart*, who scarce know yet you have one? nor, 'till Love has first told you it, or some faithless shepherd has made it ache, canst thou ever be sure it is so.——— *Le Dieu m'en garde!* said the girl.———With reason, said I; for it is a good one, 'tis a pity it should be stolen; 'tis a little treasure to thee, and gives a better air to your face, than if it was dressed out with pearls.

The young girl listened with a submissive attention,

holding her satin purse by its riband in her hand all the time.——'Tis a very small one, said I, taking hold of the bottom of it—(she held it towards me)—and there is very little in it, my dear, said I; but be but as good as thou art handsome, and Heaven will fill it. I had a parcel of crowns in my hand to pay for Shakespeare; and as she had let go the purse entirely, I put a single one in; and tying up the riband in a bow knot, returned it to her.

The young girl made me more a humble curtsey than a low one:—'twas one of those quiet, thankful sinkings, where the spirit bows itself down,—the body does no more than tell it. I never gave a girl a crown in my life which gave me half the pleasure.

My advice, my dear, would not have been worth a pin to you, said I, if I had not given this along with it: but now, when you see the crown, you'll remember it;—so don't, my dear, lay it out in ribands.

——Upon my word, sir, said the girl earnestly, I am incapable;—in saying which, as is usual in little bargains of honour, she gave me her hand:—*En verité, Monsieur, je mettrai cet argent apart*, said she.

When a virtuous convention is made betwixt man and woman, it sanctifies their most private walks; so, notwithstanding it was dusky, yet as both our roads lay the same way, we made no scruple of walking along the Quai de Conti together.

She made me a second curtsey in setting off; and before we got twenty yards from the door, as if she had not done enough before, she made a sort of a little stop, to tell me again—she thanked me.

—It was a small tribute, I told her, which I could not avoid paying to virtue, and would not be mistaken in the person I had been rendering it to for the world; but I see innocence, my dear, in your face,—and foul befall the man who ever lays a snare in its way!

The girl seemed affected, some way or other, with what I said;—she gave a low sigh:—I found I was not empowered to inquire at all after it,—so said nothing more till I got to the corner of the Rue de Nevers, where we were to part.

——But, is this the way, my dear, said I, to the Hotel de Modene?——She told me it was;—or that I might go by the Rue de Guenegualt, which was the next turn.——Then I'll go, my dear, by the Rue de Guenegualt, said I, for two reasons: first, I shall please myself; and next, I shall give you the protection of my company as far on your way as I can.——The girl was sensible I was civil,—and said, She wished the Hotel de Modena was in the Rue de St. Pierre.—— You live there? said I.——She told me she was *fille de chambre* to Madame R——.——Good God! said I, 'tis the very lady for whom I have brought a letter from Amiens.——The girl told me that Madame R——, she believed, expected a stranger with a letter, and was impatient to see him.——So I desired the girl to present my compliments to Madame R——, and say I would certainly wait upon her in the morning.

We stood still at the corner of the Rue de Nevers whilst this passed.—We then stopped a moment whilst she disposed of her *Egarements du Cœur*, &c., more commodiously than carrying them in her hand:—they were two volumes; so I held the second for her whilst she put the first into her pocket; and then she held her pocket, and I put in the other after it.

'Tis sweet to feel by what fine-spun threads our affections are drawn together.

We set off afresh; and as she took her third step, the girl put her hand within my arm.——I was just bidding her,—but she did it of herself, with that undeliberating simplicity, which showed it was out of her head that she had never seen me before. For my own part, I felt the conviction of consanguinity so strongly, that I could not help turning half round to look in her face, and see if I could trace out anything in it of a family likeness.—Tut! said I, are we not all relations?

When we arrived at the turning up of the Rue de Gueneguault, I stopped to bid her adieu for good and all: the girl would thank me again for my company and kindness.—She bid me adieu twice;—I repeated it as often; and so cordial was the parting between us, that had it happened anywhere else, I'm not sure but I should have signed it with a kiss of charity, as warm and holy as an apostle.

But in Paris as none kiss each other but the men,—I did what amounted to the same thing,—I bid God bless her!

THE PASSPORT.

PARIS.

WHEN I got home to my hotel, La Fleur told me I had been inquired after by the Lieutenant de Police.

——The deuce take it, said I,—I know the reason. It is time the reader should know it; for in the order of things in which it happened, it was omitted; not that it was out of my head, but, that had I told it then it might have been forgot now;—and now is the time I want it.

I had left London with so much precipitation, that it never entered my mind that we were at war with France; and had reached Dover, and looked through my glass at the hills beyond Boulogne, before the idea presented itself; and with this in its train, that there was no getting there without a passport. Go but to the end of a street, I have a mortal aversion for returning back no wiser than I set out; and as this was one of the greatest efforts I had ever made for knowledge, I could less bear the thoughts of it; so hearing the Count de —— had hired the packet, I begged he would take me in his *suite*. The count had some little knowledge of me, so made little or no difficulty,—only said, his inclination to serve me could reach no farther than Calais, as he was to return by way of Brussels to Paris; however, when I had once passed there, I might get to Paris without interruption; but that in Paris I must make friends and shift for myself.——Let me get to Paris, Monsieur le Count, said I,—and I shall do very well. So I embarked, and never thought more of the matter.

When La Fleur told me the Lieutenant de Police had been inquiring after me,—the thing instantly recurred;—and by the time La Fleur had well told me, the master of the hotel came into my room to tell me the same thing, with this addition to it, that my passport had been particularly asked after: the master of the hotel concluded with saying he hoped I had one. ——Not I, faith! said I.

The master of the hotel retired three steps from me, as from an infected person, as I declared this;—and poor La Fleur advanced three steps towards me, and with that sort of movement which a good soul makes to succour a distressed one: the fellow won my heart by it; and from that single trait I knew his character as perfectly, and could rely upon it as firmly, as if he had served me with fidelity for seven years.

Mon Seigneur! cried the master of the hotel;—but recollecting himself as he made the exclamation, he instantly changed the tone of it—If Monsieur, said he, has not a passport (*apparemment*), in all likelihood he he has friends in Paris who can procure him one.—Not that I know of, quoth I, with an air of indifference. ——Then certes, replied he, you'll be sent to the Bastile, or the Chatelet, *au moins*.——Poo, said I, the King of France is a good-natured soul,—he'll hurt nobody.——*Cela n'empeche pas*, said he,—you will certainly be sent to the Bastile to-morrow morning.——But I've taken your lodgings for a month, answered I; and I'll not quit them a day before the time for all the kings of France in the world.——La Fleur whispered in my ear that nobody could oppose the King of France.

Pardi, said my host, *ces Messieurs Anglois sont des gens tres extraordinaires;*—and having both said and sworn it,—he went out.

THE PASSPORT.

THE HOTEL AT PARIS.

I COULD not find in my heart to torture La Fleur's with a serious look upon the subject of my embarrassment, which was the reason I had treated it so cavalierly; and to show him how light it lay upon my mind, I dropped the subject entirely; and whilst he waited upon me at supper, talked to him with more than usual gaiety about Paris, and of the *Opera Comique.*—La Fleur had been there himself, and had followed me through the streets as far as the bookseller's shop; but seeing me come out with the young *fille de chambre,* and that we walked down the Quai de Conti together, La Fleur deemed it unnecessary to follow me a step further,—so making his own reflections upon it, he took a shorter cut,—and got to the hotel in time to be informed of the affair of the police against my arrival.

As soon as the honest creature had taken away, and gone down to sup himself, I then began to think a little seriously about my situation.

—And here, I know, Eugenius, thou wilt smile at the remembrance of a short dialogue which passed betwixt us the moment I was going to set out:—I must tell it here.

Eugenius, knowing that I was as little subject to be overburdened with money as thought, had drawn me aside to interrogate me how much I had taken care for. Upon telling him the exact sum, Eugenius shook his head, and said it would not do; so pulled out his purse, in order to empty it into mine.——I've enough, in conscience, Eugenius, said I.——Indeed, Yorick, you have not, replied Eugenius;—I know France and Italy better than you.——But you don't consider, Eugenius, said I, refusing his offer, that before I have been three days in Paris I shall take care to say or do something or other for which I shall get clapped up into the Bastile, and that I shall live there a couple of months entirely at the King of France's expense.——I beg pardon, said Eugenius dryly: really, I had forgot that resource.

Now the event I treated gaily, came seriously to my door.

Is it folly, or *nonchalance*, or philosophy, or pertinacity;—or what is it in me, that, after all, when La Fleur had gone downstairs, and I was quite alone, I could not bring down my mind to think of it otherwise than I had then spoken of it to Eugenius?

—And as for the Bastile,—the terror is in the word.—Make the most of it you can, said I to myself, the Bastile is but another word for a tower;—and a tower is but another word for a house you can't get out of.—Mercy on the gouty! for they are in it twice a year.—But with nine livres a-day, and pen and ink and paper and patience, albeit a man can't get out, he may do very well within,—at least for a month or six weeks; at the end of which, if he is a harmless fellow, his innocence appears, and he comes out a better and wiser man than he went in.

I had some occasion (I forgot what) to step into the courtyard, as I settled this account; and remember I walked downstairs in no small triumph with the conceit of my reasoning.——Beshrew the *sombre* pencil! said I, vauntingly,—for I envy not its power, which paints the evils of life with so hard and deadly a colouring. The mind sits terrified at the objects she has magnified herself, and blackened: reduce them to their proper size and hue, she overlooks them.——'Tis true, said I, correcting the proposition,—the Bastile is not an evil to be despised.—But strip it of its towers,—fill up the foss,—unbarricade the doors,—call it simply a confinement, and suppose 'tis some tyrant of a distemper, —and not of a man, which holds you in it,—the evil vanishes, and you bear the other half without complaint.

I was interrupted in the hey-day of this soliloquy, with a voice which I took to be of a child, which complained " it could not get out."—I looked up and down the passage, and seeing neither man, woman, nor child, I went out without further attention.

In my return back through the passage, I heard the same words repeated twice over; and looking up, I saw it was a starling hung in a little cage.—" I can't get out,—I can't get out," said the starling.

I stood looking at the bird: and to every person who came through the passage, it ran fluttering to the side towards which they approached it, with the same lamentation of its captivity,—" I can't get out," said the starling.——God help thee! said I,—but I'll let thee out, cost what it will; so I turned about the cage to get the door: it was twisted and double twisted so fast with wire, there was no getting it open without pulling the cage to pieces.—I took both hands to it.

The bird flew to the place where I was attempting his deliverance, and thrusting his head through the trellis, pressed his breast against it, as if impatient.—I fear, poor creature, said I, I cannot set thee at liberty.
——" No," said the starling; " I can't get out,—I can't get out," said the starling.

I vow I never had my affections more tenderly awakened; nor do I remember an incident in my life where the dissipated spirits to which my reason had been a bubble, were so suddenly called home. Mechanical as the notes were, yet so true in tune to nature were they chanted, that in one moment they overthrew all my systematic reasonings upon the Bastile; and I heavily walked upstairs, unsaying every word I had said in going down them.

Disguise thyself as thou wilt, still, Slavery, said I,— still thou art a bitter draught! and though thousands in all ages have been made to drink of thee, thou art no less bitter on that account.—'Tis thou, thrice sweet and gracious goddess, addressing myself to *Liberty*, whom all in public or in private worship, whose taste is grateful, and ever will be so, till Nature herself shall change. No *tint* of words can spot thy snowy mantle, or chymic power turn thy sceptre into iron;—with thee, to smile upon him as he eats his crust, the swain is happier than his monarch, from whose court thou art exiled.— Gracious Heaven! cried I, kneeling down upon the last step but one in my ascent, grant me but health, thou great Bestower of it, and give me but this fair goddess as my companion,—and shower down thy mitres, if it seems good unto thy Divine Providence, upon those heads which are aching for them!

THE CAPTIVE.

PARIS.

THE bird in his cage pursued me into my room. I sat down close by my table, and, leaning my head upon my hand, I began to figure to myself the miseries of confinement. I was in a right frame for it, and so I gave full scope to my imagination.

I was going to begin with the millions of my fellow-creatures born to no inheritance but slavery: but finding, however affecting the picture was, that I could not bring it near me, and that the multitude of sad groups in it did but distract me—

—I took a single captive; and having first shut him up in his dungeon, I then looked through the twilight of his grated door to take his picture.

I beheld his body half wasted away with long expectation and confinement, and felt what kind of sickness of the heart it was which arises from hope deferred. Upon looking nearer, I saw him pale and feverish; in thirty years the western breeze had not once fanned his blood;—he had seen no sun, no moon, in all that time; —nor had the voice of friend or kinsman breathed through his lattice!—His children!——

But here my heart began to bleed; and I was forced to go on with another part of the portrait.

He was sitting upon the ground upon a little straw,

in the furthest corner of his dungeon, which was alternately his chair and bed: a little calendar of small sticks were laid at the head, notched all over with the dismal days and nights he had passed there:—he had one of these little sticks in his hands, and, with a rusty nail, he was etching another day of misery to add to the heap. As I darkened the little light he had, he lifted up a hopeless eye towards the door, then cast it down,—shook his head, and went on with his work of affliction. I heard his chains upon his legs, as he turned his body to lay his little stick upon the bundle.—He gave a deep sigh.—I saw the iron enter into his soul! —I burst into tears.——I could not sustain the picture of confinement which my fancy had drawn.—I started up from my chair, and calling La Fleur,—I bid him bespeak me a remise, and have it ready at the door of the hotel by nine in the morning.

—I'll go directly, said I, myself to Monsieur le Duc de Choiseul.

La Fleur would have put me to bed; but not willing he should see anything upon my cheek which would cost the honest fellow a heart-ache, I told him I would go to bed by myself,—and bid him go do the same.

THE STARLING.
ROAD TO VERSAILLES.

I GOT into my remise the hour I proposed. La Fleur got up behind, and I bid the coachman make the best of his way to Versailles.

As there was nothing in this road, or rather nothing

which I look for in travelling, I cannot fill up the blank better than with a short history of this self-same bird, which became the subject of the last chapter.

Whilst the Honourable Mr. —— was waiting for a wind at Dover, it had been caught upon the cliffs, before it could well fly, by an English lad who was his groom; who, not caring to destroy it, had taken it in his breast into the packet;—and, by course of feeding it, and taking it once under his protection, in a day or two grew fond of it, and got it safe along with him to Paris.

At Paris, the lad had laid out a livre in a little cage for the starling; and as he had little to do better the five months his master stayed there, he taught it in his mother's tongue the four simple words — (and no more), to which I owned myself so much its debtor.

Upon his master's going on for Italy, the lad had given it to the master of the hotel. But his little song for liberty being in an *unknown* language at Paris, the bird had little or no store set by him:—so La Fleur bought both him and his cage for me for a bottle of Burgundy.

In my return from Italy, I brought him with me to the country in whose language he had learned his notes; and telling the story of him to Lord A., Lord A. begged the bird of me; in a week Lord A. gave him to Lord B.; Lord B. made a present of him to Lord C.; and Lord C.'s gentleman sold him to Lord D.'s for a shilling: Lord D. gave him to Lord E., and so on, half round the alphabet. From that rank he passed into the lower house, and passed the hands of as many commoners. But as all these wanted to get in, and my bird wanted to get out, he had almost as little store set by him in London as in Paris.

It is impossible but many of my readers must have heard of him; and if any by mere chance have ever seen him,—I beg leave to inform them that that bird was my bird,—or some vile copy set up to represent him.

I have nothing further to add upon him, but that from that time to this, I have borne this poor starling as the crest to my arms.——And let the herald's officers twist his neck about if they dare.

THE ADDRESS.

VERSAILLES.

I SHOULD not like to have my enemy take a view of my mind when I am going to ask protection of any man; for which reason I generally endeavour to protect myself: but this going to Monsieur le Duc de C——, was an act of compulsion;—had it been an act of choice, I should have done it, I suppose, like other people.

How many mean plans of dirty address, as I went along, did my servile heart form! I deserved the Bastile for every one of them.

Then nothing would serve me, when I got within sight of Versailles, but putting words and sentences together, and conceiving attitudes and tones to writhe myself into Monsieur le Duc de C——'s good graces. —This will do, said I.—Just as well, retorted I again, as a coat carried up to him by an adventurous tailor, without taking his measure.—Fool! continued I,—see Monsieur le Duc's face first;—observe what character is written in it;—take notice in what posture he stands to hear you;—mark the turns and expressions of his body and limbs;—and for the tone,—the first sound which comes from his lips will give it you; and from all these together you'll compound an address at once upon the spot, which cannot disgust the Duke;—the ingredients are his own, and most likely to go down.

Well! said I, I wish it well over.—Coward again! as if man to man was not equal throughout the whole surface of the globe; and if in the field, why not face to face in the cabinet too? and trust me, Yorick, whenever it is not so, man is false to himself, and betrays his own succours ten times where nature does it once. Go to the Duc de C—— with the Bastile in thy looks;—my life for it, thou wilt be sent back to Paris in half an hour with an escort.

I believe so, said I.—Then I'll go to the Duke, by Heaven! with all the gaiety and debonairness in the world.

—And there you are wrong again, replied I.——A heart at ease, Yorick, flies into no extremes,—'tis ever on its centre.—Well! well! cried I, as the coachman turned in at the gates, I find I shall do very well: and by the time he had wheeled round the court, and brought me up to the door, I found myself so much the better for my own lecture, that I neither ascended the steps like a victim to justice, who was to part with life upon the topmast,—nor did I mount them with a skip and a couple of strides, as I do when I fly up, Eliza! to thee, to meet it.

As I entered the door of the saloon, I was met by a person who possibly might be the *maitre d'hotel*, but had more the air of one of the under-secretaries, who told me the Duc de C—— was busy.—I am utterly ignorant, said I, of the forms of obtaining an audience, being an absolute stranger, and, what is worse in the present conjuncture of affairs, being an Englishman too.——He replied, that did not increase the difficulty.— I made him a slight bow, and told him, I had something of importance to say to Monsieur le Duc. The secretary looked towards the stairs, as if he was about to leave me to carry up this account to some one.—But I must not mislead you, said I,—for what I have to say is of no manner of importance to Monsieur le Duc de C——, but of great importance to myself.——*C'est une autre affaire*, replied he.——Not at all, said I, to a man of gallantry. But pray, good sir, continued I, when can a stranger hope to have *accesse?*——In not less than two hours, said he, looking at his watch.——The number of equipages in the courtyard seemed to justify the calculation, that I could have no nearer a prospect;— and as walking backwards and forwards in the saloon, without a soul to commune with, was for the time as bad as being in the Bastile itself, I instantly went back to my remise, and bid the coachman drive me to the *Cordon Bleu*, which was the nearest hotel.

I think there is a fatality in it;—I seldom go to the place I set out for.

THE CHEVALIER DE SAINT LOUIS

LE PATISSER.

VERSAILLES.

BEFORE I had got half-way down the street, I changed my mind: as I am at Versailles, thought I, I might as well take a view of the town; so I pulled the cord, and ordered the coachman to drive round some of the principal streets.—I suppose the town is not very large, said I.—The coachman begged pardon for setting me right, and told me it was very superb; and that numbers of the first dukes and marquises and counts had hotels.—The Count de B——, of whom the bookseller at the Quai de Conti had spoke so handsomely the night before, came instantly into my mind.—And why should I not go, thought I, to the Count de B——, who has so high an idea of English books and Englishmen,—and tell him my story? So I changed my mind a second time. In truth, it was the third; for I had intended that day for Madame de R——, in the Rue St. Pierre, and had devoutly sent her word by her *fille de chambre* that I would assuredly wait upon her;—but I am governed by circumstances;—I cannot govern them: so seeing a man standing with a basket on the other side of the street, as if he had something to sell, I bid La Fleur go up to him, and inquire for the Count's hotel.

La Fleur returned a little pale; and told me it was a Chevalier de St. Louis selling *patés*.—It is impossible, La Fleur, said I.—La Fleur could no more account for the phenomenon than myself; but persisted in his story: he had seen the croix set in gold, with its red riband, he said, tied to his buttonhole; and had looked into the basket, and seen the *patés* which the Chevalier was selling; so could not be mistaken in that.

Such a reverse in a man's life awakens a better principle than curiosity: I could not help looking for some time at him as I sat in the remise. The more I looked at him, his croix, and his basket, the stronger they wove themselves into my brain.—I got out of the remise, and went towards him.

He was begirt with a clean linen apron, which fell below his knees, and with a sort of a bib that went half way up his breast. Upon the top of this, but a little below the hem, hung his croix. His basket of little *patés* was covered over with a white damask napkin: another of the same kind was spread at the bottom; and there was such a look of *propreté* and neatness throughout, that one might have bought his *patés* of him as much from appetite as sentiment.

He made an offer of them to neither; but stood still with them at the corner of a hotel, for those to buy who chose it, without solicitation.

He was about forty-eight;—of a sedate look, something approaching to gravity. I did not wonder.—I went up rather to the basket than him, and having lifted up the napkin, and taken one of his *patés* into my hand,—I begged he would explain the appearance which affected me.

He told me in a few words, that the best part of his life had passed in the service; in which, after spending a small patrimony, he had obtained a company and the croix with it; but that, at the conclusion of the last peace, his regiment being re-formed, and the whole corps, with those of some other regiments, left without any provision, he found himself in a wide world without friends, without a livre;—and indeed, said he, without anything but this:—(pointing, as he said it, to his croix.)——The poor Chevalier won my pity; and he finished the scene by winning my esteem too.

The King, he said, was the most generous of princes; but his generosity could neither relieve nor reward every one; and it was only his misfortune to be amongst the number. He had a little wife, he said, whom he loved, who did the *patisserie;* and added, he felt no dishonour in defending her and himself from want in this way,— unless Providence had offered him a better.

It would be wicked to withhold a pleasure from the good, in passing over what happened to this poor Chevalier of St. Louis about nine months after.

It seems he usually took his stand near the iron gates which lead up to the palace; and as his croix had caught the eye of numbers, numbers had made the same inquiry which I had done.—He had told the same story, and always with so much modesty and good sense, that it had reached at last the king's ears; —who hearing the Chevalier had been a gallant officer, and respected by the whole regiment as a man of honour and integrity,—he broke up his little trade by a pension of fifteen hundred livres a-year.

As I have told this to please the reader, I beg he will allow me to relate another, out of its order, to please myself;—the two stories reflect light upon each other,—and 'tis a pity they should be parted.

THE SWORD.

RENNES.

WHEN states and empires have their periods of declension, and feel in their turns what distress and poverty is,—I stop not to tell the causes which gradually brought the house d'E—— in Britanny into decay. The Marquis d'E—— had fought up against his condition with great firmness; wishing to preserve, and still show to the world some little fragments of what his ancestors had been; their indiscretions had put it out of his power. There was enough left for the little exigencies of obscurity. But he had two boys who looked up to him for light; he thought they deserved it. He had tried his sword,—it could not open the way,—the mounting was too expensive,—and simple economy was not a match for it:—there was no resource but commerce.

In any other province in France save Britanny, this was smiting the root for ever of the little tree his pride and affection wished to see re-blossom.—But in Britanny, there being a provision for this, he availed himself of it; and taking an occasion when the states were assembled at Rennes, the Marquis, attended with his two boys, entered the court; and having pleaded the right of an ancient law of the duchy, which, though seldom claimed, he said, was no less in force, he took his sword from his side;—Here, said he, take it; and be trusty guardians of it till better times put me in condition to reclaim it.

The president accepted the Marquis's sword;—he stayed a few minutes to see it deposited in the archives of his house, and departed.

The Marquis and his whole family embarked the next day for Martinico, and in about nineteen or twenty years of successful application to business, with some unlooked-for bequests from distant branches of his house, returned home to reclaim his nobility, and to support it.

It was an incident of good fortune which will never happen to any traveller but a sentimental one, that I should be at Rennes at the very time of this solemn requisition. I call it solemn;—it was so to me.

The Marquis entered the court with his whole family: he supported his lady;—his eldest son supported his sister, and his youngest was at the other extreme of the line next his mother;—he put his handkerchief to his face twice.—

—There was a dead silence. When the Marquis had approached within six paces of the tribunal, he gave the Marchioness to his youngest son, and advancing three steps before his family,—he reclaimed his sword. His sword was given him: and the moment he got it into his hand, he drew it almost out of the scabbard:—'twas the shining face of a friend he had once given up:—he looked attentively along it, beginning at the hilt, as if to see whether it was the same,—when observing a little rust which it had contracted near the point, he brought it near his eye, and bending his head down over it,—I think I saw a tear fall upon the place. I could not be deceived by what followed.

"I shall find," said he, "some other way to get it off."

When the Marquis had said this, he returned his sword into its scabbard, made a bow to the guardians of it,—and, with his wife and daughter, and his two sons following him, walked out.

Oh how I envied him his feelings!

THE PASSPORT.

VERSAILLES.

I FOUND no difficulty in getting admittance to Monsieur le Count de B——. The set of Shakespeare was laid upon the table, and he was tumbling them over. I walked up close to the table, and giving first such a look at the books as to make him conceive I knew what they were,—I told him I had come without any one to present me, knowing I should meet with a friend in his apartment, who, I trusted, would do it for me. —It is my countryman, the great Shakespeare, said I, pointing to his works; *et ayez la bonté, mon cher ami,* apostrophising his spirit, added I, *de me faire cet honneur-là.*—

The Count smiled at the singularity of the introduction; and seeing I looked a little pale and sickly, insisted upon my taking an arm-chair; so I sat down; and to save him conjectures upon a visit so out of all rule, I told him simply of the incident in the bookseller's shop, and how that had impelled me rather to go to him with the story of a little embarrassment I was under, than to any other man in France.——And what is your embarrassment? let me hear it, said the Count. ——So I told him the story just as I have told it the reader.

——And the master of my hotel, said I, as I concluded it, will needs have it, Monsieur le Count, that I should be sent to the Bastile;—but I have no apprehensions, continued I,—for in falling into the hands of the most polished people in the world, and being conscious I was a true man, and not come to spy the nakedness of the land, I scarce thought I lay at their mercy. It does not suit the gallantry of the French, Monsieur le Count, said I, to show it against invalids.

An animated blush came into the Count de B——'s cheeks as I spoke this—*Ne craignez rien*—Don't fear, said he.—Indeed I don't, replied I again.—Besides, continued I a little sportingly, I have come laughing all the way from London to Paris; and I do not think Monsieur le Duc de Choiseul is such an enemy to mirth, as to send me back crying for my pains.

—My application to you, Monsieur le Count de B—— (making him a low bow), is to desire he will not.

The Count heard me with great good nature, or I had not said half so much,—and once or twice said,—*C'est bien dit.* So I rested my cause there,—and determined to say no more about it.

The Count led the discourse: we talked of indifferent things,—of books, and politics, and men; and then of women.——God bless them all! said I, after much discourse about them,—there is not a man upon earth who loves them so much as I do. After all the foibles I have seen, and all the satires I have read against them, still I love them; being firmly persuaded that a man who has not a sort of an affection for the whole sex, is incapable of ever loving a single one as he ought.

Heh bien! Monsieur l'Anglois, said the Count gaily;—you are not come to spy the nakedness of the land;—I believe you;—*ni encore,* I daresay, *that* of our women: but permit me to conjecture,—if, *par hazard,* they fell into your way, that the prospect would not affect you.

I have something within me which cannot bear the shock of the least indecent insinuation: in the sportability of chit-chat I have often endeavoured to conquer it, and with infinite pain have hazarded a thousand things to a dozen of the sex together,—the least of which I could not venture to a single one to gain Heaven.

Excuse me, Monsieur le Count, said I:—as for the nakedness of your land, if I saw it, I should cast my eyes over it with tears in them;—and for that of your women (blushing at the idea he had excited in me) I am so evangelical in this, and have such a fellow-feeling for whatever is *weak* about them, that I would cover it with a garment, if I knew how to throw it on;—but I could wish, continued I, to spy the *nakedness* of their hearts, and, through the different disguises of customs, climates, and religion, find out what is good in them to fashion my own by;—and therefore am I come.

It is for this reason, Monsieur le Count, continued I,

that I have not seen the Palais Royal,—nor the Luxembourg,—nor the Façade of the Louvre,—nor have attempted to swell the catalogues we have of pictures, statues, and churches.—I conceive every fair being as a temple, and would rather enter in, and see the original drawings, and loose sketches hung up in it, than the Transfiguration of Raphael itself.

The thirst of this, continued I, as impatient as that which inflames the breast of the connoisseur, has led me from my own home into France,—and from France will lead me through Italy;—'tis a quiet journey of the heart in pursuit of Nature, and those affections which arise out of her, which make us love each other,—and the world, better than we do.

The Count said a great many civil things to me upon the occasion, and added, very politely, how much he stood obliged to Shakespeare for making me known to him.——But, *à-propos*, said he;—Shakespeare is full of great things;—he forgot the small punctilio of announcing your name:—it puts you under a necessity of doing it yourself.

THE PASSPORT.

VERSAILLES.

THERE is not a more perplexing affair in life to me than to set about telling any one who I am,—for there is scarce anybody I cannot give a better account of than myself; and I have often wished I could do it in a single word,—and have an end of it. It was the only time and occasion in my life I could accomplish this to any purpose;—for Shakespeare lying upon the table, and recollecting I was in his books, I took up Hamlet, and turning immediately to the gravediggers' scene in the fifth act, I laid my finger upon Yorick; and advancing the book to the Count, with my finger all the way over the name,—*Me voici!* said I.

Now, whether the idea of poor Yorick's skull was put out of the Count's mind by the reality of my own, or by what magic he could drop a period of seven or eight hundred years, makes nothing in this account; 'tis certain, the French conceive better than they combine; —I wonder at nothing in this world, and the less at this; inasmuch as one of the first of our own church, for whose candour and paternal sentiments I have the highest veneration, fell into the same mistake in the very same case:—" He could not bear," he said, " to look into sermons wrote by the King of Denmark's jester."—Good, my lord! said I; but there are two Yoricks. The Yorick your lordship thinks of has been dead and buried eight hundred years ago: he flourished in Horwendillus's court;—the other Yorick is myself, who have flourished, my lord, in no court.——He shook his head.——Good God! said I, you might as well confound Alexander the Great with Alexander the Coppersmith, my lord!——'Twas all one, he replied.

——If Alexander, King of Macedon, could have translated your lordship, said I, I'm sure your lordship would not have said so.

The poor Count de B—— fell but into the same *error*.

——*Et, Monsieur, est il Yorick?* cried the Count.

———*Je le suis*, said I.———*Vous?*———*Moi*———*moi qui ai l'honneur de vous parler, Monsieur le Comte.*———*Mon Dieu!* said he, embracing me,—*Vous êtes Yorick?*

The Count instantly put the Shakespeare into his pocket, and left me alone in his room.

THE PASSPORT.

VERSAILLES.

I COULD not conceive why the Count de B—— had gone so abruptly out of the room, any more than I could conceive why he had put the Shakespeare into his pocket.—*Mysteries which must explain themselves, are not worth the loss of time which a conjecture about them takes up:* 'twas better to read Shakespeare; so taking up "*Much Ado about Nothing*," I transported myself instantly from the chair I sat in to Messina in Sicily, and got so busy with Don Pedro, and Benedict, and Beatrice, that I thought not of Versailles, the Count, or the passport.

Sweet pliability of man's spirit, that can at once surrender itself to illusions which cheat expectation and sorrow of their weary moments!—Long,—long since had ye numbered out my days, had I not trod so great a part of them upon this enchanted ground. When my way is too rough for my feet, or too steep for my strength, I get off it, to some smooth velvet path which fancy has scattered over with rosebuds of delight; and, having taken a few turns in it, come back strengthened and refreshed.—When evils press sore upon me, and there is no retreat from them in this world, then I take a new course;—I leave it,—and, as I have a clearer idea of the Elysian Fields than I have of Heaven, I force myself, like Æneas, into them;—I see him meet the pensive shade of his forsaken Dido, and wish to recognise it;—I see the injured spirit wave her head, and turn off silent from the author of her miseries and dishonours;—I lose the feelings for myself in hers, and in those affections which were wont to make me mourn for her when I was at school.

Surely, this is not walking in a vain shadow,—nor does man disquiet himself in vain by it:—he oftener does so in trusting the issue of his commotions to reason only.—I can safely say for myself, I was never able to conquer any one single bad sensation in my heart so decisively, as by beating up as fast as I could for some kindly and gentle sensation to fight it upon its own ground.

When I had got to the end of the third act, the Count de B—— entered with my passport in his hand. Mons. le Duc de C——, said the Count, is as good a prophet, I daresay, as he is a statesman.——*Un homme qui rit*, said the Duke, *ne sera jamais dangereux.*——Had it been for any one but the King's jester, added the Count, I could not have got it these two hours.——*Pardonnez moi*, Mons. le Count, said I, I am not the King's jester.——But you are Yorick?——Yes.—— *Et vous plaisantez?*——I answered, Indeed I did jest,—but was not paid for it;—'twas entirely at my own expense.

We have no jester at court, Mons. le Count, said I;

the last we had was in the licentious reign of Charles II.;—since which time our manners have been so gradually refining, that our court at present is full of patriots, who wish for *nothing* but the honours and wealth of our country;—and our ladies are all so chaste, so spotless, so good, so devout,—there is nothing for a jester to make a jest of.

Voila un persiflage! cried the Count.

THE PASSPORT.

VERSAILLES.

As the passport was directed to all lieutenant-governors, governors, and commandants of cities, generals of armies, justiciaries, and all officers of justice, to let Mr. Yorick the King's jester, and his baggage, travel quietly along,—I own the triumph of obtaining the passport was not a little tarnished by the figure I cut in it.—But there is nothing unmixed in this world; and some of the gravest of our divines have carried it so far as to affirm, that enjoyment itself was attended even with a sigh,—and that the greatest *they knew of* terminated, *in a general way,* in little better than a convulsion.

I remember the grave and learned Bevoriskius, in his Commentary upon the Generations from Adam, very naturally breaks off in the middle of a note, to give an account to the world of a couple of sparrows upon the outedge of his window, which had incommoded him all the time he wrote; and, at last, had entirely taken him off from his genealogy.

———'Tis strange! writes Bevoriskius, but the facts

are certain; for I have had the curiosity to mark them down, one by one, with my pen;—but the cock-sparrow, during the little time that I could have finished the other half of this note, has actually interrupted me with the reiteration of his caresses three-and-twenty times and a half.

How merciful, adds Bevoriskius, is Heaven to his creatures!

Ill-fated Yorick! that the gravest of thy brethren should be able to write that to the world, which stains thy face with crimson to copy, even in thy study.

But this is nothing to my travels;—so I twice,— twice beg pardon for it.

CHARACTER.

VERSAILLES.

AND how do you find the French? said the Count de B——, after he had given me the passport.

The reader may suppose, that, after so obliging a proof of courtesy, I could not be at a loss to say something handsome to the inquiry.

——*Mais passe pour cela.*——Speak frankly, said he; do you find all the urbanity in the French which the world give us the honour of?——I had found everything, I said, which confirmed it.——*Vraiment,* said the Count, *les François sont polis.*——To an excess, replied I.

The Count took notice of the word *excesse:* and would have it I meant more than I said. I defended myself a long time, as well as I could against it:——

he insisted I had a reserve, and that I would speak my opinion frankly.

I believe, Mons. le Compte, said I, that man has a certain compass, as well as an instrument; and that the social and other calls have occasion, by turns, for every key in him: so that, if you begin a note too high or too low, there must be a want either in the upper or under part, to fill up the system of harmony.——The Count de B—— did not understand music; so desired me to explain it some other way.——A polished nation, my dear Count, said I, makes every one its debtor; and besides, urbanity itself, like the fair sex, has so many charms, it goes against the heart to say it can do ill; and yet, I believe, there is but a certain line of perfection that man, take him altogether, is empowered to arrive at; if he gets beyond, he rather exchanges qualities than gets them. I must not presume to say how far this has affected the French in the subject we are speaking of;—but should it ever be the case of the English, in the progress of their refinements, to arrive at the same polish which distinguishes the French, if we did not lose the *politesse du cœur*, which inclines men more to humane actions than courteous ones,—we should at least lose that distinct variety and originality of character, which distinguishes them not only from each other, but from all the world besides.

I had a few of King William's shillings, as smooth as glass, in my pocket, and foreseeing they would be of use in the illustration of my hypothesis, I had got them into my hand, when I had proceeded so far:——

See, Mons. le Compte, said I, rising up, and laying

them before him upon the table,—by jingling and rubbing one against another for seventy years together in one body's pocket or another's, they are become so much alike you can scarce distinguish one shilling from another.

The English, like ancient medals, kept more apart, and passing but few people's hands, preserve the first sharpness which the fine hand of Nature has given them;—they are not so pleasant to feel,—but, in return, the legend is so visible, that, at the first look, you see whose image and superscription they bear. But the French, Mons. le Compte, added I (wishing to soften what I had said), have so many excellences, they can the better spare this;—they are a loyal, a gallant, a generous, an ingenious, and a good-tempered people, as is under Heaven;—if they have a fault, they are too *serious*.

Mon Dieu! cried the Count, rising out of his chair.

Mais vous plaisantez, said he, correcting his exclamation.——I laid my hand upon my breast, and, with earnest gravity, assured him it was my most settled opinion.

——The Count said he was mortified he could not stay to hear my reasons, being engaged to go that moment to dine with the Duc de C——.

But, if it is not too far to come to Versailles to eat your soup with me, I beg, before you leave France, I may have the pleasure of knowing you retract your opinion,—or in what manner you support it.—But if you do support it, *Mons. Anglois*, said he, you must do it with all your powers, because you have the whole world against you.——I promised the Count I would do myself the honour of dining with him before I set out for Italy;—so took my leave.

THE TEMPTATION.

PARIS.

When I alighted at the hotel, the porter told me a young woman with a band-box had been that moment inquiring for me.——I do not know, said the porter, whether she is gone away or not.—I took the key of my chamber of him, and went upstairs; and, when I had got within ten steps of the top of the landing before my door, I met her coming easily down.

It was the fair *fille de chambre* I had walked along the Quai de Conti with: Madame de R—— had sent her upon some commission to a *merchante des modes* within a step or two of the hotel de Modene; and, as I had failed in waiting upon her, had bid her inquire if I had left Paris; and, if so, whether I had not left a letter addressed to her.

As the fair *fille de chambre* was so near my door, she returned back, and went into the room with me for a moment or two, whilst I wrote a card.

It was a fine still evening in the latter end of the month of May,—the crimson window-curtains (which were of the same colour as those of the bed) were drawn close,—the sun was setting, and reflected through them so warm a tint into the fair *fille de chambre's* face,—I thought she blushed;—the idea of it made me blush myself;—we were quite alone, and that superinduced a second blush before the first could get off.

There is a sort of a pleasing half-guilty blush, where the blood is more in fault than the man;—'tis sent impetuous from the heart, and virtue flies after it,—not to call it back, but to make the sensation of it more delicious to the nerves. It is associated——

But I'll not describe it;—I felt something at first within me which was not in strict unison with the lesson of virtue I had given her the night before:—I sought five minutes for a card; I knew I had not one. I took up a pen,—I laid it down again,—my hand trembled:—the devil was in me.

I know as well as any one he is an adversary, whom, if we resist, he will fly from us; but I seldom resist him at all, from a terror that, though I may conquer, I may still get a hurt in the combat; so I give up the triumph for security; and, instead of thinking to make him fly, I generally fly myself.

The fair *fille de chambre* came close up to the bureau, where I was looking for a card,—took up first the pen I cast down, then offered to hold me the ink; she offered it so sweetly, I was going to accept it, but I durst not;——I have nothing, my dear, said I, to write upon.——Write it, said she, simply, upon anything.

——I was just going to cry out, Then I will write it, fair girl, upon thy lips!

——If I do, said I, I shall perish; so I took her by the hand, and led her to the door, and begged she would not forget the lesson I had given her.——She said, indeed, she would not, and as she uttered it with some earnestness, she turned about, and gave me both her hands, closed together, into mine;—it was impossible not to compress them in that situation;—I wished to let them go; and all the time I held them, I kept arguing within myself against it,—and still I held them on.—In two minutes I found I had all the battle to fight over again;—and I felt my legs and every limb about me tremble at the idea.

The foot of the bed was within a yard and a half of the place where we were standing.—I had still hold of her hands—(and how it happened, I can give no account); but I neither asked her, nor drew her, nor did I think of the bed;—but so it did happen, we both sat down.

I'll just show you, said the fair *fille de chambre*, the little purse I have been making to-day to hold your crown. So she put her hand into her right pocket, which was next me, and felt for it some time;—then into the left.——" She had lost it."——I never bore expectation more quietly;—it was in her right pocket at last; she pulled it out; it was of green taffeta, lined with a little bit of white quilted satin, and just big enough to hold the crown:—she put it into my hand: it was pretty; and I held it ten minutes, with the back of my hand resting upon her lap, looking sometimes at the purse, sometimes on one side of it.

A stitch or two had broke out in the gathers of my stock; the fair *fille de chambre*, without saying a word, took out her little housewife, threaded a small needle, and sewed it up. I foresaw it would hazard the glory of the day, and, as she passed her hand in silence across and across my neck in the manœuvre, I felt the laurels shake which fancy had wreathed about my head.

A strap had given way in her walk, and the buckle of her shoe was just falling off.——See, said the *fille de chambre*, holding up her foot.——I could not from my soul but fasten the buckle in return; and, putting in the strap,—and lifting up the other foot with it, when I had done, to see both were right, in doing it so suddenly, it unavoidably threw the fair *fille de chambre* off her centre,—and then ——

THE CONQUEST.

YES,—and then——Ye, whose clay-cold heads and lukewarm hearts can argue down or mask your passions, tell me, what trespass is it that man should have them? or how his spirit stands answerable to the Father of spirits, but for his conduct under them?

If Nature has so wove her web of kindness, that some threads of love and desire are entangled with the piece,—must the whole web be rent in drawing them out?—Whip me such stoics, great Governor of Nature! said I to myself;—wherever thy Providence shall place me for the trials of my virtue; whatever is my danger;—whatever is my situation,—let me feel the movements which rise out of it, and which belong to me as a man,—and, if I govern them as a good one, I will trust the issues to thy justice; for thou hast made us, and not we ourselves.

As I finished my address, I raised the fair *fille de chambre* up by the hand, and led her out of the room:

—she stood by me till I locked the door and put the key in my pocket,—*and then*,—the victory being quite decisive,—and not till then, I pressed my lips to her cheek, and, taking her by the hand again, led her safe to the gate of the hotel.

THE MYSTERY.

PARIS.

IF a man knows the heart, he will know it was impossible to go back instantly to my chamber;—it was touching a cold key with a flat third to it, upon the close of a piece of music, which had called forth my affections; therefore, when I let go the hand of the *fille de chambre*, I remained at the gate of the hotel for some time, looking at every one who passed by, and forming conjectures upon them, till my attention got fixed upon a single object which confounded all kind of reasoning upon him.

It was a tall figure, of a philosophic, serious, adust look, which passed and repassed sedately along the street, making a turn of about sixty paces on each side of the gate of the hotel.—The man was about fifty-two, had a small cane under his arm, was dressed in a dark drab-coloured coat, waistcoat, and breeches, which seemed to have seen some years' service;—they were still clean, and there was a little air of frugal *propreté* throughout him. By his pulling off his hat, and his attitude of accosting a good many in his way, I saw he was asking charity; so I got a sous or two out of my pocket ready to give him, as he took me in his turn.

He passed by me without asking anything,—and yet did not go five steps farther before he asked charity of a little woman.—I was much more likely to have given of the two. He had scarce done with the woman, when he pulled his hat off to another who was coming the same way. An ancient gentleman came slowly, and, after him, a young smart one. He let them both pass, and asked nothing: I stood observing him half an hour; in which time he had made a dozen turns backwards and forwards, and found that he invariably pursued the same plan.

There were two things very singular in this, which set my brain to work, and to no purpose;—the first was, Why the man should *only* tell his story to the sex;—and secondly, What kind of story it was, and what species of eloquence it could be, which softened the hearts of the women, which he knew 'twas to no purpose to practise upon the men.

There were two other circumstances which entangled this mystery:—the one was, He told every woman what he had to say, in her ear, and in a way which had much more the air of a secret than a petition:—the other was, It was always successful;—he never stopped a woman but she pulled out her purse, and immediately gave him something.

I could form no system to explain the phenomenon.

I had got a riddle to amuse me for the rest of the evening; so I walked upstairs to my chamber.

THE CASE OF CONSCIENCE.

PARIS.

I WAS immediately followed up by the master of the hotel, who came into my room to tell me I must provide lodgings elsewhere.——How so, friend? said I.——He answered, I had a young woman locked up with me two hours that evening in my bedchamber, and 'twas against the rules of his house.——Very well, said I, we'll all part friends then,—for the girl is no worse,—and I am no worse,—and you will be just as I found you.—It was enough, he said, to overthrow the credit of his hotel.—*Voyez vous, Monsieur,* said he, pointing to the foot of the bed we had been sitting upon.——I own it had something of the appearance of an evidence; but my pride not suffering me to enter into any detail of the case, I exhorted him to let his soul sleep in peace, as I resolved to let mine do that night, and that I would discharge what I owed him at breakfast.

——I should not have minded, Monsieur, said he, if you had had twenty girls——'Tis a score more, replied I, interrupting him, than I ever reckoned upon.—— Provided, added he, it had been but in a morning.—— And does the difference of the time of the day at Paris make a difference in the sin?——It made a difference, he said, in the scandal.——I like a good distinction in my heart; and cannot say I was intolerably out of temper with the man.——I own it necessary, resumed the master of the hotel, that a stranger at Paris should have the opportunities presented to him of buying lace and silk stockings, and ruffles, *et tout cela;*—and 'tis nothing if a woman comes with a band-box.——O' my conscience, said I, she had one; but I never looked into it.——Then, Monsieur, said he, has bought nothing. ——Not one earthly thing, replied I.——Because, said he, I could recommend you to one who would use you *en conscience.*——But I must see her this night, said I. ——He made me a low bow, and walked down.

Now shall I triumph over this *maitre d'hotel,* cried I;—and what then? Then I shall let him see I know he is a dirty fellow.—And what then?—What then!— I was too near myself to say it was for the sake of others.—I had no good answer left;—there was more of spleen than of principle in my project, and I was sick of it before the execution.

In a few minutes the *grisette* came in with her box of lace.——I'll buy nothing, however, said I, within myself.

The *grisette* would show me everything. I was hard to please; she would not seem to see it. She opened her little magazine, and laid all her laces, one after another, before me;—unfolded and folded them up again, one by one, with the most patient sweetness. —I might buy,—or not;—she would let me have everything at my own price;—the poor creature seemed anxious to get a penny; and laid herself out to win me, and not so much in a manner which seemed artful, as in one I felt simple and caressing.

If there is not a fund of honest cullibility in man, so much the worse;—my heart relented, and I gave up my second resolution as quietly as the first. Why should I chastise one for the trespass of another? If thou art tributary to this tyrant of an host, thought I, looking up in her face, so much harder is thy bread.

If I had not had more than four louis d'ors in my purse, there was no such thing as rising up and showing her the door till I had first laid three of them out in a pair of ruffles.

—The master of the hotel will share the profit with her;—no matter,—then I have only paid, as many a poor soul has *paid* before me, for an act he *could* not do, or think of.

THE RIDDLE.

PARIS.

WHEN La Fleur came up to wait upon me at supper, he told me how sorry the master of the hotel was, for his affront to me in bidding me change my lodgings.

A man who values a good night's rest will not lie down with enmity in his heart, if he can help it.—So I bid La Fleur tell the master of the hotel, that I was sorry, on my side, for the occasion I had given him;—and you may tell him, if you will, La Fleur, added I, that if the young woman should call again, I shall not see her.

This was a sacrifice not to him, but myself, having resolved, after so narrow an escape, to run no more risks, but to leave Paris, if it was possible, with all the virtue I entered it.

C'est deroger à noblèsse, Monsieur, said La Fleur, making me a bow down to the ground as he said it.—

Et encore, Monsieur, said he, may change his sentiments;—and if (*par hazard*) he should like to amuse himself,——I find no amusement in it, said I, interrupting him.

——*Mon Dieu!* said La Fleur,—and took away.

In an hour's time he came to put me to bed, and was more than commonly officious:—something hung upon his lips to say to me, or ask me, which he could not get off; I could not conceive what it was; and indeed gave myself little trouble to find it out, as I had another riddle so much more interesting upon my mind, which was that of the man's asking charity before the door of the hotel.—I would have given anything to have got to the bottom of it; and that not out of curiosity,—'tis so low a principle of inquiry, in general, I would not purchase the gratification of it with a two-sous piece; —but a secret, I thought, which so soon and so certainly softened the heart of every woman you came near, was a secret at least equal to the philosopher's stone; had I had both the Indies, I would have given up one to have been master of it.

I tossed and turned it almost all night long in my brains, to no manner of purpose; and when I awoke in the morning, I found my spirits as much troubled with my *dreams,* as ever the King of Babylon had been with his; and I will not hesitate to affirm, it would have puzzled all the wise men of Paris as much as those of Chaldea, to have given its interpretation.

LE DIMANCHE.

PARIS.

It was Sunday; and when La Fleur came in, in the morning, with my coffee and roll and butter, he had got himself so gallantly arrayed, I scarce knew him.

I had covenanted at Montreuil to give him a new hat with a silver button and loop, and four louis d'ors *pour s'adoniser*, when we got to Paris; and the poor fellow, to do him justice, had done wonders with it.

He had bought a bright, clean, good scarlet coat, and a pair of breeches of the same.——They were not a crown worse, he said, for the wearing.—I wished him hanged for telling me.——They looked so fresh, that though I knew the thing could not be done, yet I would rather have imposed upon my fancy with thinking I had bought them new for the fellow, than that they had come out of the Rue de Friperie.

This is a nicety which makes not the heart sore at Paris.

He had purchased, moreover, a handsome blue satin waistcoat, fancifully enough embroidered;—this was, indeed, something the worse for the service it had done, but 'twas clean scoured,—the gold had been touched up, and, upon the whole, was rather showy than otherwise;—and as the blue was not violent, it suited with the coat and breeches very well; he had squeezed out of the money, moreover, a new bag and a *solitaire;* and had insisted with the *fripier* upon a gold pair of garters to his breeches knees.—He had purchased muslin ruffles *bien brodées*, with four livres of his own money;

—and a pair of white silk stockings for five more;—and, to top all, Nature had given him a handsome figure, without costing him a sous.

He entered the room thus set off, with his hair dressed in the first style, and with a handsome *bouquet* in his breast.—In a word, there was that look of festivity in everything about him, which at once put me in mind it was Sunday—and by combining both together, it instantly struck me that the favour he wished to ask of me the night before, was to spend the day as everybody in Paris spent it besides. I had scarce made the conjecture, when La Fleur, with infinite humility, but with a look of trust, as if I should not refuse him, begged I would grant him the day, *pour faire la gallant vis-à-vis de sa maîtresse.*

Now it was the very thing I intended to do myself *vis-à-vis* Madame de R———.—I had retained the remise on purpose for it, and it would not have mortified my vanity to have had a servant so well dressed as La Fleur was, to have got up behind it: I never could have worse spared him.

But we must *feel*, not argue, in these embarrassments;—the sons and daughters of Service part with liberty, but not with nature, in their contracts; they are flesh and blood, and have their little vanities and wishes in the midst of the house of bondage, as well as their task-masters;—no doubt they have set their self-denials at a price,—and their expectations are so unreasonable, that I would often disappoint them, but that their condition puts it so much in my power to do it.

Behold,—Behold, I am thy servant,—disarms me at once of the powers of a master.

——Thou shalt go, La Fleur, said I.

—And what mistress, La Fleur, said I, canst thou have picked up in so little a time at Paris?——La Fleur laid his hand upon his breast, and said, 'Twas a *petite demoiselle*, at Monsieur le Count de B——'s.—La Fleur had a heart made for society; and to speak the truth of him, let as few occasions slip him as his master,—so that, somehow or other,—but how,—Heaven knows,—he had connected himself with the *demoiselle* upon the landing of the staircase, during the time I was taken up with my passport; and as there was time enough for me to win the Count to my interest, La Fleur had contrived to make it do to win the maid to his. The family, it seems, was to be at Paris that day, and he had made a party with her, and two or three more of the Count's household, upon the *Boulevards*.

Happy people! that once a-week at least are sure to lay down all your cares together, and dance and sing, and sport away the weights of grievance, which bow down the spirit of other nations to the earth.

THE FRAGMENT.

PARIS.

LA FLEUR had left me something to amuse myself with for the day more than I had bargained for, or could have entered either into his head or mine.

He had brought the little print of butter upon a

currant-leaf; and, as the morning was warm, and he had a good step to bring it, he had begged a sheet of waste paper to put betwixt the currant-leaf and his hand.—As that was plate sufficient, I bade him lay it upon the table as it was; and as I resolved to stay within all day, I ordered him to call upon the *traiteur*, to bespeak my dinner, and leave me to breakfast by myself.

When I had finished the butter, I threw the currant-leaf out of the window, and was going to do the same by the waste paper;—but, stopping to read a line first, and that drawing me on to a second and third,—I thought it better worth; so I shut the window, and drawing a chair up to it, I sat down to read it.

It was in the old French of Rabelais's time; and, for aught I know, might have been wrote by him: it was, moreover, in a Gothic letter, and that so faded and gone off by damps and length of time, it cost me infinite trouble to make anything of it.—I threw it down; and then wrote a letter to Eugenius,—then I took it up again, and embroiled my patience with it afresh:—and then, to cure that, I wrote a letter to Eliza.—Still it kept hold of me; and the difficulty of understanding it increased but the desire.

I got my dinner; and after I had enlightened my mind with a bottle of Burgundy, I at it again;—and after two or three hours poring upon it, with almost as deep attention as ever Gruter or Jacob Spon did upon a nonsensical inscription, I thought I made sense of it; but to make sure of it, the best way, I imagined, was to turn it into English, and see how it would look then;—so I went on leisurely as a trifling man does, sometimes writing a sentence,—then taking a turn or two,—and then looking how the world went, out of the window; so that it was nine o'clock at night before I had done it.—I then began, and read it as follows:—

THE FRAGMENT.

PARIS.

——Now as the Notary's wife disputed the point with the Notary with too much heat,——I wish, said the Notary (throwing down the parchment), that there was another Notary here, only to set down and attest all this.

——And what would you do then, Monsieur? said she, rising hastily up.—The Notary's wife was a little fume of a woman, and the Notary thought it well to avoid a hurricane by a mild reply——I would go, answered he, to bed.——You may go to the devil, answered the Notary's wife.

Now there happening to be but one bed in the house, the other two rooms being unfurnished, as is the custom at Paris, and the Notary not caring to lie in the same bed with a woman who had but that moment sent him pell-mell to the devil, went forth with his hat, and cane, and short cloak, the night being very windy, and walked out ill at ease towards the Pont Neuf.

Of all the bridges which ever were built, the whole world who have passed over the Pont Neuf must own, that it is the noblest,—the finest,—the grandest,—the lightest,—the longest,—the broadest, that ever conjoined land and land together upon the face of the terraqueous globe.—

By this it seems as if the author of the fragment had not been a Frenchman.

The worst fault which divines and the doctors of the Sorbonne can allege against it is, that if there is but a capful of wind in or about Paris, 'tis more blasphemously *sacre Dieu'd* there than in any other aperture of the whole city,—and with reason good and cogent, Messieurs; for it comes against you without crying *garde d'eau*, and with such unpremeditable puffs, that of the few who cross it with their hats on, not one in fifty but hazards two livres and a half, which is its full worth.

The poor Notary, just as he was passing by the sentry, instinctively clapped his cane to the side of it; but in raising it up, the point of his cane catching hold of the loop of the sentinel's hat, hoisted it over the spikes of the balustrade clear into the Seine.

——'Tis an ill wind, said a boatman, who catched it, which blows nobody any good.

The sentry, being a Gascon, incontinently twirled up his whiskers, and levelled his arquebuss.

Arquebusses in those days went off with matches; and an old woman's paper lantern at the end of the bridge happening to be blown out, she had borrowed the sentry's match to light it;—it gave a moment's time for the Gascon's blood to run cool, and turn the accident better to his advantage.—*'Tis an ill wind*, said he, catching off the Notary's castor, and legitimating the capture with the boatman's adage.

The poor Notary crossed the bridge, and passing

along the Rue de Dauphine into the Fauxbourg of St. Germain, lamented himself as he walked along in this manner :—

Luckless man that I am! said the Notary, to be the sport of hurricanes all my days!—to be born to have the storm of ill language levelled against me and my profession wherever I go!—to be forced into marriage by the thunder of the church to a tempest of a woman! —to be driven forth out of my house by domestic winds, and despoiled of my castor by pontific ones!—to be here, bare-headed, in a windy night, at the mercy of the ebbs and flows of accidents!—Where am I to lay my head?—Miserable man! what wind in the two-and-thirty points in the whole compass can blow unto thee, as it does to the rest of thy fellow-creatures, good!

As the Notary was passing on by a dark passage, complaining in this sort, a voice called out to a girl, to bid her run for the next Notary.—Now the Notary being the next, and availing himself of his situation, walked up the passage to the door, and passing through an old sort of a saloon, was ushered into a large chamber, dismantled of everything but a long military pike, —a breastplate,—a rusty old sword, and bandoleer, hung up equidistant in four different places against the wall.

An old personage, who had heretofore been a gentleman, and, unless decay of fortune taints the blood along with it, was a gentleman at that time, lay supporting his head upon his hand, in his bed; a little table with a taper burning was set close beside it, and close by the table was placed a chair. The Notary sat him down in it; and pulling out his ink-horn and a sheet or two of paper which he had in his pocket, he placed them before him, and dipping his pen in his ink, and leaning his breast over the table, he disposed everything to make the gentleman's last will and testament.

———Alas! Monsieur le Notaire, said the gentleman, raising himself up a little, I have nothing to bequeath, which will pay the expense of bequeathing, except the history of myself, which I could not die in peace unless I left it as a legacy to the world; the profits arising out of it I bequeath to you for the pains of taking it from me. It is a story so uncommon, it must be read by all mankind;—it will make the fortunes of your house.

———The Notary dipped his pen into his ink-horn.——— Almighty Director of every event in my life!—said the old gentleman, looking up earnestly, and raising his hands towards Heaven,—Thou, whose hand has led me on through such a labyrinth of strange passages down into this scene of desolation, assist the decaying memory of an old, infirm, and broken-hearted man!— Direct my tongue by the spirit of thy eternal truth, that this stranger may set down nought but what is written in that *Book*, from whose records, said he, clasping his hands together, I am to be condemned or acquitted!———The Notary held up the point of his pen betwixt the taper and his eye.

———It is a story, Monsieur le Notaire, said the gentleman, which will rouse up every affection in nature;—it will kill the humane, and touch the heart of Cruelty herself with pity.———

The Notary was inflamed with a desire to begin, and

put his pen a third time into his ink-horn; and the old gentleman, turning a little more towards the Notary, began to dictate his story in these words:——

——And where is the rest of it, La Fleur? said I,—as he just then entered the room.

THE FRAGMENT, AND THE BOUQUET.
PARIS.

WHEN La Fleur came close up to the table, and was made to comprehend what I wanted, he told me there were only two other sheets of it, which he had wrapped round the stalks of a *bouquet* to keep it together, which he had presented to the *demoiselle* upon the *Boulevards.*
——Then prithee, La Fleur, said I, step back to her, to the Count de B——'s hotel, and *see if thou canst get it.*——There is no doubt of it, said La Fleur;—and away he flew.

In a very little time the poor fellow came back, quite out of breath, with deeper marks of disappointment in his looks, than could arise from the simple irreparability of the fragment. *Juste ciel!* in less than two minutes that the poor fellow had taken his last tender farewell of her,—his faithless mistress had given his *gage d'amour* to one of the Count's footmen,—the footman to a young sempstress,—and the sempstress to a fiddler, with my fragment at the end of it.—Our misfortunes were involved together;—I gave a sigh,—and La Fleur echoed it back again to my ear.

——How perfidious! cried La Fleur.——How unlucky! said I.

——I should not have been mortified, Monsieur, quoth La Fleur, if she had lost it.——Nor I, La Fleur, said I, had I found it.

Whether I did or no will be seen hereafter.

THE ACT OF CHARITY.
PARIS.

The man who either disdains or fears to walk up a dark entry, may be an excellent good man, and fit for a hundred things; but he will not do to make a good Sentimental Traveller. I count little of the many things I see pass at broad noonday, in large and open streets.—Nature is shy, and hates to act before spectators; but in such an unobserved corner you sometimes see a single short scene of hers, worth all the sentiments of a dozen French plays compounded together,—and yet they are *absolutely* fine;—and whenever I have a more brilliant affair upon my hands than common, as they suit a preacher just as well as a hero, I generally make my sermon out of 'em;—and for the text,—" Cappadocia, Pontus and Asia, Phrygia and Pamphylia,"—is as good as any one in the Bible.

There is a long dark passage issuing out from the *Opera Comique* into a narrow street; 'tis trod by a few who humbly wait for a *fiacre*, or wish to get off quietly o'foot when the opera is done. At the end of it, towards the theatre, 'tis lighted by a small candle, the light of which is almost lost before you get half-way down, but near the door;—'tis more for ornament than use: you see it as a fixed star of the least magnitude;

it burns,—but does little good to the world, that we know of.

In returning along this passage, I discerned, as I approached within five or six paces of the door, two ladies standing, arm-in-arm, with their backs against the wall, waiting, as I imagined, for a *fiacre* :—as they were next the door, I thought they had a prior right; so edged myself up within a yard or little more of them, and quietly took my stand.—I was in black, and scarce seen.

The lady next me was a tall lean figure of a woman, of about thirty-six; the other, of the same size and make, of about forty: there was no mark of wife or widow in any one part of either of them;—they seemed to be two upright vestal sisters, unsapped by caresses, unbroke in upon by tender salutations. I could have wished to have made them happy;—their happiness was destined, that night, to come from another quarter.

A low voice, with a good turn of expression, and sweet cadence at the end of it, begged for a twelve-sous piece betwixt them, for the love of Heaven. I thought it singular that a beggar should fix the quota of an alms,—and that the sum should be twelve times as much as what is usually given in the dark. They both seemed astonished at it as much as myself.——Twelve sous! said one.——A twelve-sous piece! said the other, —and made no reply.

—The poor man said, he knew not how to ask less of ladies of their rank; and bowed down his head to the ground.

——Poo! said they,—we have no money.

The beggar remained silent for a moment or two, and renewed his supplication.

———Do not, my fair young ladies, said he, stop your good ears against me.———Upon my word, honest man! said the younger, we have no change.———Then God bless you! said the poor man, and multiply those joys which you can give to others, without change!———I observed the elder sister put her hand into her pocket. ———I'll see, said she, if I have a sous!———A sous! give twelve, said the supplicant; Nature has been bountiful to you; be bountiful to a poor man.

———I would, friend, with all my heart, said the younger, if I had it.

———My fair charitable! said he, addressing himself to the elder,—what is it but your goodness and humanity which makes your bright eyes so sweet, that they outshine the morning, even in this dark passage! and what was it which made the Marquis de Santerre and his brother say so much of you both as they just passed by?

The two ladies seemed much affected; and impulsively at the same time they both put their hands into their pocket, and each took out a twelve-sous piece.

The contest betwixt them and the poor supplicant was no more,—it was continued betwixt themselves, which of the two should give the twelve-sous piece in charity;—and, to end the dispute, they both gave it together, and the man went away.

THE RIDDLE EXPLAINED.

PARIS.

I STEPPED hastily after him: it was the very man whose success in asking charity of the women before the door of the hotel had so puzzled me;—and I found at once his secret, or at least the basis of it:—'twas flattery.

Delicious essence! how refreshing art thou to Nature! how strongly are all its powers and all its weaknesses on thy side! how sweetly dost thou mix with the blood, and help it through the most difficult and tortuous passages to the heart!

The poor man, as he was not straitened for time, had given it here in a larger dose: 'tis certain he had a way of bringing it into less form, for the many sudden cases he had to do with in the streets; but how he contrived to correct, sweeten, concentre, and qualify it,—I vex not my spirit with the inquiry;—it is enough, the beggar gained two twelve-sous pieces,—and they can best tell the rest who have gained much greater matters by it.

PARIS.

WE get forwards in the world, not so much by doing services as receiving them: you take a withering twig, and put it into the ground; and then you water it, because you have planted it.

Mons. le Count de B——, merely because he had done me one kindness in the affair of my passport, would go on and do me another, the few days he was at Paris, in making me known to a few people of rank; and they were to present me to others, and so on.

I had got master of my *secret* just in time to turn these honours to some little account; otherwise, as is commonly the case, I should have dined or supped a single time or two round; and then, by *translating* French looks and attitudes into plain English, I should presently have seen that I had got hold of the *couvert* * of some more entertaining guest; and, in course, should have resigned all my places, one after another, merely upon the principle that I could not keep them.—As it was, things did not go much amiss.

I had the honour of being introduced to the old Marquis de B——. In days of yore he had signalised himself by some small feats of chivalry in the *Cour d'Amour*, and had dressed himself out to the idea of tilts and tournaments ever since.—The Marquis de B—— wished to have it thought the affair was somewhere else than in his brain. "He could like to take a trip to England:" and asked much of the English ladies.——Stay where you are, I beseech you, Mons. le Marquis, said I.——*Les Messieurs Anglois* can scarce get a kind look from them as it is.——The Marquis invited me to supper.

Mons. P——, the farmer-general, was just as inquisitive about our taxes.—They were very considerable, he heard.——If we knew but how to collect them, said I, making him a low bow.

I could never have been invited to Mons. P——'s concerts upon any other terms.

---

* Plate, napkin, knife, fork, and spoon.

I had been misrepresented to Madame de Q―― as an *esprit*.―Madame de Q―― was an *esprit* herself: she burnt with impatience to see me, and hear me talk. I had not taken my seat, before I saw she did not care a sous whether I had any wit or no―I was let in to be convinced she had.―I call Heaven to witness I never once opened the door of my lips.

Madame de Q―― vowed to every creature she met, ―" She had never had a more improving conversation with a man in her life."

There are three epochas in the empire of a French woman:―She is coquette,―then deist,―then *devoté*: the empire during these is never lost;―she only changes her subjects; when thirty-five years and more have unpeopled her dominions of the slaves of love, she re-peoples it with the slaves of infidelity, and then with the slaves of the church.

Madame de V―― was vibrating betwixt the first of these epochas: the colour of the rose was fading fast away;―she ought to have been a deist five years before the time I had the honour to pay my first visit.

She placed me upon the same sofa with her, for the sake of disputing the point of religion more closely.―In short, Madame de V―― told me she believed nothing.―I told Madame de V―― it might be her principle; but I was sure it could not be her interest to level the out-works, without which I could not conceive how such a citadel as hers could be defended;―that there was not a more dangerous thing in the world than for a beauty to be a deist;―that it was a debt I owed my creed, not to conceal it from her;―that I had not been five minutes sat upon the sofa beside her, but I had began to form designs;—and what is it but the sentiments of religion, and the persuasion they had excited in her breast, which could have checked them as they rose up?

——We are not adamant, said I, taking hold of her hand;—and there is need of all restraints, till Age in his own time steals in and lays them on us.—But, my dear lady, said I, kissing her hand,—'tis too—too soon.—

I declare I had the credit all over Paris of unperverting Madame de V——. ——She affirmed to Mons. D—— and the Abbé M—— that in one half hour I had said more for revealed religion than all their Encyclopedia had said against it,—I was lifted directly into Madame de V——'s *coterie;*—and she put off the epocha of deism for two years.

I remember it was in this *coterie,* in the middle of a discourse, in which I was showing the necessity of a *first cause,* that the young Count de Faineant took me by the hand to the farthest corner of the room, to tell me my *solitaire* was pinned too strait about my neck. ——It should be *plus badinant,* said the Count, looking down upon his own;—but a word, Mons. Yorick, *to the wise.*

——And *from the wise,* Mons. le Count, replied I, making him a bow,—*is enough.*

The Count de Faineant embraced me with more ardour than ever I was embraced by mortal man.

For three weeks together, I was of every man's opinion I met.——*Pardi! ce Mons. Yorick a autant d'esprit que nous autres.*——*Il raisonne bien,* said another.——*C'est un bon enfant,* said a third.—And at this price I could have eaten and drank and been merry all the days of my life at Paris; but 'twas a dishonest *reckoning;*—I grew ashamed of it.—It was the gain of a slave :—every sentiment of honour revolted against it;—the higher I got, the more was I forced upon my *beggarly system;* —the better the *coterie,*—the more children of Art,—I languished for those of Nature; and one night, after a most vile prostitution of myself to half-a-dozen different people, I grew sick,—went to bed;—ordered La Fleur to get me horses in the morning, to set out for Italy.

MARIA.

MOULINES.

I NEVER felt what the distress of plenty was in any one shape till now,—to travel it through the Bourbonnois, the sweetest part of France, in the hey-day of the vintage, when Nature is pouring her abundance into every one's lap, and every eye is lifted up,—a journey through each step of which music beats time to *Labour,* and all her children are rejoicing as they carry in their clusters;—to pass through this with my affections flying out, and kindling at every group before me,—and every one of them was pregnant with adventures.—

Just Heaven!—it would fill up twenty volumes;— and alas! I have but a few small pages left of this to crowd it into,—and half of these must be taken up with the poor Maria, my friend Mr. Shandy met with near Moulines.

The story he had told of that disordered maid affected me not a little in the reading; but when I got within the neighbourhood where she lived, it returned so strong into my mind, that I could not resist an impulse which prompted me to go half a league out of the road, to the village where her parents dwelt, to inquire after her.

'Tis going, I own, like the Knight of the Woeful Countenance, in quest of melancholy adventures;—I know not how it is, but I am never so perfectly conscious of the existence of a soul within me, as when I am entangled in them.

The old mother came to the door; her looks told me the story before she opened her mouth.—She had lost her husband; he had died, she said, of anguish, for the loss of Maria's sense, about a month before.—She had feared at first, she added, that it would have plundered her poor girl of what little understanding was left; but, on the contrary, it had brought her more to herself;—still she could not rest.—Her poor daughter, she said, crying, was wandering somewhere about the road.

—Why does my pulse beat languid as I write this? and what made La Fleur, whose heart seemed only to be tuned to joy, to pass the back of his hand twice across his eyes, as the woman stood and told it? I beckoned to the postillion to turn back into the road.

When we had got within half a league of Moulines, at a little opening in the road, leading to a thicket, I discovered poor Maria sitting under a poplar. She was sitting with her elbow in her lap, and her head leaning on one side within her hand :—a small brook ran at the foot of the tree.

I bid the postillion go on with the chaise to Moulines; —and La Fleur to bespeak my supper; and that I would walk after him.

She was dressed in white, and much as my friend described her, except that her hair hung loose, which before was twisted with a silken net. She had superadded likewise to her jacket a pale green riband, which fell across her shoulder to the waist; at the end of which hung her pipe.—Her goat had been as faithless as her lover; and she had got a little dog in lieu of him, which she kept tied by a string to her girdle. As I looked at her dog, she drew him towards her with the string.——" Thou shalt not leave me, Sylvio," said she. I looked in Maria's eyes, and saw she was thinking more of her father than of her lover, or her little goat; for as she uttered them, the tears trickled down her cheeks.

I sat down close by her; and Maria let me wipe them away as they fell, with my handkerchief.—I then steeped it in my own,—and then in hers,—and then in mine,—and then I wiped hers again;—and as I did it, I felt such undescribable emotions within me, as I am sure could not be accounted for from any combinations of matter and motion.

I am positive I have a soul; nor can all the books with which materialists have pestered the world, ever convince me to the contrary.

MARIA.

When Maria had come a little to herself, I asked her if she remembered a pale thin person of a man, who had sat down betwixt her and her goat about two years before?——She said, she was unsettled much at that time, but remembered it upon two accounts:— That, ill as she was, she saw the person pitied her; and next, That her goat had stolen his handkerchief, and she had beat him for the theft;—she had washed it, she said, in the brook, and kept it ever since in her pocket, to restore it to him, in case she should ever see him again; which, she added, he had half promised her. As she told me this, she took the handkerchief out of her pocket, to let me see it; she had folded it up neatly in a couple of vine-leaves, tied round with a tendril.— On opening it, I saw an *S.* marked in one of the corners.

——She had since that, she told me, strayed as far as Rome, and walked round St. Peter's once,—and returned back:—that she found her way alone across the Apennines,—had travelled over all Lombardy without money, —and through the flinty roads of Savoy without shoes: —how she had borne it, and how she had got supported, she could not tell;—but *God tempers the winds*, said Maria, *to the shorn lamb*.

——Shorn indeed; and to the quick, said I:—and wast thou in my own land, where I have a cottage, I would take thee to it, and shelter thee; thou shouldst eat of my own bread, and drink of my own cup;—I would be kind to thy Sylvio;—in all thy weaknesses and wanderings I would seek after thee, and bring thee back;—when the sun went down I would say my prayers; and when I had done, thou shouldst play thy evening-song upon thy pipe: nor would the incense of my sacrifice be worse accepted for entering Heaven along with that of a broken heart!

Nature melted within me as I uttered this; and Maria observing, as I took out my handkerchief, that it was steeped too much already to be of use, would needs go wash it in the stream.——And where will you dry it, Maria? said I.—I'll dry it in my bosom, said she;—'twill do me good.

——And is your heart still so warm, Maria? said I.

I touched upon the string on which hung all her sorrows; she looked with wistful disorder for some time in my face; and then, without saying anything, took her pipe, and played her service to the Virgin.—The string I had touched ceased to vibrate; in a moment or two Maria returned to herself,—let her pipe fall,—and rose up.

——And where are you going, Maria? said I.——She said, to Moulines.——Let us go, said I, together.—Maria put her arm within mine, and lengthening the string to let the dog follow,—in that order we entered Moulines.

MARIA.

MOULINES.

THOUGH I hate salutations and greetings in the market-place, yet when we got into the middle of this,

I stopped to take my last look and last farewell of Maria.

Maria, though not tall, was nevertheless of the first order of fine forms:—affliction had touched her looks with something that was scarce earthly; still she was feminine; and so much was there about her of all that the heart wishes, or the eye looks for in woman, that could the traces be ever worn out of her brain, and those of Eliza out of mine, she should *not only eat of my bread and drink of my own cup*, but Maria should lie in my bosom, and be unto me as a daughter.

Adieu, poor luckless maiden!—Imbibe the oil and wine which the compassion of a stranger, as he journeyeth on his way, now pours into thy wounds;—the Being who has twice bruised thee can only bind them up for ever.

THE BOURBONNOIS.

There was nothing from which I had painted out for myself so joyous a riot of the affections, as in this journey in the vintage, through this part of France; but pressing through this gate of sorrow to it, my sufferings have totally unfitted me. In every scene of festivity I saw Maria in the background of the piece, sitting pensive under her poplar; and I had got almost to Lyons before I was able to cast a shade across her.

—Dear Sensibility! source inexhausted of all that's precious in our joys, or costly in our sorrows!—thou chainest thy martyr down upon his bed of straw,—and 'tis thou who liftest him up to Heaven!—Eternal fountain of our feeling!—'tis here I trace thee,—and this is thy "*divinity which stirs within me;*" —not that, in some sad and sickening moments, "*my soul shrinks back upon herself, and startles at destruction!*"—mere pomp of words!—but that I feel some generous joys and generous cares beyond myself;—all comes from thee, great, —great *Sensorium* of the world! which vibrates, if a hair of our heads but falls upon the ground in the remotest desert of thy creation.—Touched with thee, Eugenius draws my curtain when I languish,—hears my tale of symptoms, and blames the weather for the disorder of his nerves. Thou givest a portion of it sometimes to the roughest peasant who traverses the bleakest mountains.—He finds the lacerated lamb of another's flock;—this moment I behold him leaning with his head against his crook, with piteous inclination looking down upon it!—Oh! had I gone one moment sooner!—it bleeds to death!—his gentle heart bleeds with it!

Peace to thee, generous swain!—I see thou walkest off with anguish,—but thy joys shall balance it; for happy is thy cottage,—and happy is the sharer of it,— and happy are the lambs which sport about you.

THE SUPPER.

A SHOE coming loose from the fore-foot of the thill-horse at the beginning of the ascent of Mount Taurira, the postillion dismounted, twisted the shoe off, and put it in his pocket. As the ascent was of five or six miles, and that horse our main dependence, I made a point of having the shoe fastened on again as well as we could; but the postillion had thrown away the nails; and the hammer in the chaise-box being of no great use without them, I submitted to go on.

He had not mounted half a mile higher, when coming to a flinty piece of road, the poor devil lost a second shoe, and from off his other fore-foot. I then got out of the chaise in good earnest; and seeing a house about a quarter of a mile to the left hand, with a great deal to do I prevailed upon the postillion to turn up to it. The look of the house, and of everything about it, as we drew nearer, soon reconciled me to the disaster.—It was a little farm-house, surrounded with about twenty acres of vineyard, about as much corn; and close to the house, on one side, was a *potagerie* of an acre and a half, full of everything which could make plenty in a French peasant's house; and on the other side was a little wood, which furnished wherewithal to dress it. It was about eight in the evening when I got to the house, —so I left the postillion to manage his point as he could; and, for mine, I walked directly into the house.

The family consisted of an old grey-headed man and his wife, with five or six sons and sons-in-law, and their several wives, and a joyous genealogy out of them.

They were all sitting down together to their lentil-soup; a large wheaten loaf was in the middle of the table; and a flagon of wine at each end of it promised joy through the stages of the repast:—'twas a feast of love.

The old man rose up to meet me, and, with a respectful cordiality, would have me sit down at the table;

my heart was set down the moment I entered the room: so I sat down at once, like a son of the family; and, to invest myself in the character as speedily as I could, I instantly borrowed the old man's knife, and, taking up the loaf, cut myself a hearty luncheon; and, as I did it, I saw a testimony in every eye, not only of an honest welcome, but of a welcome mixed with thanks that I had not seemed to doubt it.

Was it this? or tell me, Nature, what else it was, that made this morsel so sweet,—and to what magic I owe it, that the draught I took of their flagon was so delicious with it, that they remain upon my palate to this hour?

If the supper was to my taste, the grace which followed it was much more so.

THE GRACE.

WHEN supper was over, the old man gave a knock upon the table with the haft of his knife, to bid them prepare for the dance; the moment the signal was given, the women and girls ran altogether into a back apartment to tie up their hair,—and the young men to the door to wash their faces, and change their *sabots;* and in three minutes, every soul was ready upon a little esplanade before the house to begin.—The old man and his wife came out last, and, placing me betwixt them, sat down upon a sofa of turf by the door.

The old man had some fifty years ago been no mean performer upon the *vielle*,—and, at the age he was then of, touched it well enough for the purpose.

His wife sung now and then a little to the tune,—then intermitted,—and joined her old man again as their children and grand-children danced before them.

It was not till the middle of the second dance, when, for some pauses in the movement wherein they all seemed to look up, I fancied I could distinguish an elevation of spirit different from that which is the cause or the effect of simple jollity. In a word, I thought I beheld Religion mixing in the dance;—but, as I had never seen her so engaged, I should have looked upon it now as one of the illusions of an imagination which is eternally misleading me, had not the old man, as soon as the dance ended, said that this was their constant way; and that all his life long he had made it a rule, after supper was over, to call out his family to dance and rejoice; believing, he said, that a cheerful and contented mind was the best sort of thanks to Heaven that an illiterate peasant could pay——

——Or a learned prelate either, said I.

THE CASE OF DELICACY.

WHEN you have gained the top of Mount Taurira, you run presently down to Lyons;—adieu then to all rapid movements!—'tis a journey of caution; and it fares better with sentiments, not to be in a hurry with them; so I contracted with a *voiturin* to take his time with a couple of mules, and convey me in my own chase safe to Turin, through Savoy.

Poor, patient, quiet, honest people! fear not; your poverty, the treasury of your simple virtues, will not be envied you by the world, nor will your vallies be invaded by it.—Nature! in the midst of thy disorders, thou art still friendly to the scantiness thou hast created : with all thy great works about thee, little hast thou left to give, either to the scythe or to the sickle—but to that little thou grantest safety and protection ; and sweet are the dwellings which stand so sheltered!

Let the way-worn traveller vent his complaints upon the sudden turns and dangers of your roads, your rocks, your precipices; the difficulties of getting up, the horrors of getting down, mountains impracticable,—and cataracts, which roll down great stones from their summits, and block up his road. The peasants had been all day at work in removing a fragment of this kind between St. Michael and Madane; and, by the time my *voiturin* got to the place, it wanted full two hours of completing, before a passage could anyhow be gained. There was nothing but to wait with patience;—'twas a wet and tempestuous night; so that by the delay and that together, the *voiturin* found himself obliged to put up five miles short of his stage, at a little decent kind of an inn by the roadside.

I forthwith took possession of my bedchamber, got a good fire, ordered supper, and was thanking Heaven it was no worse,—when a *voiturin* arrived with a lady in it, and her servant-maid.

As there was no other bedchamber in the house, the hostess, without much nicety, led them into mine, telling them, as she ushered them in, that there was nobody in it but an English gentleman ;—that there were two good beds in it, and a closet within the room which held another. The accent in which she spoke of this third bed; did not say much for it—however, she said there were three beds, and but three people,—and she durst say the gentleman would do anything to accommodate matters.——I left not the lady a moment to make a conjecture about it, so instantly made a declaration that I would do anything in my power.

As this did not amount to an absolute surrender of my bed-chamber, I still felt myself so much the proprietor, as to have a right to do the honours of it;—so I desired the lady to sit down, pressed her into the warmest seat, called for more wood, desired the hostess to enlarge the plan of the supper, and to favour us with the very best wine.

The lady had scarce warmed herself five minutes at the fire, before she began to turn her head back and to give a look at the beds: and the oftener she cast her eyes that way, the more they returned perplexed.—I felt for her—and for myself; for in a few minutes, what by her looks, and the case itself, I found myself as much embarrassed as it was possible the lady could be herself.

That the beds we were to lie in were in one and the same room, was enough simply by itself to have excited all this;—but the position of them (for they stood parallel, and so very close to each other, as only to allow a space for a small wicker-chair betwixt them) rendered the affair still more oppressive to us;—they were fixed up, moreover, near the fire, and the projection of the chimney on one side; and a large beam which crossed the room on the other, formed a kind of recess for them that was no way favourable to the nicety of our sensations:—if anything could have added to it, it was that the two beds were both of them so very small, as to cut us off from every idea of the lady and the maid lying together; which, in either of them, could it have been feasible, my lying beside them, though a thing not to be wished, yet there was nothing in it so terrible which the imagination might not have passed over without torment.

As for the little room within, it offered little or no consolation to us: 'twas a damp, cold closet, with a half dismantled window-shutter, and with a window which had neither glass nor oil-paper in it to keep out the tempest of the night. I did not endeavour to stifle my cough when the lady gave a peep into it; so it reduced the case in course to this alternative,—That the lady should sacrifice her health to her feelings, and take up with the closet herself, and abandon the bed next mine to her maid,—or, that the girl should take the closet, &c.

The lady was a Piedmontese of about thirty, with a glow of health in her cheeks. The maid was a Lyonoise of twenty, and as brisk and lively a French girl as ever moved. There were difficulties every way,—and the obstacle of the stone in the road, which brought us into the distress, great as it appeared whilst the peasants were removing it, was but a pebble to what lay in our way now—I have only to add, that it did not lessen the weight which hung upon our spirits, that we were both too delicate to communicate what we felt to each other upon the occasion.

We sat down to supper; and, had we not had more

generous wine to it than a little inn in Savoy could have furnished, our tongues had been tied up till Necessity herself had set them at liberty;—but the lady having a few bottles of Burgundy in her voiture, sent down her *fille de chambre* for a couple of them; so that by the time supper was over, and we were left alone, we felt ourselves inspired with a strength of mind sufficient to talk, at least, without reserve upon our situation. We turned it every way, and debated and considered it in all kinds of lights in the course of a two hours' negotiation; at the end of which the articles were settled finally betwixt us, and stipulated for in form and manner of a treaty of peace,—and, I believe, with as much religion and good faith on both sides, as in any treaty which has yet had the honour of being handed down to posterity.

They were as follows:—

First, As the right of the bed-chamber is in Monsieur, —and he thinking the bed next to the fire to be the warmest, he insists upon the concession on the lady's side of taking up with it.

Granted on the part of Madame; with a proviso, That, as the curtains of that bed are of a flimsy transparent cotton, and appear likewise too scanty to draw close, that the *fille de chambre* shall fasten up the opening, either by corking-pins or needle and thread, in such a manner as shall be deemed a sufficient barrier on the side of Monsieur.

2dly, It is required on the part of Madame, that Monsieur shall lie the whole night through in his *robe de chambre*.

Rejected: inasmuch as Monsieur is not worth a *robe de chambre;* he having nothing in his portmanteau but six shirts and a black silk pair of breeches.

The mentioning the silk pair of breeches made an entire change of the article,—for the breeches were accepted as an equivalent for the *robe de chambre;* and so it was stipulated and agreed upon, that I should lie in my black silk breeches all night.

3dly, It was insisted upon, and stipulated for by the lady, that after Monsieur was got to bed, and the candle and fire extinguished, that Monsieur should not speak one single word the whole night.

Granted, provided Monsieur's saying his prayers might not be deemed an infraction of the treaty.

There was but one point forgot in this treaty, and that was the manner in which the lady and myself should be obliged to undress and get to bed;—there was one way of doing it, and that I leave to the reader to devise, protesting as I do it, that if it is not the most delicate in nature,—'tis the fault of his own imagination,—against which this is not my first complaint.

Now when we were got to bed, whether it was the novelty of the situation, or what it was, I know not, but so it was, I could not shut my eyes; I tried this side and that, and turned and turned again, till a full hour after midnight, when Nature and Patience both wearing out,—O my God! said I.

——You have broke the treaty, Monsieur, said the lady, who had no more slept than myself.—I begged a thousand pardons; but insisted it was no more than an ejaculation.——She maintained 'twas an entire infraction of the treaty.——I maintained it was provided for in the clause of the third article.

The lady would by no means give up the point, though she weakened her barrier by it; for, in the warmth of the dispute, I could hear two or three corking pins fall out of the curtain to the ground.

——Upon my word and honour, Madame, said I, stretching my arm out of bed by way of asseveration,—

(I was going to have added, that I would not have trespassed against the remotest idea of decorum for the world)—

—But the *fille de chambre* hearing there were words between us, and fearing that hostilities would ensue in course, had crept silently out of her closet; and it being totally dark, had stolen so close to our beds, that she had got herself into the narrow passage which separated them, and had advanced so far up as to be in a line betwixt her mistress and me;—

So that, when I stretched out my hand, I caught hold of the *fille de chambre's*——

THE POSITION OF DELICACY

A TALE OF A TUB.

THE AUTHOR'S APOLOGY.

IF good and ill nature equally operated upon mankind, I might have saved myself the trouble of this apology; for it is manifest, by the reception the following discourse hath met with, that those who approve it are a great majority among the men of taste; yet there have been two or three treatises written expressly against it, besides many others that have flirted at it occasionally, without one syllable having been ever published in its defence, or even quotation to its advantage, that I can remember, except by the polite author of a late discourse between a deist and a Socinian.

Therefore, since the book seems calculated to live at least as long as our language, and our taste admits no great alterations, I am content to convey some apology along with it.

The greatest part of that book was finished about thirteen years since (1696), which is eight years before it was published. The author was then young, his invention at the height, and his reading fresh in his head. By the assistance of some thinking, and much conversation, he had endeavoured to strip himself of as many real prejudices as he could; I say real ones, because under the notion of prejudices he knew to what dangerous heights some men have proceeded. Thus prepared, he thought the numerous and gross corruptions in religion and learning might furnish matter for a satire that would be useful and diverting: he resolved to proceed in a manner that should be altogether new, the world having been already too long nauseated with endless repetitions upon every subject. The abuses in religion he proposed to set forth in the allegory of the coats and the three brothers, which was to make up the body of the discourse. Those in learning he chose to introduce by way of digressions. He was then a young gentleman much in the world, and wrote to the taste of those who were like himself; therefore in order to allure them, he gave a liberty to his pen which might not suit with maturer years or graver characters, and which he could have easily corrected with a very few blots, had he been master of his papers for a year or two before their publication.

Not that he would have governed his judgment by the ill-placed cavils of the sour, the envious, the stupid, and the tasteless, which he mentions with disdain. He acknowledges there are several youthful sallies, which from the grave and the wise may deserve a rebuke. But he desires to be answerable no farther than he is guilty, and that his faults may not be multiplied by the ignorant, the unnatural and uncharitable applications of those who have neither candour to suppose good meanings, nor palate to distinguish true ones: after which, he will forfeit his life if any one opinion can be fairly deduced from that book which is contrary to religion or morality.

Why should any clergyman of our Church be angry to see the follies of fanaticism and superstition exposed, though in the most ridiculous manner, since that is perhaps the most probable way to cure them, or at least to hinder them from farther spreading? Besides, though it was not intended for their perusal, it rallies nothing but what they preach against. It contains nothing to provoke them by the least scurrility upon their persons or their functions. It celebrates the Church of England as the most perfect of all others in discipline and doctrine; it advances no opinion they reject, nor condemns any they receive. If the clergy's resentments lay upon their hands, in my humble opinion they might have found more proper objects to employ them on: *nondum tibi defuit hostis;* I mean those heavy, illiterate scribblers, prostitute in their reputations, vicious in their lives, and ruined in their fortunes, who, to the shame of good sense as well as piety, are greedily read, merely upon the strength of bold, false, impious assertions, mixed with unmannerly reflections upon the priesthood, and openly intended against all religion, in short, full of such principles as are kindly received, because they are levelled to remove those terrors that religion tells men will be the consequence of immoral lives: nothing like which is to be met with in this discourse, though some of them are pleased so freely to censure it. And I wish there were no other instance of what I have too frequently observed, that many of that reverend body are not always very nice in distinguishing between their enemies and their friends.

Had the author's intentions met with a more candid interpretation from some, whom out of respect he forbears to name, he might have been encouraged to an examination of books written by some of those authors above described, whose errors, ignorance, dulness, and villany he thinks he could have detected and exposed in such a manner, that the persons who are most conceived to be infected by them would soon lay them aside and be ashamed: but he has now given over those thoughts, since the weightiest men* in the weightiest stations are pleased to think it a more dangerous point to laugh at those corruptions in religion which they themselves must disapprove, than to endeavour pulling up those very foundations wherein all Christians have agreed.

He thinks it no fair proceeding that any person should offer determinately to fix a name upon the author of this discourse, who hath all along concealed himself from most of his nearest friends: yet several have gone a farther step, and pronounced another book † to have been the work of the same hand with this, which the author directly affirms to be a thorough mistake, he having yet never so much as read that discourse—a plain instance how little truth there often is in general surmises, or in conjectures drawn from a similitude of style or way of thinking.

Had the author written a book to expose the abuses in law or in physic, he believes the learned professors in either faculty would have been so far from resenting it as to have given him thanks for his pains, especially if he had made an honourable reservation for the true practice of either science.

---

* Alluding to Dr. Sharp's (the Archbishop of York) representation of the author.—*Hawkesworth*.

† *Letter concerning Enthusiasm.*

But religion, they tell us, ought not to be ridiculed; and they tell us truth: yet surely the corruptions in it may; for we are taught by the tritest maxim in the world, that religion being the best of things, its corruptions are likely to be the worst.

There is one thing which the judicious reader cannot but have observed, that some of those passages in this discourse, which appear most liable to objection, are what they call parodies, where the author personates the style and manner of other writers whom he has a mind to expose. I shall produce one instance; it is towards the end of the Introduction. Dryden, L'Estrange, and some others I shall not name, are here levelled at, who, having spent their lives in faction and apostacies and all manner of vice, pretended to be sufferers for loyalty and religion. So Dryden tells us in one of his prefaces of his merits and sufferings, he thanks God that he possesses his soul in patience: in other places he talks at the same rate, and L'Estrange often uses the like style, and I believe the reader may find more persons to give that passage an application: but this is enough to direct those who may have overlooked the author's intention.

There are three or four other passages which prejudiced or ignorant readers have drawn by great force to hint at ill meanings, as if they glanced at some tenets in religion. In answer to all which, the author solemnly protests he is entirely innocent, and never had it once in his thoughts that anything he said would in the least be capable of such interpretation, which he will engage to deduce full as fairly from the most innocent book in the world. And it will be obvious to every reader that this was not any part of his scheme or design, the abuses he notes being such as all Church of England men agree in; nor was it proper for his subject to meddle with other points than such as have been perpetually controverted since the Reformation.

To instance only in that passage about the three wooden machines mentioned in the introduction: in the original manuscripts there was a description of a fourth, which those who had the papers in their power blotted out, as having something in it of satire that I suppose they thought was too particular, and therefore they were forced to change it to the number three, from whence some have endeavoured to squeeze out a dangerous meaning that was never thought on. And indeed the conceit was half spoiled by changing the numbers, that of four being much more cabalistic, and therefore better exposing the pretended virtue of numbers, a superstition there intended to be ridiculed.

Another thing to be observed is, that there generally runs an irony through the thread of the whole book, which the men of taste will observe and distinguish, and which will render some objections that have been made very weak and insignificant.

This apology being chiefly intended for the satisfaction of future readers, it may be thought unnecessary to take any notice of such treatises as have been writ against the ensuing discourse, which are already sunk into waste paper and oblivion, after the usual fate of common answerers to books which are allowed to have any merit: they are, indeed, like annuals that grow about a young tree, and seem to vie with it for a summer, but fall and die with the leaves in autumn, and are never heard of any more. When Dr. Echard writ his book about the contempt of the clergy, numbers of these answers immediately started up, whose memory if he had not kept alive by his replies, it would now be utterly unknown that he were ever answered at all. There is, indeed, an exception when any great genius thinks it worth his while to expose a foolish piece; so we still read Marvel's answer to Parker* with pleasure, though the book it answers be sunk long ago: so the Earl of Orrery's *Remarks*

---

* Parker, afterwards Bishop of Oxford, wrote many treatises against the Dissenters, with insolence and contempt (says Burnet) that enraged them beyond measure; for which he was chastised by Andrew Marvel, under-secretary to Milton, in a little book called, *The Rehearsal Transposed.*—*Hawkes.*

will be read with delight, when the *Dissertation* he exposes will be neither sought nor found :* but these are no enterprises for common hands, nor to be hoped for above once or twice in an age. Men would be more cautious of losing their time in such an undertaking, if they did but consider that to answer a book effectually requires more pains and skill, more wit, learning, and judgment, than were employed in the writing it. And the author assures those gentlemen who have given themselves that trouble with him, that his discourse is the product of the study, the observation, and the invention of several years; that he often blotted out much more than he left, and if his papers had not been a long time out of his possession, they must have still undergone more severe corrections: and do they think such a building is to be battered with dirt-pellets, however envenomed the mouths may be that discharge them? He had seen the productions but of two answerers, one of which at first appeared as from an unknown hand, but since avowed by a person † who, upon some occasions, hath discovered no ill vein of humour.

---

* Boyle's Remarks upon Bentley's *Dissertation on the Epistles of Phalaris.—Hawkes.*

† Supposed to be Dr. William King, the civilian, author of an *Account of Denmark*, a *Dissertation on Samplars*, and other pieces of burlesque on the Royal Society, and the *Art of Cookery*, in imitation of Horace's *Art of Poetry*, etc.—*Hawkes.*

'Tis a pity any occasion should put him under a necessity of being so hasty in his productions, which otherwise might often be entertaining. But there were other reasons obvious enough for his miscarriage in this; he writ against the conviction of his talent, and entered upon one of the wrongest attempts in nature, to turn into ridicule by a week's labour a work which had cost so much time, and met with so much success in ridiculing others; the manner how he handled his subject I have now forgot, having just looked it over when it first came out, as others did, merely for the sake of the title.*

The other answer is from a person of a graver character, and is made up of half invective and half annotation,† in the latter of which he hath generally succeeded well enough. And the project at that time was not amiss, to draw in readers to his pamphlet, several having appeared desirous that there might be some explication of the more difficult passages. Neither can he be altogether blamed for offering at

* This we cannot recover at present, it being so absolutely forgotten, the oldest booksellers in trade remember nothing of it.—*Hawkes.*

† Wotton's *Defence of his Reflections upon Ancient and Modern Learning.* From the annotations are selected the notes signed W. Wotton. Thus Wotton appears busied to illustrate a work he laboured to condemn, and adds force to a satire pointed against himself: as captives were bound to the chariot-wheel of the victor, and compelled to increase the pomp of his triumph, whom they had in vain attempted to defeat.—*Hawkes.*

the invective part, because it is agreed on all hands that the author had given him a sufficient provocation. The great objection is against his manner of treating it, very unsuitable to one of his function. It was determined by a fair majority that this answerer had, in a way not to be pardoned, drawn his pen against a certain great man then alive, and universally reverenced for every good quality that could possibly enter into the composition of the most accomplished person; it was observed how he was pleased and affected to have that noble writer called his adversary, and it was a point of satire well directed; for I have been told Sir W. Temple was sufficiently mortified at the term. All the men of wit and politeness were immediately up in arms, through indignation, which prevailed over their contempt by the consequences they apprehended from such an example, and it grew to be Porsenna's case, *idem trecenti juravimus.* In short, things were ripe for a general insurrection, till my Lord Orrery had a little laid the spirit and settled the ferment. But his lordship being principally engaged with another antagonist,[*] it was thought necessary in order to quiet the minds of men, that this opposer should receive a reprimand, which partly occasioned that discourse of the *Battle of the Books*, and the author was further at the pains

---

[*] Bentley, concerning Phalaris and Æsop.—*Hawkes.*

to insert one or two remarks on him in the body of the book.

This answerer has been pleased to find fault with about a dozen passages, which the author will not be at the trouble of defending, further than by assuring the reader that for the greater part the reflector is entirely mistaken, and forces interpretations which never once entered into the writer's head, nor will, he is sure, into that of any reader of taste and candour; he allows two or three at most there produced to have been delivered unwarily, for which he desires to plead the excuse offered already—of his youth and frankness of speech, and his papers being out of his power at the time they were published.

But this answerer insists, and says, what he chiefly dislikes is the design: what that was I have already told, and I believe there is not a person in England, who can understand that book, that ever imagined it to have been anything else but to expose the abuses and corruptions in learning and religion.

But it would be good to know what design this reflector was serving, when he concludes his pamphlet by a caution to readers to beware of thinking the author's wit was entirely his own. Surely this must have had some alloy of personal animosity, at least, mixed with the design of serving the public by so useful a discovery; and it indeed touches the author in a very tender point, who insists upon it, that through the whole book he has not borrowed one single hint from any writer in the world; and he thought of all criticisms that would never have been one. He conceived it was never disputed to be an original, whatever faults it might have. However, this answerer produces three instances to prove this author's wit is not his own in many places. The first is, that the names of Peter, Martin, and Jack are borrowed from a letter of the late Duke of Buckingham.* Whatever wit is contained in those three names the author is content to give it up, and desires his readers will substract as much as they placed upon that account; at the same time protesting solemnly that he never once heard of that letter, except in this passage of the answerer: so that the names were not borrowed, as he affirms, though they should happen to be the same, which, however, is odd enough, and what he hardly believes, that of Jack being not quite so obvious as the other two. The second instance to show the author's wit is not his own, is Peter's banter, as he calls it, in his Alsatian phrase, upon transubstantiation, which is taken from the same duke's conference with an Irish priest, where a cork is turned into a horse. This the author confesses to have seen about ten years after his book

* Villiers.

was writ, and a year or two after it was published. Nay, the answerer overthrows this himself; for he allows the tale was writ in 1697, and I think that pamphlet was not printed till many years after. It was necessary that corruption should have some allegory as well as the rest; and the author invented the properest he could, without inquiring what other people had written; and the commonest reader will find there is not the least resemblance between the two stories. The third instance is in these words: "I have been assured that the *Battle in St. James' Library* is, *mutatis mutandis*, taken out of a French book, entitled *Combat des Livres*, if I misremember not." In which passage there are two clauses observable, "I have been assured," and "if I misremember not." I desire first to know whether, if that conjecture proves an utter falsehood, those two clauses will be a sufficient excuse for this worthy critic. The matter is a trifle; but would he venture to pronounce at this rate upon one of greater moment? I know nothing more contemptible in a writer than the character of a plagiary, which he here fixes at a venture, and this not for a passage, but a whole discourse taken out from another book, only *mutatis mutandis*. The author is as much in the dark about this as the answerer, and will imitate him by an affirmation at random, that if there be a word of truth in this reflection, he is a paltry imitating pedant, and the answerer is a person of wit, manners, and truth. He takes his boldness from never having seen any such treatise in his life, nor heard of it before; and he is sure it is impossible for two writers of different times and countries to agree in their thoughts after such a manner, that two continued discourses shall be the same, only *mutatis mutandis*. Neither will he insist upon the mistake on the title; but let the answerer and his friend produce any book they please, he defies them to show one single particular where the judicious reader will affirm he has been obliged for the smallest hint, giving only allowance for the accidental encountering of a single thought, which he knows may sometimes happen, though he has never yet found it in that discourse, nor has heard it objected by anybody else.

So that if ever any design was unfortunately executed, it must be that of this answerer, who, when he would have it observed that the author's wit is none of his own, is able to produce but three instances, two of them mere trifles, and all three manifestly false. If this be the way these gentlemen deal with the world in those criticisms where we have not leisure to defeat them, their readers had need be cautious how they rely upon their credit; and whether this proceeding can be reconciled to humanity or truth.

let those who think it worth their while determine.

It is agreed this answerer would have succeeded much better if he had stuck wholly to his business as a commentator upon the *Tale of a Tub*, wherein it cannot be denied that he hath been of some service to the public, and has given very fair conjectures towards clearing up some difficult passages; but it is the frequent error of those men (otherwise very commendable for their labours) to make excursions beyond their talent and their office, by pretending to point out the beauties and the faults, which is no part of their trade, which they always fail in, which the world never expected from them, nor gave them any thanks for endeavouring at. The part of Minellius or Farnaby* would have fallen in with his genius, and might have been serviceable to many readers who cannot enter into the abstruser parts of that discourse; but *optat ephippia bos piger*, the dull, unwieldy, ill-shaped ox would needs put on the furniture of a horse, not considering he was born to labour, to plough the ground for the sake of superior beings, and that he has neither the shape, mettle, nor speed of that nobler animal he would affect to personate.

* Low commentators, who wrote notes upon classic authors for the use of schoolboys.—*Hawkes.*

It is another pattern of this answerer's fair dealing to give us hints that the author is dead, and yet to lay the suspicion upon somebody, I know not who, in the country; to which can only be returned, that he is absolutely mistaken in all his conjectures; and surely conjectures are at best too light a pretence to allow a man to assign a name in public. He condemns a book, and consequently the author, of whom he is utterly ignorant, yet at the same time fixes in print what he thinks a disadvantageous character upon those who never deserve it. A man who receives a buffet in the dark may be allowed to be vexed; but it is an odd kind of revenge to go to cuffs in broad day with the first that he meets, and lay the last night's injury at his door. And thus much for this discreet, candid, pious, and ingenious answerer.

How the author came to be without his papers is a story not proper to be told, and of very little use, being a private fact, of which the reader would believe as little or as much as he thought good. He had, however, a blotted copy by him, which he intended to have written over with many alterations, and this the publishers were well aware of, having put it into the bookseller's preface that they apprehended a surreptitious copy, which was to be altered, &c. This, though not regarded by readers, was a real truth, only the surreptitious copy was rather that which was printed; and they made all the haste they could, which indeed was needless, the author not being at all prepared; but he has been told the bookseller was in much pain, having given a good sum for the copy.

In the author's original copy there were not so many chasms as appear in the book; and why some of them were left he knows not: had the publication been trusted to him, he would have made several corrections of passages against which nothing 'hath ever been objected. He would likewise have altered a few of those that seem with any reason to be excepted against; but, to deal freely, the greatest number he should have left untouched, as never suspecting it possible any wrong interpretations could be made of them.

The author observes at the end of the book there is a discourse called *A Fragment*, which he more wondered to see in print than all the rest. Having been a most imperfect sketch, with the addition of a few loose hints which he once lent a gentleman who had designed a discourse of somewhat the same subject, he never thought of it afterwards, and it was sufficient surprise to see it pieced up together wholly out of the method and scheme he had intended; for it was the groundwork of a much larger discourse, and he was sorry to observe the materials so foolishly employed.

There is one further objection made by those who have answered this book, as well as by some others, that Peter is frequently made to repeat oaths and curses. Every reader observes, it was necessary to know that Peter did swear and curse. The oaths are not printed out, but only supposed, and the idea of an oath is not immoral, like the idea of a profane or immodest speech. A man may laugh at the popish folly of cursing people to hell, and imagine them swearing, without any crime; but lewd words or dangerous opinions, though printed by halves, fill the reader's mind with ill ideas; and of these the author cannot be accused. For the judicious reader will find that the severest strokes of satire in his book are levelled against the modern custom of employing wit upon those topics, of which there is a remarkable instance in the seventh section, as well as in several others, though perhaps once or twice expressed in too free a manner, excusable only for the reasons already alleged. Some overtures have been made by a third hand to the bookseller for the author's altering those passages which he thought might require it. But it seems the bookseller will not hear of any such thing, being apprehensive it might spoil the sale of the book.

The author cannot conclude this apology without making this one reflection, that as wit is the noblest and most useful gift of human nature, so humour is the most agreeable; and where these two enter far into the composition of any work, they will render it always acceptable to the world. Now the greater part of those who have no share or taste of either, but by their pride, pedantry, and ill manners lay themselves bare to the lashes of both, think the blow is weak because they are insensible; and where wit hath any mixture of raillery, 'tis but calling it banter, and the work is done. This polite word of theirs was first borrowed from the bullies in Whitefriars, then fell among the footmen, and at last retired to the pedants, by whom it is applied as properly to the productions of wit, as if I should apply it to Sir Isaac Newton's mathematics. But if this bantering, as they call it, be so despisable a thing, whence comes it to pass they have such a perpetual itch towards it themselves? To instance only in the answerer already mentioned; it is grievous to see him, in some of his writings, at every turn going out of his way to be waggish, to tell us of *a cow that pricked up her tail:* and in his answer to this discourse he says *it is all a farce and a ladle*, with other passages equally shining. One may say of these *impedimenta literarum*, that wit owes them a shame;

and they cannot take wiser counsel than to keep out of harm's way, or at least not to come till they are sure they are called.

To conclude: with those allowances above required this book should be read, after which, the author conceives, few things will remain which may not be excused in a young writer. He wrote only to the men of wit and taste, and he thinks he is not mistaken in his accounts when he says they have been all of his side, enough to give him the vanity of telling his name, wherein the world, with all its wise conjectures, is yet very much in the dark; which circumstance is no disagreeable amusement either to the public or himself.

The author is informed that the bookseller has prevailed on several gentlemen to write some explanatory notes, for the goodness of which he is not to answer, having never seen any of them, nor intending it till they appear in print, when it is not unlikely he may have the pleasure to find twenty meanings which never entered into his imagination.

June 3, 1709.

POSTSCRIPT.

SINCE the writing of this, which was about a year ago, a prostitute bookseller hath published a foolish paper, under the name of *Notes on the Tale of a Tub*, with some account of the author; and with an insolence, which I suppose is punishable by law, hath presumed to assign certain names. It will be enough for the author to assure the world that the writer of that paper is utterly wrong in all his conjectures upon that affair. The author further asserts that the whole work is entirely of one hand, which every reader of judgment will easily discover, the gentleman who gave the copy to the bookseller being a friend of the author, and using no other liberties besides that of expunging certain passages, where now the chasms appear under the name of desiderata. But if any person will prove his claim to three lines in the whole book, let him step forth and tell his name and titles, upon which the bookseller shall have orders to prefix them to next edition, and the claimant shall from henceforward be acknowledged the undisputed author.

TO THE RIGHT HONOURABLE

JOHN LORD SOMERS.

―――o―――

My Lord,—Although the author has written a large dedication, yet that being addressed to a prince whom I am never likely to have the honour of being known to—a person, besides, as far as I can observe, not at all regarded or thought on by any of our present writers; and being wholly free from that slavery which booksellers usually lie under to the caprices of authors, I think it a wise piece of presumption to inscribe these papers to your Lordship, and to implore your Lordship's protection of them. God, and your Lordship, know their faults and their merits; for as to my own particular, I am altogether a stranger to the matter; and though everybody else should be equally ignorant, I do not fear the sale of the book at all the worse upon that score. Your Lordship's name on the front in capital letters will at any time get off one edition; neither would I desire any other help to grow an alderman than a patent for the sole privilege of dedicating to your Lordship.

I should now, in right of a dedicator, give your Lordship a list of your own virtues, and at the same time be very unwilling to offend your modesty; but chiefly I should celebrate your liberality towards men of great parts and small fortunes, and give you broad hints that I mean myself. And I was just going on in the usual method, to peruse a hundred or two of dedications, and transcribe an abstract, to be applied to your Lordship, but I was diverted by a certain accident. For upon the covers of these papers I casually observed, written in large letters, the two following words, DETUR DIGNISSIMO, which, for aught I knew, might contain some important meaning. But it unluckily fell out that none of the authors I employ understood Latin, though I have them often in pay to translate out of that language; I was therefore compelled to have recourse to the curate of our parish, who Englished it thus, *Let it be given to the worthiest.* And his comment was, that the author meant his work should be dedicated to the sublimest genius of the age for wit, learning, judgment, eloquence, and wisdom. I called at a poet's chamber (who works for my shop) in an alley hard by, showed him the translation, and desired his opinion who it was that the author could mean: he told me, after some consideration, that vanity was a thing he abhorred; but by the description he thought himself to be the person aimed at, and at the same time he very kindly offered his own assistance *gratis* towards penning a dedication to himself. I desired him, however, to give a second guess; why then, said he, it must be I, or my Lord Somers. From thence I went to several other wits of my acquaintance, with no small hazard and weariness to my person, from a prodigious number of dark, winding stairs, but found them all in the same story, both of your Lordship and themselves. Now your Lordship is to understand that this proceeding was not of my own invention; for I have somewhere heard it is a maxim, that those to whom everybody allows the second place have an undoubted title to the first.

This infallibly convinced me that your Lordship was the person intended by the author. But being very unacquainted in the style and form of dedications, I employed those wits aforesaid to furnish me with hints and materials towards a panegyric upon your Lordship's virtues.

In two days they brought me ten sheets of paper filled up on every side. They swore to me that they had ransacked whatever could be found in the characters of Socrates, Aristides, Epaminondas, Cato,

Tully, Atticus, and other hard names which I cannot now recollect. However, I have reason to believe they imposed upon my ignorance, because, when I came to read over their collections, there was not a syllable there but what I and everybody else knew as well as themselves. Therefore I grievously suspect a cheat, and that these authors of mine stole and transcribed every word from the universal report of mankind. So that I look upon myself as fifty shillings out of pocket to no manner of purpose.

If by altering the title I could make the same materials serve for another dedication, as my betters have done, it would help to make up my loss: but I have made several persons dip here and there in those papers, and before they read three lines they have all assured me plainly that they cannot possibly be applied to any person besides your Lordship.

I expected, indeed, to have heard of your Lordship's bravery at the head of an army; of your undaunted courage in mounting a breach, or scaling a wall; or to have had your pedigree traced in a lineal descent from the house of Austria; or your wonderful talent at dress and dancing; or your profound knowledge in algebra, metaphysics, and the oriental tongues. But to ply the world with an old beaten story of your wit, and eloquence, and learning, and wisdom, and justice, and politeness, and candour, and evenness of temper in all scenes of life; of that great discernment in discovering, and readiness in favouring deserving men, with forty other common topics, I confess I have neither conscience nor countenance to do it. Because there is no virtue, either of a public or private life, which some circumstances of your own have not often produced upon the stage of the world; and those few which, for want of occasions to exert them, might otherwise have passed unseen or unobserved by your *friends*, your *enemies* * have at length brought to light.

It is true, I should be very loth that the bright example of your Lordship's virtues should be lost to after-ages, both for their sake and your own, but chiefly because they will be so very necessary to adorn the history of a late reign; † and that is another reason why I would forbear to make a recital of them here, because I have been told by wise men, that as dedications have run for some years past, a good historian will not be apt to have recourse thither in search of characters.

---

* In 1701 Lord Somers was impeached by the Commons, who, either finding their proofs defective, or, for other reasons, delayed coming to trial, and the Lords thereupon proceeded to the trial without them, and acquitted him.—*Hawkes.*

† King William's, whose memory he defended in the House of Lords against some invidious reflections of the Earl of Nottingham. —*Hawkes.*

There is one point wherein I think we dedicators would do well to change our measures; I mean, instead of running on so far upon the praise of our patrons' *liberality*, to spend a word or two in admiring their *patience.* I can put no greater compliment on your Lordship's, than by giving you so ample an occasion to exercise it at present. Though perhaps I shall not be apt to reckon much merit to your Lordship upon that score, who having been formerly used to tedious harangues,* sometimes to as little purpose, will be the readier to pardon this, especially when it is offered by one who is, with all respect and veneration,—My LORD,

   Your Lordship's most obedient

   And most faithful servant,

    THE BOOKSELLER.

---

* Sir John Somers was Attorney-General, then made Lord Keeper of the Seals in 1692, and Lord High Chancellor and Baron of Evesham in April 1697.—*Hawkes.*

THE BOOKSELLER TO THE READER.

---o---

IT is now six years * since these papers came first to my hand, which seems to have been about a twelvemonth after they were written. For the author tells us in his preface to the first treatise, that he had calculated it for the year 1697, and in several passages of that discourse, as well as the second, it appears they were written about that time.

As to the author, I can give no manner of satisfaction; however, I am credibly informed that this publication is without his knowledge, for he concludes the copy is lost, having lent it to a person since dead, and being never in possession of it after. So that whether the work received his last hand, or whether he intended to fill up the defective places, is like to remain a secret.

If I should go about to tell the reader by what

---

* The *Tale of a Tub* was first published in 1704.—*Hawkes.*

accident I became master of these papers it would in this unbelieving age pass for little more than the cant or jargon of the trade. I therefore gladly spare both him and myself so unnecessary a trouble. There yet remains a difficult question why I published them no sooner. I forebore upon two accounts: first, because I thought I had better work upon my hands; and secondly, because I was not without some hope of hearing from the author, and receiving his directions. But I have been lately alarmed with intelligence of a surreptitious copy, which a certain great wit had new polished and refined, or, as our present writers express themselves, fitted to the humour of the age, as they have already done with great felicity to Don Quixote, Boccalini, La Bruyere, and other authors. However, I thought it fairer dealing to offer the whole work in its naturals. If any gentleman will please to furnish me with a key, in order to explain the more difficult parts, I shall very gratefully acknowledge the favour, and print it by itself.

THE EPISTLE DEDICATORY.

---o---

TO HIS ROYAL HIGHNESS
PRINCE POSTERITY.*

---o---

SIR, I here present your Highness with the fruits of a very few leisure hours stolen from the short intervals of a world of business, and of an employment quite alien from such amusements as this: the poor production of that refuse of time which has lain heavy upon my hands during a long prorogation of

---

* The citation out of Irenæus which originally appeared in the title-page to the *Tale of a Tub, &c.*, and is here suppressed, seems to be all gibberish; it is a form of initiation, used anciently by the Marcosian heretics.—*W. Wotton.*

It is the usual style of decried writers to appeal to Posterity, who is here represented as a prince in his nonage, and *Time* as his governor; and the author begins in a way very frequent with him, by personating other writers, who sometimes offer such reasons and excuses for publishing their works as they ought chiefly to conceal and be ashamed of.

Parliament, a great dearth of foreign news, and a tedious fit of rainy weather: for which, and other reasons, it cannot choose extremely to deserve such a patronage as that of your Highness, whose numberless virtues in so few years make the world look upon you as the future example to all princes. For although your Highness is hardly got clear of infancy, yet has the universal learned world already resolved upon appealing to your future dictates with the lowest and most resigned submission, fate having decreed you sole arbiter of the productions of human wit in this polite and most accomplished age. Methinks the number of appellants were enough to shock and startle any judge of a genius less unlimited than yours. But, in order to prevent such glorious trials, the person, it seems, to whose care the education of your Highness is committed, has resolved, I am told, to keep you in almost universal ignorance of your studies, which it is your inherent birthright to inspect.

It is amazing to me that this person should have assurance, in the face of the sun, to go about persuading your Highness that our age is almost wholly illiterate, and has hardly produced one writer upon any subject. I know very well that when your Highness shall come to riper years, and have gone through the learning of antiquity, you will be too curious to neglect inquiring into the authors of the very age before you. And to think that this *Insolent*, in the account he is preparing for your view, designs to reduce them to a number so insignificant as I am ashamed to mention, it moves my zeal and my spleen for the honour and interest of our vast flourishing body, as well as of myself, for whom I know by long experience he has professed, and still continues, a peculiar malice.

It is not unlikely, that when your Highness will one day peruse what I am now writing, you may be ready to expostulate with your governor upon the credit of what I here affirm, and command him to show you some of our productions: to which he will answer (for I am well informed of his designs) by asking your Highness where they are, and what is become of them? and pretend it a demonstration that there never were any, because they are not then to be found. Not to be found! Who has mislaid them? Are they sunk in the abyss of things? It is certain that in their own nature they were light enough to swim upon the surface for all eternity, therefore the fault is in him who tied weights so heavy to their heels as to depress them to the centre. Is their very essence destroyed? who has annihilated them? were they drowned by purges or martyred by pipes? who administered them to the posteriors of —— ? But that it may no longer be a doubt with your Highness who is to be the author of this universal ruin, I beseech you to observe that large and terrible scythe which your governor affects to bear continually about him. Be pleased to remark the length and strength, the sharpness and hardness of his nails and teeth; consider his baneful, abominable breath, enemy to life and matter, infectious, and corrupting, and then reflect whether it be possible for any mortal ink or paper of this generation to make a suitable resistance. Oh that your Highness would one day resolve to disarm this usurping *maire du palais** of his furious engines, and bring your empire *hors de page*.†

It were endless to recount the several methods of tyranny and destruction which your governor is pleased to practise on this occasion. His inveterate malice is such to the writings of our age, that of several thousands produced yearly from this renowned city, before the next revolution of the sun there is not one to be heard of. Unhappy infants, many of them barbarously destroyed before they have so

---

* Comptroller. The kingdom of France had a race of kings which they call *les rois fainéans*, from their doing nothing, who lived lazily in their apartments, while the kingdom was administered by the *maire de palais*, till Charles Martel, the last mayor, put his master to death, and took the kingdom into his own hand.—*Hawkes.*

† Out of guardianship.

much as learned their mother tongue to beg for pity! Some he stifles in their cradles, others he frights into convulsions, whereof they suddenly die: some he flays alive, others he tears limb from limb. Great numbers are offered to Moloch, and the rest, tainted by his breath, die of a languishing consumption.

But the concern I have most at heart is for our corporation of poets, from whom I am preparing a petition to your Highness, to be subscribed with the names of one hundred and thirty-six of the first rate, but whose immortal productions are never likely to reach your eyes, though each of them is now humble and an earnest appellant for the laurel, and has large comely volumes to show for a support to his pretensions. The never-dying works of these illustrious persons, your governor, sir, has devoted to unavoidable death; and your Highness is to be made believe that our age has never arrived at the honour to produce one single poet.

We confess immortality to be a great and powerful goddess: but in vain we offer up to her our devotions, and our sacrifices, if your Highness' governor, who has usurped the priesthood, must, by an unparalleled ambition and avarice, wholly intercept and devour them.

To affirm that our age is altogether unlearned, and

devoid of writers in any kind, seems to be an assertion so bold and so false, that I have been sometimes thinking the contrary may almost be provoked by uncontrollable demonstration. It is true, indeed, that although their numbers be vast, and their productions numerous in proportion, yet they are hurried so hastily off the scene that they escape our memory and elude our sight. When I first thought of this address, I had prepared a copious list of titles to present your Highness, as an undisputed argument for what I affirm: the originals were posted fresh upon all gates and corners of streets; but returning in a very few hours to take a review, they were all torn down, and fresh ones in their places. I inquired after them among readers and booksellers, but I inquired in vain; the *memorial of them was lost among men, their place was no more to be found;* and I was laughed to scorn for a clown and a pedant, without all taste and refinement, little versed in the course of present affairs, and that knew nothing of what had passed in the best companies of court and town. So that I can only avow in general to your Highness that we do abound in learning and wit; but to fix upon particulars is a task too slippery for my slender abilities. If I should venture, in a windy day, to affirm to your Highness that there is a large cloud near the horizon in the form of a bear, another in the zenith with the head of an ass, a third to the westward with claws like a dragon, and your Highness should in a few minutes think fit to examine the truth, it is certain they would all be changed in figure and position : new ones would arise, and all we could agree upon would be, that clouds there were, but that I was grossly mistaken in the zoography and topography of them.

But your governor, perhaps, may still insist, and put the question, What is, then, become of those immense bales of paper which must have needs been employed in such numbers of books? Can these, also, be wholly annihilate, and so of a sudden as I pretend? What shall I say in return of so invidious an objection? it ill befits the distance between your Highness and me to send you for ocular conviction to a jakes or an oven, to the windows of a brothel, or to a sordid lantern. Books, like men, their authors, have no more than one way of coming into the world, but there are ten thousand to go out of it and return no more.

I profess to your Highness, in the integrity of my heart, that what I am going to say is literally true this minute I am writing. What revolutions may happen before it shall be ready for your perusal I can by no means warrant. However, I beg of you to accept it as a specimen of our learning, our politeness, and our wit. I do therefore affirm, upon the word of a sincere man, that there is now actually in being a certain poet, called John Dryden, whose translation of Virgil was lately printed in a large folio, well bound, and if diligent search were made, for aught I know is yet to be seen. There is another called Nahum Tate, who is ready to make oath that he has caused many reams of verse to be published, whereof both himself and his bookseller (if lawfully required) can still produce authentic copies, and therefore wonders why the world is pleased to make such a secret of it. There is a third, known by the name of Tom Durfey, a poet of a vast comprehension, and universal genius, and most profound learning. There are also one Mr. Rymer, and one Mr. Dennis, most profound critics. There is a person styled Dr. B—tl—y, who has written near a thousand pages of immense erudition, giving a full and true account of a certain squabble of wonderful importance between himself and a bookseller.* He is a writer of infinite wit and humour; no man rallies with a better grace, and in more sprightly turns. Further, I avow to your Highness that with these eyes I have beheld the

---

* Bentley, in his controversy with Lord Orrery upon the genuineness of Phalaris' epistles, has given in a preface a long account of his dialogues with a bookseller about the loan and restitution of a MS.— *Hawkes.*

person of William W—tt—n, B.D., who has written a good sizeable volume against a friend of your governor * (from whom, alas! he must therefore look for little favour) in a most gentlemanly style, adorned with the utmost politeness and civility, replete with discoveries equally valuable for their novelty and use, and embellished with *traits* of wit so poignant and so apposite, that he is a worthy yokemate to his fore-mentioned friend.

Why should I go upon farther particulars, which might fill a volume with the just eulogies of my contemporary brethren? I shall bequeath this piece of justice to a larger work, wherein I intend to write a character of the present set of wits in our nation. Their persons I shall describe particularly and at length, their genius and understanding in miniature.

In the meantime, I do here make bold to present your Highness with a faithful abstract, drawn from the universal body of all arts and sciences, intended wholly for your service and instruction. Nor do I doubt in the least but your Highness will peruse it as carefully, and make as considerable improvements as other young princes have already done, by the

---

* Sir William Temple.

many volumes of late years written for a help to their studies.*

That your Highness may advance in wisdom and virtue, as well as years, and at last outshine all your royal ancestors, shall be the daily prayer of,

Sir,

Your Highness'

Most devoted, &c.

December 1697.

---

* There were innumerable books printed for the use of the Dauphin of France.—*Hawkes.*

THE AUTHOR'S PREFACE.

THE wits of the present age being so very numerous and penetrating, it seems the grandees of Church and State begin to fall under horrible apprehensions lest these gentlemen, during the intervals of a long peace, should find leisure to pick holes in the weak sides of religion and government: to prevent which there has been much thought employed of late upon certain projects for taking off the force and edge of those formidable inquirers from canvassing and reasoning upon such delicate points. They have at length fixed upon one which will require some time as well as cost to perfect. Meanwhile the danger is hourly increasing by new levies of wits, all appointed, as there is reason to fear, with pen, ink, and paper, which may, at an hour's warning, be drawn out into pamphlets and other offensive weapons ready for immediate execution, it was judged of absolute necessity that some present expedient be thought on till the main design can be brought to maturity. To this end, at a grand committee some days ago this important discovery was made by a certain curious and refined observer: that seamen have a custom, when they meet a whale, to fling him out an empty tub, by way of amusement, to divert him from laying violent hands upon the ship. This parable was immediately mythologised. The whale was interpreted to be Hobbes' *Leviathan*, which tosses and plays with all schemes of religion and government, whereof a great many are hollow, and dry, and empty, and noisy, and wooden, and given to rotation. This is the Leviathan from whence the terrible wits of our age are said to borrow their weapons. The ship in danger is easily understood to be its old antitype, the commonwealth. But how to analyse the tub was a matter of difficulty; when, after long inquiry and debate, the literal meaning was preserved: and it was decreed that, in order to prevent these leviathans from tossing and sporting with the commonwealth, which of itself is too apt to fluctuate, they should be diverted from that game by a TALE OF A TUB. And my genius being conceived to lie not unhappily that way, I had the honour done me to be engaged in the performance.

This is the sole design in publishing the following treatise, which I hope will serve for an *interim* of some months to employ those unquiet spirits, till the perfecting of that great work, into the secret of which it is reasonable the courteous reader should have some little light.

It is intended that a large academy be erected, capable of containing nine thousand seven hundred forty and three persons, which, by modest computation, is reckoned to be pretty near the current number of wits in this island. These are to be disposed into the several schools of this academy, and there pursue those studies to which their genius most inclines them. The undertaker himself will publish his proposals with all convenient speed, to which I shall refer the curious reader for a more particular account, mentioning at present only a few of the principal schools. There is, first, a large *pæderastic* school, with French and Italian masters; there is also the *spelling* school, *a very spacious building;* the school of *looking-glasses;* the school of *swearing;* the school of *critics;* the school of *salvation;* the school of *hobby-horses;* the school of *poetry;* the school of *tops;* * the school of *spleen;* the school of *gaming;* and many others too tedious to recount. No person

---

* This, I think, the author should have omitted, it being of the very same nature with the school of *hobby-horses*, if one may venture to censure one who is so severe a censurer of others, perhaps with too little distinction.]

to be admitted member into any of these schools without an attestation, under two sufficient persons' hands, certifying him to be a wit.

But to return: I am sufficiently instructed in the principal duty of a preface, if my genius were capable of arriving at it. Thrice have I forced my imagination to make the tour of its invention, and thrice it has returned empty, the latter having been wholly drained by the following treatise. Not so my more successful brethren, the moderns, who will by no means let slip a preface or dedication without some notable distinguishing stroke to surprise the reader at the entry, and kindle a wonderful expectation of what is to ensue. Such was that of a most ingenious poet, who, soliciting his brain for something new, compared himself to the hangman and his patron to the patient. This was *insigne, recens, indictum ore alio.** When I went through that necessary and noble course of study,† I had the happiness to observe many such egregious touches, which I shall not injure the authors by transplanting, because I have remarked that nothing is so very tender as a *modern* piece of wit, and which is very apt to suffer so much in the carriage. Some things are extremely witty to-day, or fasting, or in this place, or at eight

---

* Horace. Something extraordinary new, and never hit upon before.
† Reading prefaces, &c.

o'clock, or over a bottle, or spoken by Mr. What-d'-ye-call-'m, or in a summer's morning, any of the which, by the smallest transposal or misapplication, is utterly annihilate. Thus, wit has its walks and purlieus, out of which it may not stray the breadth of a hair upon peril of being lost. The moderns have artfully fixed this mercury, and reduced it to the circumstances of time, place, and person. Such a jest there is that will not pass out of Covent Garden, and such a one that is nowhere intelligible but at Hyde Park Corner. Now, though it sometimes tenderly affects me to consider that all the towardly passages I shall deliver in the following treatise will grow quite out of date and relish with the first shifting of the present scene, yet I must needs subscribe to the justice of this proceeding, because I cannot imagine why we should be at expense to furnish wit for succeeding ages, when the former have made no sort of provision for ours; wherein I speak the sentiment of the very newest, and consequently the most orthodox refiners, as well as my own. However, being extremely solicitous that every accomplished person who has got into the taste of wit calculated for this present month of August 1697, should descend to the very bottom of all the sublime throughout this treatise, I hold fit to lay down this general maxim: whatever reader desires to have a thorough comprehension of an author's thoughts cannot take a better method than by putting himself into the circumstances and postures of life that the writer was in upon every important passage as it flowed from his pen, for this will introduce parity and strict correspondence of ideas between the reader and the author. Now, to assist the diligent reader in so delicate an affair, as far as brevity will permit, I have recollected that the shrewdest pieces of this treatise were conceived in bed in a garret. At other times, for a reason best known to myself, I thought fit to sharpen my intention with hunger; and, in general, the whole work was begun, continued, and ended under a long course of physic and a great want of money. Now I do affirm, it will be absolutely impossible for the candid peruser to go along with me in a great many bright passages, unless, upon the several difficulties emergent, he will please to capacitate and prepare himself by these directions. And this I lay down as my principal *postulatum*.

Because I have professed to be a most devoted servant of all *modern* forms, I apprehend some curious wit may object against me for proceeding thus far in a preface without declaiming, according to the custom, against the multitude of writers whereof the whole multitude of writers most reasonably complain. I am just come from perusing some hundreds of prefaces, wherein the authors do at the very beginning address the gentle reader concerning this enormous grievance. Of these I have preserved a few examples, and shall set them down as near as my memory has been able to retain them.

One begins thus: "For a man to set up for a writer when the press swarms with," &c.

Another: "The tax upon paper does not lessen the number of scribblers who daily pester," &c.

Another: "When every little would-be-wit takes pen in hand 'tis in vain to enter the list," &c.

Another: "To observe what trash the press swarms with," &c.

Another: "Sir, it is merely in obedience to your commands that I venture into the public; for who, upon a less consideration, would be of a party with such a rabble of scribblers?" &c.

Now, I have two words in my own defence against this objection. First, I am far from granting the number of writers a nuisance to our nation, having strenuously maintained the contrary in several parts of the following discourse. Secondly, I do not well understand the justice of this proceeding, because I observe many of these polite prefaces to be not only from the same hand, but from those who are most voluminous in their several productions. Upon which I shall tell the reader a short tale.

A mountebank in Leicester-Fields had drawn a huge assembly about him. Among the rest, a fat, unwieldy fellow, half stifled in the press, would be every fit crying out, "Lord, what a filthy crowd is here! Pray, good people, give way a little. Bless me! what devil has raked this rabble together? Zounds! what squeezing is this? Honest friend, remove your elbow." At last a weaver that stood next him could hold no longer. "A plague confound you," said he, "for an overgrown sloven! and who, I wonder, helps to make up the crowd half so much as yourself? Don't you consider that you take up more room with that carcass than any five here? Is not the place as free for us as for you? Bring your own body to a reasonable compass, and then I'll engage we shall have room enough for us all."

There are certainly common privileges of a writer, the benefit whereof I hope there will be no reason to doubt; particularly that where I am not understood it shall be concluded that something very useful and profound is couched underneath; and again, that whatever word or sentence is printed in a different character shall be judged to contain something extraordinary, either of wit or sublimity.

As for the liberty I have thought fit to take of praising myself upon some occasions or none, I am sure it will need no excuse if a multitude of great examples be allowed sufficient authority. For it is here to be noted, that praise was originally a pension paid by the world: but the moderns finding the trouble and charge too great in collecting it, have lately bought out the fee-simple, since which time the right of presentation is wholly in ourselves. For this reason it is, that when an author makes his own eulogy, he uses a certain form to declare and insist upon his title, which is commonly in these or the like words, " I speak without vanity," which I think plainly shows it to be a matter of right and justice. Now, I do here once for all declare, that in every encounter of this nature through the following treatise the form aforesaid is implied, which I mention to save the trouble of repeating it on so many occasions.

It is a great ease to my conscience that I have written so elaborate and useful a discourse without one grain of satire intermixed, which is the sole point wherein I have taken leave to dissent from the famous originals of our age and country. I have observed some satirists to use the public much at the rate that pedants do a naughty boy ready horsed for discipline: first expostulate the case, then plead the necessity of the rod from great provocations, and conclude every period with a lash. Now, if I know anything of mankind, these gentlemen might very well spare their reproof and correction; for there is not, through all nature, another so callous and insensible a member as the world's posteriors, whether you apply to it the toe or the birch. Besides most of our late satirists seem to lie under a sort of mistake, that because nettles have the prerogative to sting, therefore all other weeds must do so too. I make not this comparison out of the least design to detract from these worthy writers; for it is well known among mythologists that weeds have the pre-eminence over all other vegetables; and therefore the first monarch of this island, whose taste and judgment were so acute and refined, did very wisely root the roses from the collar of the *order*, and plant the thistles in their stead, as the nobler flower of the two. For which reason it is conjectured by profound antiquaries, that the satirical itch, so prevalent in this part of our island, was first brought among us from beyond the Tweed. Here may it long flourish and abound! May it survive, and neglect the scorn of the world with as much ease and contempt as the world is insensible to the lashes of it! May their own dulness, or that of their party, be no discouragement for the authors to proceed! but let them remember it is with wits as with razors, which are never so apt to cut those they are employed on as when they have *lost their edge*. Besides, those whose teeth are too rotten to bite are best of all others qualified to revenge that defect with their breath.

I am not, like other men, to envy or undervalue the talents I cannot reach, for which reason I must needs bear a true honour to this large eminent sect of our British writers. And I hope this little panegyric will not be offensive to their ears, since it has the advantage of being only designed for themselves. Indeed, Nature herself has taken order, that fame and honour should be purchased at a better pennyworth by satire than by any other productions of the brain, the world being soonest provoked to praise by lashes as men are to love. There is a problem in an ancient author why dedications, and other bundles of flattery, run all upon stale, musty topics, without the smallest tincture of anything new, not only to the torment and nauseating of the Christian reader, but, if not suddenly prevented, to the universal spreading of that pestilent disease, the lethargy, in this island: whereas there is very little satire which has not something in it untouched before. The defects of the former are usually imputed to the want of invention among those who are dealers in that kind, but, I think, with a great deal of injustice, the solution being easy and natural. For the materials of panegyric, being very few in number, have been long since exhausted. For as health is but one thing, and has been always the same, whereas diseases are by thousands, besides new and daily additions; so all the virtues that have been ever in mankind are to be counted upon a few fingers, but his follies and vices are innumerable, and time adds hourly to the heap. Now, the utmost a poor poet can do is to get by heart a list of the cardinal virtues, and deal them with his utmost liberality to his hero or his patron. He may ring the changes as far as it will go, and vary his phrase till he has talked round; but the reader quickly finds it is all pork,* with a little variety of sauce. For there is no inventing terms of art beyond our ideas, and when our ideas are exhausted terms of art must be so too.

But though the matter for panegyric were as fruitful as the topics of satire, yet would it not be hard to find out a sufficient reason why the latter will be always better received than the first. For this, being bestowed only upon one or a few persons at a time, is sure to raise envy, and consequently ill words, from the rest, who have no share in the blessing. But satire, being levelled at all, is never resented for an offence by any, since every individual person makes bold to understand it of others, and very wisely removes his particular part of the burden upon the shoulders of the world, which are broad

* Plutarch.

enough, and able to bear it. To this purpose I have sometimes reflected upon the difference between Athens and England with respect to the point before us. In the Attic commonwealth * it was the privilege and birthright of every citizen and poet to rail aloud and in public, or to expose upon the stage by name any person they pleased, though of the greatest figure, whether a Creon, a Hyperbolus, an Alcibiades, or a Demosthenes. But, on the other side, the least reflecting word let fall against the people in general was immediately caught up and revenged upon the authors, however considerable for their quality or their merits. Whereas in England it is just the reverse of all this. Here you may securely display your utmost rhetoric against mankind, in the face of the world; tell them that all are gone astray; that here is none that doeth good, no, not one; that we live in the very dregs of time; that knavery and atheism are epidemic as the small-pox; that honesty is fled with Astræa; with any other commonplaces, equally new and eloquent, which are furnished by the *splendida bilis;* † and when you have done, the whole audience, far from being offended, shall return you thanks as a deliverer of precious and useful truths. Nay, farther; it is but to venture your lungs, and you may preach in Covent Garden against

---

* *Vide* Xenophon. † Horace. Spleen.

foppery and fornication, and *something else ;* against pride and dissimulation and bribery at Whitehall: you may expose rapine and injustice in the *inns of court* chapel, and in a *city* pulpit be as fierce as you please against avarice, hypocrisy, and extortion. It is but a ball bandied to and fro, and every man carries a racket about him to strike it from himself among the rest of the company. But on the other side, whoever should mistake the nature of things so far as to drop but a single hint in public how such a one starved half the fleet, and half poisoned the rest; how such a one, from a true principle of love and honour, pays no debts but for women and play; how such a one has got a running sore and runs out of his estate; how Paris, bribed by Juno and Venus,* loth to offend either party, slept out the whole cause on the bench; or how such an orator makes long speeches in the senate with much thought, little sense, and to no purpose: whoever, I say, should venture to be thus particular must expect to be imprisoned for *scandalum magnatum*, to have challenges sent him, to be sued for defamation, and to be brought before the bar of the house.

But I forgot that I am expatiating on a subject

---

* Juno and Venus are money and a mistress, very powerful bribes to a judge, if scandal says true. I remember such reflections were cast about at that time, but I cannot fix the person intended here.

wherein I have no concern, having neither a talent nor an inclination for satire. On the other side, I am so entirely satisfied with the whole present procedure of human things, that I have been some years preparing materials towards *A Panegyric upon the World*, to which I intended to add a second part, intituled, *A Modest Defence of the Proceedings of the Rabble in all Ages.* Both these I had thought to publish by way of appendix to the following treatise; but finding my commonplace book fill much slower than I had reason to expect, I have chosen to defer them to another occasion. Besides, I have been unhappily prevented in that design by a certain domestic misfortune, in the particulars whereof, though it would be very seasonable and much in the modern way to inform the gentle reader, and would also be of great assistance towards extending this preface into the size now in vogue, which by rule ought to be as large in proportion as the subsequent volume is small, yet I shall now dismiss our impatient reader from any farther attendance at the porch, and having duly prepared his mind by a preliminary discourse, shall gladly introduce him to the sublime mysteries that ensue.

A TALE OF A TUB.

SECTION I.

THE INTRODUCTION.

WHOEVER hath an ambition to be heard in a crowd must press and squeeze and thrust and climb with indefatigable pains, till he has exalted himself to a certain degree of altitude above them. Now, in all assemblies, though you wedge them ever so close, we may observe this peculiar property, that over their heads there is room enough, but how to reach it is the difficult point, it being as hard to get quit of number as of hell:

> evadere ad auras,
> Hoc opus, hic labor est.*

To this end, the philosopher's way in all ages has been by erecting certain edifices in the air. But

---

* But to return, and view the cheerful skies;
In this the task and mighty labour lies.

whatever practice and reputation these kind of structures have formerly possessed, or may still continue in, not excepting even that of Socrates, when he was suspended in a basket to help contemplation, I think, with due submission, they seem to labour under two inconveniences. First, That the foundations being laid too high, they have been often out of *sight*, and ever out of *hearing*. Secondly, That the materials, being very transitory, have suffered much from inclemencies of air, especially in these northwest regions. Therefore, towards the just performance of this great work there remain but three methods that I can think on, whereof the wisdom of our ancestors being highly sensible, has, to encourage all aspiring adventurers, thought fit to erect three wooden machines for the use of those orators who desire to talk much without interruption. These are the pulpit, the ladder, and the stage-itinerant. For as to the bar, though it be compounded of the same matter, and designed for the same use, it cannot however be well allowed the honour of the fourth, by reason of its level or inferior situation exposing it to the perpetual interruption from collaterals. Neither can the bench itself, though raised to a proper eminency, put in a better claim, whatever its advocates insist on. For if they please to look into the original design of its erection, and the circumstances or adjuncts subservient to that design, they will soon acknowledge the present practice exactly correspondent to the primitive institution, and both to answer the etymology of the name, which in the Phœnician tongue is a word of great signification, importing, if literally interpreted, the place of sleep, but in common acceptation, a seat well bolstered and cushioned, for the repose of old and gouty limbs (*senes ut in otia tuta recedant*), fortune being indebted to them this part of retaliation, that as formerly they have long talked whilst others slept, so now they may sleep as long whilst others talk.

But if no other argument could occur to exclude the bench and the bar from the list of oratorial machines, it were sufficient that the admission of them would overthrow a number which I was resolved to establish, whatever argument it might cost me, in imitation of that prudent method observed by many other philosophers and great clerks, whose chief art in division has been to grow fond of some proper mystical number, which their imaginations have rendered sacred to a degree, that they force common reason to find room for it in every part of nature; reducing, including, and adjusting every genus and species within that compass, by coupling some against their wills, and banishing others at any rate. Now, among all the rest, the profound number THREE is that which has most employed my sublimest speculations, nor ever without wonderful delight. There is now in the press, and will be published next term, a panegyrical essay of mine upon this number, wherein I have, by most convincing proofs, not only reduced the senses and the elements under its banner, but brought over several deserters from its two great rivals, SEVEN and NINE.

Now the first of these oratorial machines, in place as well as in dignity, is the *pulpit*. Of pulpits there are in this island several sorts, but I esteem only that made of timber from the *sylva Caledonia*, which agrees very well with our climate. If it be upon its decay, it is the better both for conveyance of sound, and for other reasons to be mentioned by and by. The degree of perfection in shape and size I take to consist in being extremely narrow, with little ornament, and best of all without a cover (for by ancient rule, it ought to be the only uncovered *vessel* in every assembly where it is rightfully used), by which means, from its near resemblance to a pillory, it will ever have a mighty influence on human ears.

Of *ladders* I need say nothing. It is observed by foreigners themselves, to the honour of our country, that we excel all nations in our practice and understanding of this machine. The ascending orators do not only oblige their audience in the agreeable delivery, but the whole world in the *early* publication of their speeches, which I look upon as the choicest treasury of our British eloquence, and whereof, I am informed, that worthy citizen and bookseller, Mr. John Dunton, hath made a faithful and a painful collection, which he shortly designs to publish in twelve volumes in folio, illustrated with copper-plates—a work highly useful and curious, and altogether worthy of such a hand.

The last engine of orators is the *stage-itinerant*,* erected with much sagacity, *sub Jove pluvio in triviis et quadriviis*.† It is the great seminary of the two former, and its orators are sometimes preferred to the one, and sometimes to the other, in proportion to their deservings, there being a strict and perpetual intercourse between all three.

From this accurate deduction it is manifest, that for obtaining attention in public there is of necessity required a *superior position of place*. But although this point be generally granted, yet the cause is little agreed in, and it seems to me that very few philosophers have fallen into a true natural solution of this phenomenon. The deepest account, and the most fairly digested of any I have yet met with is this, that air being a heavy body, and therefore, according to the system of Epicurus,‡ continually descending, must needs be more so when loaded and pressed down by words—which are also bodies of much weight and gravity, as it is manifest from those deep impressions they make and leave upon us, and therefore must be delivered from a due altitude, or else

---

* Is the mountebank's stage, whose orators the author determines either to the gallows or a conventicle.

† In the open air, and in streets where the greatest resort is.

‡ Lucretia, lib. ii.

they will neither carry a good aim nor fall down with a sufficient force.

> Corpoream quoque enim vocem constare fatendum est,
> Et sonitum, quoniam possunt impellere sensus.*

And I am the readier to favour this conjecture from a common observation, that in the several assemblies of these orators nature itself hath instructed the hearers to stand with their mouths open, and erected parallel to the horizon, so as they may be intersected by a perpendicular line from the zenith to the centre of the earth. In which position, if the audience be well compact, every one carries home a share, and little or nothing is lost.

I confess there is something yet more refined in the contrivance and structure of our modern theatres. For, first, the pit is sunk below the stage, with due regard to the institution above deduced, that whatever weighty matter shall be delivered thence, whether it be lead or gold, may fall plump into the jaws of certain critics, as I think they are called, which stand ready opened to devour them. Then the boxes are built round, and raised to a level with the scene, in deference to the ladies; because that large portion of wit laid out in raising pruriences and protuberances is observed to run much upon a line and ever in a circle. The whining passions and

---

* 'Tis certain, then, that *voice* that thus can wound
   Is all *material*, *body* every *sound*.—Lucretia, lib. iv.

little starved conceits are gently wafted up, by their own extreme levity, to the middle region, and there fixed, and are frozen by the frigid understandings of the inhabitants. Bombastry and buffoonery, by nature lofty and light, soar highest of all, and would be lost in the roof, if the prudent architect had not, with much foresight, contrived for them a fourth place, called the twelvepenny gallery, and there planted a suitable colony, who greedily intercept them in their passage.

Now, this physico-logical scheme of oratorial receptacles or machines contains a great mystery, being a type, a sign, an emblem, a shadow, a symbol, bearing analogy to the spacious commonwealth of writers, and to those methods by which they must exalt themselves to a certain eminency above the inferior world. By the pulpit are adumbrated the writings of our modern saints in Great Britain, as they have spiritualised and refined them from the dross and grossness of sense and human reason. The matter, as we have said, is of rotten wood, and that upon two considerations: because it is the quality of rotten wood to give light in the dark; and secondly, because its cavities are full of worms; which is a type with a pair of handles,* having a respect to the two principal qualifications of the

---

* The two principal qualifications of a fanatic preacher are, his inward light and his head full of maggots; and the two different fates of his writings are, to be burnt or worm-eaten.

orator, and the two different fates attending upon his works.

The *ladder* is an adequate symbol of faction and of poetry, to both of which so noble a number of authors are indebted for their fame. Of *faction*,* because . . . *Hiatus* . . . *in M.S.* Of poetry, because its orators do perorate with a song; and because, climbing up by slow degrees, Fate is sure to turn them off before they can reach within many steps of the top; and because it is a preferment attained by transferring of property and a confounding of *meum* and *tuum*.

Under the *stage-itinerant* are couched those productions designed for the pleasure and delight of mortal man, such as, *Sixpennyworth of Wit*, *Westminster Drolleries*, *Delightful Tales*, *Complete Jesters*, and the like, by which the writers of and for GRUB STREET have, in these latter ages, so nobly triumphed over *Time*—have clipped his wings, pared his nails, filed his teeth, turned back his hour-glass, blunted his scythe, and drawn the hobnails out of his shoes. It is under this class I have presumed to list my present treatise, being just come from having the honour conferred upon me to be adopted a member of that illustrious fraternity.

* Here is pretended a defect in the manuscript; and this is very frequent with our author, either when he thinks he cannot say anything worth reading, or when he has no mind to enter on the subject, or when it is a matter of little moment; or perhaps to amuse his reader, whereof he is frequently very fond, or, lastly, with some satirical intention.

Now, I am not unaware how the productions of the Grub Street brotherhood have of late years fallen under many prejudices, nor how it has been the perpetual employment of two *junior* start-up societies to ridicule them and their authors, as unworthy their established post in the commonwealth of wit and learning. Their own consciences will easily inform them whom I mean. Nor has the world been so negligent a looker-on as not to observe the continual efforts made by the societies of Gresham * and of Wills's † to edify a name and reputation upon the ruins of OURS. And this is yet a more feeling grief to us, upon the regards of tenderness as well as of justice, when we reflect on their proceedings not only as unjust, but as ungrateful, undutiful, and unnatural. For how can it be forgot by the world or themselves, to say nothing of our own records, which are full and clear in the point, that they both are seminaries not only of our planting, but our watering too? I am informed that our two rivals have lately made an offer to enter into the lists with united forces, and challenge us to a comparison of books, both as to weight and number. In return to which, with license from our president, I humbly offer two

---

* Gresham College was the place where the Royal Society then met, from whence they removed to Crane Court in Fleet Street.

† Wills's coffee-house, in Covent Garden, was formerly the place where the poets usually met; which, though it be yet fresh in memory, in some years may be forgotten, and want this explanation.

answers. First, we say the proposal is like that which Archimedes made upon a smaller affair,* including an impossibility in the practice; for where can they find scales of capacity enough for the first, or an arithmetician of capacity enough for the second? Secondly, we are ready to accept the challenge, but with this condition, that a third indifferent person be assigned, to whose impartial judgment it should be left to decide which society each book, treatise, or pamphlet does most properly belong to. This point, God knows, is very far from being fixed at present; for we are ready to produce a catalogue of some thousands which, in all common justice, ought to be entitled to our fraternity, but by the revolted and new-fangled writers most perfidiously ascribed to the others. Upon all which we think it very unbecoming our prudence that the determination should be remitted to the authors themselves, when our adversaries, by briguing † and caballing, have caused so universal a defection from us, that the greatest part of our society hath already deserted to them, and our nearest friends begin to stand aloof, as if they were half ashamed to own us.

This is the utmost I am authorised to say upon so ungrateful and melancholy a subject, because we are extremely unwilling to inflame a controversy whose continuance may be so fatal to the interests of us all, desiring much rather that things be amicably

---

* *Viz.*, about moving the earth.   † Quarrelling, disputing.

composed; and we shall so far advance on our side, as to be ready to receive the two prodigals with open arms whenever they shall think fit to return from their husks and their harlots—which, I think, from the present course of their studies,* they most properly may be said to be engaged in—and, like an indulgent parent, continue to them our affection and our blessing.

But the greatest maim given to that general reception which the writings of our society have formerly received, next to the transitory state of all sublunary things, hath been a superficial vein among many readers of the present age, who will by no means be persuaded to inspect beyond the surface and the rind of things: whereas, wisdom is a fox, who, after long hunting, will at last cost you the pains to dig out: it is a cheese, which, by how much the richer, has the thicker, the homelier, and the coarser coat, and whereof, to a judicious palate, the maggots are the best: it is a sack-posset, wherein the deeper you go you will find it the sweeter. Wisdom is a hen, whose cackling we must value and consider, because it is attended with an egg. But then, lastly, it is a nut, which, unless you choose with judgment, may cost you a tooth and pay you with nothing but a worm. In consequence of these momentous truths, the Grubæan sages have always chosen to convey their precepts and their arts shut up within the

* Virtuoso experiments and modern comedies.

vehicles of types and fables, which having been perhaps more careful and curious in adorning than was altogether necessary, it has fared with these vehicles after the usual fate of coaches over-finely painted and gilt, that the transitory gazers have so dazzled their eyes and filled their imaginations with the outward lustre, as neither to regard nor consider the person or the parts of the owner within—a misfortune we undergo with somewhat less reluctancy, because it has been common to us with Pythagoras, Æsop, Socrates, and other of our predecessors.

However, that neither the world nor ourselves may any longer suffer by such misunderstandings, I have been prevailed on, after much importunity from my friends, to travel in a complete and laborious dissertation upon the prime productions of our society, which, besides their beautiful externals for the gratification of superficial readers, have darkly and deeply couched under them the most finished and refined systems of all sciences and arts; as I do not doubt to lay open by untwisting or unwinding, and either to draw up by exhalation or display by incision.

This great work was entered upon some years ago by one of our most eminent members. He began with the history of Reynard the fox,* but neither

---

* The author seems here to be mistaken, for I have seen a Latin edition of Reynard the fox above a hundred years old, which I take to be the original; for the rest, it has been thought by many people to contain some satirical design in it.

lived to publish his essay, nor to proceed farther in so useful an attempt: which is very much to be lamented, because the discovery he made and communicated with his friends is now universally received: nor do I think any of the learned will dispute that famous treatise to be a complete body of civil knowledge, and the revelation, or rather the apocalypse, of all state *arcana*. But the progress I have made is much greater, having already finished my annotations upon several dozens, from some of which I shall impart a few hints to the candid reader, as far as will be necessary to the conclusion at which I aim.

The first piece I have handled is that of *Tom Thumb*, whose author was a Pythagorean philosopher. This dark treatise contains the whole scheme of the *metempsychosis*, deducing the progress of the soul through all her stages.

The next is *Dr. Faustus*, penned by Artephius, an author *bonæ notæ*, and an *adeptus*.

He published it in the nine-hundredth-eighty-fourth year of his age.* This writer proceeds wholly by *reincrudation*, or in the *via humida*, and the marriage between Faustus and Helen does most conspicuously dilucidate the fermenting of the male and female dragon.

Whittington and his Cat is the work of that mysterious rabbi, Jeruba Hannasi, containing a defence

* The chymists say of him in their books, that he prolonged his life to a thousand years, and then died voluntarily.—*Hawkes.*

of the *Gemara* of the *Jerusalem Misna*,* and its just preference to that of Babylon, contrary to the vulgar opinion.

The *Hind and Panther*. This is the masterpiece of a famous writer now living,† intended for a complete abstract of sixteen thousand schoolmen, from Scotus to Bellarmine.

Tommy Pots. Another piece, supposed by the same hand, by way of supplement to the former.

The *Wise Men of Gotham, cum appendice*. This is a treatise of immense erudition, being the great original and fountain of those arguments, bandied about both in France and England, for a just defence of the *moderns*' learning and wit against the presumption, the pride, and ignorance of the *ancients*. This unknown author hath so exhausted the subject, that a penetrating reader will easily discover whatever hath been written since upon that dispute to be little more than repetition. An abstract of this treatise hath been lately published by a worthy member of our society.‡

These notices may serve to give the learned reader an idea, as well as a taste, of what the whole work is likely to produce, wherein I have now altogether

---

* The *Gemara* is the decision, explanation, or the interpretation of the Jewish rabbis; and the *Misna* is, properly, the code or body of the Jewish civil or common law.—*Hawkes.*

† *Viz.*, in 1698.

‡ This I suppose to be understood of Mr. Wotton's discourse of ancient and modern learning.

circumscribed my thoughts and my studies, and if I can bring it to a perfection before I die, shall reckon I have well employed the poor remains of an unfortunate life.* This, indeed, is more than I can justly expect from a quill worn to the pith in the service of the State, in pros and cons upon popish plots and mealtubs,† and exclusion bills and passive obedience, and addresses of lives and fortunes, and prerogative, and property, and liberty of conscience, and letters to a friend; from an understanding and a conscience threadbare and ragged with perpetual turning; from a head broken in a hundred places by the malignants of the opposite factions; and from a body spent with diseases ill cured by trusting to quacks and surgeons, who, as it afterwards appeared, were professed enemies to me and the government, and revenged their party's quarrel upon my nose and shins. Fourscore and eleven pamphlets have I written under three reigns, and for the service of six-and-thirty factions. But finding the State has no further occasion for me and my ink, I retire willingly to draw it out into speculations more becoming a philosopher, having, to my unspeakable comfort, passed a long life with a conscience void of offence.

* Here the author seems to personate L'Estrange, Dryden, and some others, who, after having passed their lives in vices, faction, and falsehood, have the impudence to talk of merit and innocence and sufferings.

† In King Charles II.'s time there was an account of a Presbyterian plot, found in a tub, which then made much noise.

But to return: I am assured, from the reader's candour, that the brief specimen I have given will easily clear all the rest of our society's productions from an aspersion grown, as it is manifest, out of envy and ignorance, that they are of little further use or value to mankind beyond the common entertainments of their wit and their style (for these, I am sure, have never yet been disputed by our keenest adversaries), in both which, as well as the more profound and mystical part, I have throughout this treatise closely followed the most applauded originals. And to render all complete, I have, with much thought and application of mind, so ordered, that the chief title prefixed to it—I mean, that under which I design it shall pass in the common conversations of court and town, is modelled exactly after the manner peculiar to *our* society.

I confess to have been somewhat liberal in the business of titles,* having observed the humour of multiplying them to bear great vogue among certain writers, whom I exceedingly reverence. And indeed it seems not unreasonable that books, the children of the brain, should have the honour to be christened with variety of names, as well as other infants of quality. Our famous Dryden has ventured to proceed a point further, endeavouring to introduce also

---

* The title-page in the original was so torn, that it was not possible to recover several titles which the author here speaks of.

a multiplicity of *godfathers*,* which is an improvement of much more advantage, upon a very obvious account. It is a pity this admirable invention has not been better cultivated, so as to grow by this time into general imitation, when such an authority serves it for a precedent: nor have my endeavours been wanting to second so useful an example. But it seems there is an unhappy expense usually annexed to the calling of a godfather, which was clearly out of my head, as it is very reasonable to believe. Where the pinch lay I cannot certainly affirm; but having employed a world of thoughts and pains to split my treatise into forty sections, and having entreated forty lords of my acquaintance that they would do me the honour to stand, they all made it a matter of conscience, and sent me their excuses.

* See Virgil translated, &c. He dedicated the different parts of Virgil to different patrons.

SECTION II.

A TALE OF A TUB.

ONCE upon a time there was a man who had three sons by one wife,* and all at a birth, neither could the midwife tell certainly which was the eldest. Their father died while they were young, and upon his death-bed, calling the lads to him, spoke thus :—

"Sons, because I have purchased no estate, nor was born to any, I have long considered of some good legacies to bequeath you; and at last, with much care as well as expense, have provided each of you (here they are) a new coat.† Now, you are to

---

* By these three sons, Peter, Martin, and Jack, Popery, the Church of England, and our Protestant Dissenters are designed.—*W. Wotton.*

In the character of Peter we see the pope, seated on his pontifical throne, and adorned with his triple crown : in the picture of Martin we view Luther and the first Reformers : and in the description of Jack we behold John Calvin and his disciples. The author's arrows are chiefly directed against Peter and Jack. To Martin he shows all the indulgence that the laws of allegory will permit.—*Orrery.*

† By his coats, which he gave his sons, the garment of the Israelites. —*W. Wotton.*

An error (with submission) of the learned commentator ; for by the

understand that these coats have two virtues contained in them. One is, that with good wearing they will last you fresh and sound as long as you live. The other is, that they will grow in the same proportion with your bodies, lengthening and widening of themselves, so as to always fit. Here, let me see them on you before I die. So, very well; pray, children, wear them clean, and brush them often. You will find in my will* (here it is) full instructions in every particular concerning the wearing and management of your coats, wherein you must be very exact, to avoid the penalties I have appointed for every transgression or neglect, upon which your future fortunes will entirely depend. I have also commanded in my will that you should live together in one house like brethren and friends; for then you will be sure to thrive, and not otherwise."

Here, the story says, the good father died, and the three sons went altogether to seek their fortunes.

I shall not trouble you with recounting what adventures they met with for the first seven years, any further than by taking notice that they carefully observed their father's will, and kept their coats in very good order; that they travelled through several

---

coats are meant the doctrine and faith of Christianity, by the wisdom of the divine Founder fitted to all times, places, and circumstances.— *Lambin.*

* The New Testament.

countries, encountered a reasonable quantity of giants, and slew certain dragons.

Being now arrived at the proper age for producing themselves, they came up to town, and fell in love with the ladies, but especially three who about that time were in chief reputation—the Duchess d'Argent, Madame de Grands Titres, and the Countess d'Orgueil.* On their first appearance our three adventurers met with a very bad reception; and soon with great sagacity guessing out the reason, they quickly began to improve in the good qualities of the town. They wrote, and rallied, and rhymed, and sung, and said and said nothing; they drank, and fought, and slept, and swore, and took snuff: they went to new plays on the first night, haunted the chocolate houses, beat the watch, lay on bulks, and even did worse; they bilked hackney-coachmen, ran in debt with shopkeepers and lay with their wives; they killed bailiffs, kicked fiddlers down stairs, ate at Locket's, loitered at Wills's; they talked of the drawing-room, and never came there; dined with lords they never saw; whispered a duchess, and spoke never a word; exposed the scrawls of their laundress for billetdoux of quality, came ever just from court, and were never seen in it; attended the

---

* Their mistresses are the Duchess d'Argent, Mademoiselle de Grands Titres, and the Countess d'Orgueil, *i.e.*, covetousness, ambition, and pride, which were the three great vices that the ancient fathers inveighed against as the first corruptions of Christianity.—*W. Wotton.*

levee *sub dio*, got a list of peers by heart in one company, and with great familiarity retailed them in another. Above all, they constantly attended those committees of senators who are silent in the *house*, and loud in the *coffee-house*, where they nightly adjourn to chew the cud of politics, and are encompassed with a ring of disciples, who lie in wait to catch up their droppings. The three brothers had acquired forty other qualifications of the like stamp, too tedious to recount, and, by consequence, were justly reckoned the most accomplished persons in the town. But all would not suffice, and the ladies aforesaid continued still inflexible. To clear up which difficulty, I must, with the reader's good leave and patience, have recourse to some points of weight which the authors of that age not sufficiently illustrated.

For about this time it happened a sect arose, whose tenets obtained and spread very far, especially in the *grand monde* and among everybody of good fashion.* They worshipped a sort of idol † who, as their doctrine delivered, did daily create men by a kind of manufacturing operation. This idol they placed in the highest parts of the house, on an altar erected about three feet. He was shown in the posture of a Persian emperor, sitting on a superficies, with his legs

---

* This is an occasional satire upon dress and fashion, in order to introduce what follows.

† By this idol is meant a tailor.

interwoven under him. This god had a goose for his ensign, whence it is that some learned men pretend to deduce his origin from Jupiter Capitolinus. At his left hand, beneath the altar, hell seemed to open, and catch at the animals the idol was creating; to prevent which, certain of his priests hourly flung in pieces of the unformed mass or substance, and sometimes whole limbs already enlivened, which that horrid gulf insatiably swallowed, terrible to behold. The goose was also held a subaltern divinity, or *deus minorum gentium*, before whose shrine was sacrificed that creature whose hourly food is human gore, and who is in so great renown abroad for being the delight and favourite of the Egyptian Cercopithecus.* Millions of these animals were cruelly slaughtered every day to appease the hunger of that consuming deity. The chief idol was also worshipped as the inventor of the yard and needle, whether as the god of seamen, or on account of certain other mystical attributes, hath not been sufficiently cleared.

The worshippers of this deity had also a system of their belief, which seemed to turn upon the following fundamentals. They held the universe to be a large suit of clothes which invests everything: that the earth is invested by the air; the air is invested by the stars; and the stars are invested by the *primum mobile*. Look on this globe of earth, and you will

---

* The Egyptians worshipped a monkey, which animal is very fond of eating lice, styled here creatures that feed on human gore.

find it to be a very complete and fashionable dress. What is that which some call land but a fine coat faced with green? or the sea, but a waistcoat of water-tabby? Proceed to the particular works of the creation, you will find how curious journeyman Nature hath been to trim up the vegetable beaux: observe how sparkish a periwig adorns the head of a beech, and what a fine doublet of white satin is worn by the birch. To conclude from all, what is man himself but a *micro-coat*,* or rather a complete suit of clothes, with all its trimmings? As to his body there can be no dispute. But examine even the acquirements of his mind, you will find them all contribute in their order towards furnishing out an exact dress. To instance no more—is not religion a cloak? honesty a pair of shoes, worn out in the dirt? self-love a surtout? vanity a shirt? and conscience a pair of breeches, which may be made to cover or uncover that which should not be seen?

These *postulata* being admitted, it will follow in due course of reasoning that those beings which the world calls improperly *suits of clothes* are in reality the most refined species of animals; or, to proceed higher, that they are rational creatures, or men. For is it not manifest that they live, and move, and talk, and perform all other offices of human life? Are not beauty, and wit, and mien, and breeding their

---

* Alluding to the word *microcosm*, or a little world, as man has been called by philosophers.

inseparable properties? In short, we see nothing but them, hear nothing but them. Is it not they who walk the streets, fill up parliament-house, coffee-houses, play-houses, brothels? It is true, indeed, that these animals, which are vulgarly called *suits of clothes*, or *dresses*, do, according to certain compositions, receive different appellations. If one of them be trimmed up with a gold chain, and a red gown, and a white rod, and a great horse, it is called a *lord mayor;* if certain ermine and furs be placed in a certain position, we style them a *judge;* and so an apt conjunction of lawn and black satin we entitle a *bishop*.

Others of these professors, though agreeing in the main system, were yet more refined upon certain branches of it, and held that man was an animal compounded of two dresses, the natural and the celestial suit, which were the body and the soul; that the soul was the outward and the body the inward clothing; that the latter was *ex traduce*, but the former of daily creation and circumfusion. This last they proved by Scripture, because "in them we live, and move, and have our being:" as likewise by philosophy, because they are all in all, and all in every part. Besides, said they, separate these two, and you will find the body to be only a senseless, unsavoury carcass. By all which it is manifest that the outward dress must needs be the soul.

To this system of religion were tagged several

subaltern doctrines,* which were entertained with great vogue, as, particularly, the faculties of the mind were deduced by the learned among them in this manner: embroidery was sheer wit, gold fringe was agreeable conversation, gold lace was repartee, a huge long periwig was humour, and a coat full of powder was very good raillery, all which required abundance of *finesse* and *delicatesse* to manage with advantage, as well as a strict observance after times and fashions.

I have, with much pains and reading, collected out of ancient authors this short summary of a body of philosophy and divinity, which seems to have been composed by a vein and race of thinking very different from any other systems, either ancient or modern. And it was not merely to entertain or

---

* The first part of the tale is the history of Peter · thereby Popery is exposed. Everybody knows the Papists have made great additions to Christianity: that, indeed, is the great exception which the Church of England makes against them: accordingly, Peter begins his pranks with adding a shoulder-knot to his coat.—*W. Wotton.*

The actions of Peter are the actions of a man intoxicated with pride, power, rage, tyranny, and self-conceit. These passions are placed in the most ridiculous light, and the effects of them produce to us the tenets and doctrines of papal Rome, such as purgatory, penance, images, indulgences, auricular confession, transubstantiation, and those dreadful monsters, the pontifical bulls, which, according to this ludicrous author, derived their original from the famous bulls of Colchis, described by Ovid:—

> Terribiles vultus, præfixaque cornua ferro;
> Pulvereumque solum pede pulsa vere bisulco;
> Fumificisque locum mugitibus implevere.
> Met. i. vii. v. 112.

satisfy the reader's curiosity, but rather to give him light into several circumstances of the following story, that, knowing the state of dispositions and opinions in an age so remote, he may better comprehend those great events which were the issue of them. I advise, therefore, the courteous reader to peruse, with a world of application, again and again whatever I have written upon this matter. And leaving these broken ends, I carefully gather up the chief thread of my story, and proceed.

These opinions, therefore, were so universal, as well as the practices of them, among the refined part of court and town, that our three brother-adventurers, as their circumstances then stood, were strangely at a loss. For, on the one side the three ladies they addressed themselves to, whom we have named already, were ever at the very top of the fashion, and abhorred all that were below it but the breadth of a hair. On the other side, their father's will was very precise, and it was the main precept in it, with the greatest penalties annexed, not to add to or diminish from their coats one thread, without a positive command in the will. Now the coats their father had left them were, it is true, of very good cloth, and, besides, so neatly sown, you would swear they were all of a piece, but at the same time very plain, and with little or no ornament.* And it happened that

---

* His description of the cloth of which the coat was made has a farther meaning than the words may seem to import: "The coats their

before they were a month in town great shoulder-knots came up : * straight all the world wore shoulder-knots; no approaching the ladies-*ruelles* without the quota of shoulder-knots. "That fellow," cries one, "has no soul; where is his shoulder-knot?" Our three brethren soon discovered their want by sad experience, meeting in their walks with forty mortifications and indignities. If they went to the playhouse, the door-keeper showed them into the twelvepenny gallery. If they called a boat, says a waterman, "I am first sculler." If they stepped to the *Rose* to take a bottle, the drawer would cry, "Friend, we sell no ale." If they went to visit a lady, a footman met them at the door with "Pray send up your message." In this unhappy case they went immediately to consult their father's will, read it over and over, but not a word of the shoulder-knot. What should they do? What temper should they find? Obedience was absolutely necessary, and yet shoulder-knots appeared extremely requisite. After much thought, one of the brothers, who hap-

---

father had left them were of very good cloth, and, besides, so neatly sown, you would swear they were all of a piece, but at the same time very plain, and with little or no ornament." This is the distinguishing character of the Christian religion. *Christiani religio absoluta et simplex*, was Ammianus Marcellinus's description of it, who was himself a heathen.—*W. Wotton.*

* By this is understood the first introducing of pageantry and unnecessary ornaments in the church, such as were neither for convenience nor edification; as a shoulder-knot, in which there is neither symmetry nor use.

pened to be more book-learned than the other two, said he had found an expedient. "It is true," said he, "there is nothing here in this will, *totidem verbis*,* making mention of shoulder-knots; but I dare conjecture we may find them *inclusive*, or *totidem syllabis*." This distinction was immediately approved by all, and so they fell again to examine. But their evil star had so directed the matter, that the first syllable was not to be found in the whole writing: upon which disappointment, he who found the former evasion took heart, and said, "Brothers, there is yet hope; for though we cannot find them *totidem verbis*, nor *totidem syllabis*, I dare engage we shall make them out *tertio modo*, or *totidem literis*." This discovery was also highly commended, upon which they fell once more to the scrutiny, and picked out S-H-O-U-L-D-E-R, when the same planet, enemy to their repose, had wonderfully contrived that a K was not to be found. Here was a weighty difficulty! But the distinguishing brother, for whom we shall hereafter find a name, now his hand was in, proved, by a very good argument, that K was a modern illegitimate letter, unknown to the learned ages, nor anywhere to be found in ancient manuscripts.

"'Tis true," said he, "the word *Calendæ* hath in

---

* When the Papists cannot find anything which they want in Scripture they go to oral tradition. Thus Peter is introduced dissatisfied with the tedious way of looking for all the letters of any word which he has occasion for in the *will* when neither the constituent syllables, nor much less the whole word, were there *in terminis*.—*W. Wotton.*

Q. V. C.* been sometimes written with a K, but erroneously: for in the best copies it has been ever spelt with a C. And by consequence, it was a gross mistake in our language to spell *knot* with a K, but that from henceforward he would take care it should be written with a C." Upon this all farther difficulty vanished; shoulder-knots were made clearly out to be *jure paterno*, and our three gentlemen swaggered with as large and as flaunting ones as the best.

But as human happiness is of a very short duration, so in those days were human fashions, upon which it entirely depends. Shoulder-knots had their time, and we must now imagine them in their decline; for a certain lord came just from Paris, with fifty yards of gold-lace upon his coat, exactly trimmed after the court-fashion of that month. In two days all mankind appeared closed up in bars of gold-lace.† Whoever durst peep abroad without his complement of gold-lace was as scandalous as a ———, and as ill received among the women. What should our three knights do in this momentous affair? They had sufficiently strained a point already in the affair of shoulder-knots. Upon recourse to the will nothing appeared there but *altum silentium*. That of the shoulder-knots was a loose, flying, circumstantial

---

* *Quibusdam veteribus codicibus*, some ancient manuscripts.

† I cannot tell whether the author means any new innovation by this word, or whether it be only to introduce the new methods of forcing and perverting Scripture.

point, but this of gold-lace seemed too considerable an alteration without better warrant: it did *aliquo modo essemiæ adhærere,* and therefore required a positive precept. But about this time it fell out that the learned brother aforesaid had read *Aristotelis dialectica,* and especially that wonderful piece, *De interpretatione,* which has the faculty of teaching its readers to find out a meaning in everything but itself—like commentators on the Revelation, who proceed prophets without understanding a syllable of the text. "Brothers," said he, "you are to be informed that of wills *duo sunt genera,* nuncupatory* and scriptory. That in the scriptory will here before us there is no precept or mention about gold lace, *conceditur:* but *si idem affirmetur de nuncupatoria negatur.* For, brothers, if you remember, we heard a fellow say, when we were boys, that he heard my father's man say that he heard my father say, that he would advise his sons to get gold lace on their coats as soon as ever they could procure money to buy it." "By G——, that is very true," cries the other; "I remember it perfectly well," said the third. And so, without more ado, they got the largest gold-lace in the parish, and walked about as fine as lords.

A while after there came up, all in fashion, a pretty sort of flame-coloured satin † for linings, and the

---

* By this is meant tradition, allowed to have equal authority with the Scripture, or rather greater.

† This is purgatory, whereof he speaks more particularly hereafter.

mercer brought a pattern of it immediately to our three gentlemen: "An' please your worships," said he, "my Lord C—— and Sir J. W. had linings out of this very piece last night. It takes wonderfully; and I shall not have a remnant left, enough to make my wife a pincushion, by to-morrow morning at ten o'clock." Upon this they fell again to rummage the will because the present case required a positive precept, the lining being held by orthodox writers to be of the essence of the coat. After long search they could fix upon nothing to the matter in hand, except a short advice of their father in the will to take care of fire, and put out their candles before they went to sleep.* This, though a good deal for the purpose, and helping very very far towards self-conviction, yet not seeming wholly of force to establish a command, being resolved to avoid farther scruple, as well as future occasion for scandal, says he that was

but here only to show how Scripture was perverted to prove it; which was done by giving equal authority with the canon to Apocrypha, called here a codicil annexed.

It is likely the author, in every one of these changes in the brothers' dresses, refers to some particular error in the Church of Rome, though it is not easy, I think, to apply them all. But by this of flame-coloured satin is manifestly intended purgatory; by gold-lace may perhaps be understood the lofty ornaments and plate in the churches. The shoulder knots and silver fringe are not so obvious, at least to me. But the Indian figures of men, women, and children plainly relate to the pictures in the Romish churches—of God like an old man, of the virgin Mary, and our Saviour as a child.

* That is, to take care of hell; and in order to do that to subdue and extinguish their lusts.

the scholar, "I remember to have read in wills of a codicil annexed which is indeed a part of the will, and what it contains hath equal authority with the rest. Now, I have been considering, of this same will here before us, and I cannot reckon it to be complete for want of such a codicil. I will therefore fasten one in its proper place very dexterously. I have had it by me some time. It was written by a dog-keeper of my grandfather's,* and talks a great deal, as good luck would have it, of this very flame-coloured satin." The project was immediately approved by the other two; an old parchment scroll was tagged on according to art, in the form of a codicil annexed, and the satin bought and worn.

Next winter a player, hired for the purpose by the corporation of fringe-makers, acted his part in a new comedy all covered with silver fringe,† and, according to the laudable custom, gave rise to that fashion. Upon which the brothers, consulting their father's will, to their great astonishment found these words; "Item, I charge and command my said three sons to wear no sort of silver-fringe upon or about their said coats," &c., with a penalty, in case of disobedience, too long here to insert. However, after some pause, the brother so often mentioned for his erudi-

---

* I believe this refers to that part of the Apocrypha where mention is made of Tobit and his dog.

† This is certainly the farther introducing the pomps of habit and ornament.

tion, who was well skilled in criticism, had found in a certain author, which he said should be nameless, that the same word which in the will is called fringe does also signify a broom-stick,* and doubtless ought to have the same interpretation in this paragraph. This another of the brothers disliked, because of that epithet *silver*, which could not, he humbly conceived, in propriety of speech be reasonably applied to a broom-stick. But it was replied upon him that this epithet was understood in a mythological and allegorical sense. However, he objected again, why their father should forbid them to wear a *broom-stick* on their coats—a caution that seemed unnatural and impertinent; upon which he was taken up short, as one that spoke irreverently of a *mystery*, which doubtless was very useful and significant, but ought not to be over-curiously pried into or nicely reasoned upon. And, in short, their father's authority being now considerably sunk, this expedient was allowed to serve as a lawful dispensation for wearing their full proportion of silver-fringe.

A while after was revived an old fashion, long antiquated, of embroidery, with Indian figures of men, women, and children.† Here they remembered

---

* The next subject of our author's wit is the glosses and interpretations of Scripture, very many absurd ones of which are allowed in the most authentic books of the Church of Rome.—*W. Wotton.*

† The images of saints, the blessed virgin, and our Saviour an infant. *Ibid.* Images in the Church of Rome give him but too fair a handle, "the brothers remembered," &c. The allegory here is direct.—*W. Wotton.*

but too well how their father had always abhorred this fashion; that he made several paragraphs on purpose, importing his utter detestation of it, and bestowing his everlasting curse on his sons whenever they should wear it. For all this, in a few days they appeared higher in the fashion than anybody else in the town. But they solved the matter by saying that these figures were not all the *same* with those that were formerly worn, and were meant in the will. Besides, they did not wear them in the sense as forbidden by their father, but as they were a commendable custom, and of great use to the public. That these rigorous clauses in the will did therefore require some allowance, and a favourable interpretation, and ought to be understood *cum grano salis*.

But fashions perpetually altering in that age, the scholastic brother grew weary of searching farther evasions and solving everlasting contradictions. Resolved, therefore, at all hazards, to comply with the modes of the world, they concerted matters together, and agreed unanimously to lock up their father's will in a strong box,* brought out of Greece, or Italy, I have forgotten which, and trouble themselves no farther to examine it, but only refer to its authority

---

* The Papists formerly forbade the people the use of Scripture in a vulgar tongue: Peter therefore locks up his father's will in a strong box, brought out of Greece or Italy. These countries are named, because the New Testament is written in Greek, and the vulgar Latin, which is the authentic edition of the Bible in the Church of Rome, is the language of old Italy. — *W. Wotton.*

whenever they thought fit. In consequence whereof a while after it grew a general mode to wear an infinite number of points, most of them tagged with silver. Upon which the scholar pronounced *ex cathedra* * that points were absolutely *jure paterno*, as they might very well remember. It is true, indeed, the fashion prescribed somewhat more than were directly named in the will: however, that they as heirs-general of their father, had power to make and add certain clauses for public emolument, though not deducible, *totidem verbis*, from the letter of the will, or else *multa absurda sequerentur*. This was understood for canonical, and therefore on the following Sunday they came to church all covered with points.

The learned brother so often mentioned was reckoned the best scholar in all that or the next street to it, insomuch, as having run something behindhand in the world, he obtained the favour of a certain lord † to receive him into his house and to teach his children. A while after the lord died, and he, by long practice, of his father's will found the way of contriving a deed of conveyance of that house to

---

* The popes, in their decretals and bulls, have given their sanction to very many gainful doctrines, which are now received in the Church of Rome, that are not mentioned in Scripture, and are unknown to the primitive Church. Peter accordingly pronounces *ex cathedra* that points tagged with silver were absolutely *jure paterno;* and so they wore them in great numbers.—*W. Wotton.*

† This was Constantine the Great, from whom the popes pretend a donation of St. Peter's patrimony, which they have been never able to produce.

himself and his heirs. Upon which he took possession, turned the young squires out, and received his brothers in their stead.*

---

* The bishops of Rome enjoyed their privileges in Rome at first by the favour of the emperors, whom at last they shut out of their own capital city, and then forged a donation from Constantine the Great, the better to justify what they did. In imitation of this, Peter, "having run something behindhand in the world, obtained leave of a certain lord," &c.—*W. Wotton.*

SECTION III.

A DIGRESSION CONCERNING CRITICS.

ALTHOUGH I have been hitherto as cautious as I could, upon all occasions most nicely to follow the rules and methods of writing laid down by the example of our illustrious moderns, yet has the unhappy shortness of my memory led me into an error, from which I must extricate myself before I can decently pursue my principal subject. I confess, with shame, it was an unpardonable omission to proceed so far as I have already done, before I had performed the due discourses, expostulatory, supplicatory, or deprecatory with my good lords the critics. Towards some atonement for this grievous neglect, I do here make humbly bold to present them with a short account of themselves and their art, by looking into the original and pedigree of the word as it is generally understood among us, and very briefly considering the ancient and present state thereof.

By the word *critic*, at this day so frequent in all conversations, there have sometimes been distinguished three very different species of mortal men, according as I have read in ancient books and pamphlets. For, first, by this term was understood such persons as invented or drew up rules for themselves and the world, by observing which a careful reader might be able to pronounce upon the productions of the learned, from his taste to a true relish of the sublime and the admirable, and divide every beauty of matter or of style from the corruption that apes it; in their common perusal of books singling out the errors and defects—the nauseous, the fulsome, the dull, and the impertinent—with the caution of a man that walks through Edinburgh streets in a morning, who is indeed as careful as he can to watch diligently and spy out the filth in his way; not that he is curious to observe the colour and complexion of the ordure, or take its dimensions, much less to be paddling in or tasting, but only with a design to come out as cleanly as he may. These men seem, though very erroneously, to have understood the appellation of critic in a literal sense; that one principal part of his office was to praise and acquit, and that a critic who sets up to read only for an occasion of censure and reproof is a creature as barbarous as a judge who should take up a resolution to hang all men that came before him on trial.

Again, by the word *critic* have been meant the

restorers of ancient learning from the worms and graves and dust of manuscripts.

Now the races of those two have been for some ages utterly extinct; and besides, to discourse any further of them would not be at all to my purpose.

This third and noblest sort is that of the TRUE CRITIC, whose original is the most ancient of all. Every true critic is a hero born, descending in a direct line from a celestial stem by Momus and Hybris, who begat Zoilus, who begat Tigellius, who begat Etcætera the elder, who begat Bentley, and Rymer, and Wotton, and Perrault, and Dennis, who begat Etcætera the younger.

And these are the critics from whom the commonwealth of learning has in all ages received such immense benefits, that the gratitude of their admirers placed their origin in heaven, among those of Hercules, Theseus, Perseus, and other great deservers of mankind. But heroic virtue itself hath not been exempt from the obloquy of evil tongues. For it hath been objected that those ancient heroes, famous for their combating so many giants and dragons and robbers, were in their own persons a greater nuisance to mankind than any of those monsters they subdued; and therefore, to render their obligations more complete, when all other vermin were destroyed, should in conscience have concluded with the same justice upon themselves, as Hercules most generously did, and hath, upon that score, procured to himself more temples and votaries than the best of his fellows. For these reasons, I suppose, it is why some have conceived it would be very expedient for the public good of learning, that every true critic, as soon as he had finished his task assigned, should immediately deliver himself up to ratsbane or hemp, or from some convenient altitude, and that no man's pretensions to so illustrious a character should by any means be received before that operation were performed.

Now, from this heavenly descent of criticism, and the close analogy it bears to heroic virtue, it is easy to assign the proper employment of a true ancient genuine critic, which is, to travel through this vast world of writings, to pursue and hunt those monstrous faults bred within them; to drag out the lurking errors, like Cacus from his den; to multiply them like Hydra's heads; and rake them together like Augeas' dung: or else drive away a sort of dangerous fowl, who have a perverse inclination to plunder the best branches of the tree of knowledge, like those Stymphalian birds that eat up the fruit.

These reasonings will furnish us with an adequate definition of a true critic, that he is a discoverer and collector of writers' faults, which may be further put beyond dispute by the following demonstration: that whoever will examine the writings in all kinds, wherewith this ancient sect has honoured the world, shall immediately find, from the whole thread and tenor of them, that the ideas of the authors have been altogether conversant and taken up with the faults and blemishes and oversights and mistakes of other writers; and, let the subject treated on be whatever it will, their imaginations are so entirely possessed and replete with the defects of other pens, that the very quintessence of what is bad does of necessity distil into their own, by which means the whole appears to be nothing else but an abstract of the criticisms they themselves have made.

Having thus briefly considered the original and office of a critic, as the word is understood in its most noble and universal acceptation, I proceed to refute the objections of those who argue from the silence and pretermission of authors, by which they pretend to prove that the very art of criticism as now exercised and by me explained is wholly modern; and consequently, that the critics of Great Britain and France have no title to an original so ancient and illustrious as I have deduced. Now, if I can clearly make out, on the contrary, that the most ancient writers have particularly described both the person and the office of a true critic, agreeable to the definition laid down by me, their grand objection, from the silence of authors, will fall to the ground.

I confess to have for a long time borne a part in this general error, from which I should never have acquitted myself but through the assistance of our noble moderns, whose most edifying volumes I turn indefatigably over night and day, for the improvement of my mind and the good of my country. These have, with unwearied pains, made many useful searches into the weak sides of the ancients, and given a comprehensive list of them. Besides, they have proved beyond contradiction that the very finest things delivered of old have been long since invented and brought to light by much later pens;* and that the noblest discoveries those ancients ever made of art and nature have all been produced by the transcending genius of the present age, which clearly shows how little merit those ancients can justly pretend to, and takes off that blind admiration paid them by men in a corner, who have the unhappiness of conversing too little with present things. Reflecting maturely upon all this, and taking in the whole compass of human nature, I easily conclude that these agents, highly sensible of their many imperfections, must needs have endeavoured, from some passages in their works, to obviate, soften, or divert the censorious reader by satire or panegyric upon the true critics, in imitation of their masters, the moderns. Now, in the commonplaces of both these † I was plentifully instructed by a long course of useful study in prefaces and prologues, and therefore immediately resolved to try what I could discover of either by a diligent perusal of the most

---

* See Wotton, of *Ancient and Modern Learning*.
† Satire and Panegyric upon Critics.

ancient writers, and especially those who treated of the earliest times. Here I found, to my great surprise, that although they all entered, upon occasion, into particular descriptions of the true critic, according as they were governed by their fears or their hopes, yet whatever they touched of that kind was with abundance of caution, adventuring no further than mythology and hieroglyphic. This, I suppose, gave ground to superficial readers for urging the silence of authors against the antiquity of the true critic, though the types are so apposite, and the applications so necessary and natural, that it is not easy to conceive how any reader of a modern eye or taste could overlook them. I shall venture, from a great number, to produce a few, which, I am very confident, will put this question beyond dispute.

It well deserves considering, that these ancient writers, in treating enigmatically upon the subject, have generally fixed upon the very same hieroglyph, varying only the story according to their affections or their wit. For, first, Pausanias is of opinion that the perfection of writing correctly was entirely owing to the institution of critics; and that he can possibly mean no other than the true critic is, I think, manifest enough from the following description. He says,* "They were a race of men who delighted to nibble at the superfluities and excrescences of books; which the learned at length observing, took warning, of

* Lib.——

their own accord, to lop the luxuriant, the rotten, the dead, the sapless, and the overgrown branches from their works." But now all this he cunningly shades under the following allegory: "That the Nauplians in Argos learned the art of pruning their vines by observing, that when an ass had browsed upon one of them it thrived the better and bore fairer fruit." But Herodotus,* holding the very same hieroglyph, speaks much plainer, and almost *in terminis*. He hath been so bold as to tax the true critics of ignorance and malice, telling us openly, for I think nothing can be plainer, that "in the western part of Libya there were *asses* with horns." Upon which relation Ctesias † yet refines, mentioning the very same animal about India, adding "that whereas all other *asses* wanted a gall, these horned ones were so redundant in that part, that their flesh was not to be eaten because of its extreme bitterness."

Now, the reason why those ancient writers treated this subject only by types and figures was, because they durst not make open attacks against a party so potent and terrible as the critics of those ages were, whose very voice was so dreadful, that a legion of authors would tremble and drop their pens at the sound: for so Herodotus tells us expressly in another place,‡ how "a vast army of Scythians was put to flight in a panic terror by the braying of an *ass*."

---

* Lib. iv.   † *Vide* excerpta ex eo apud Photium.
‡ Lib. ix.

A DIGRESSION CONCERNING CRITICS.

From hence it is conjectured by certain profound philologers, that the great awe and reverence paid to a true critic by the writers of Britain have been derived to us from those our Scythian ancestors. In short, this dread was so universal, that in process of time those authors who had a mind to publish their sentiments more freely, in describing the true critics of their several ages, were forced to leave off the use of the former hieroglyph, as too nearly approaching the prototype, and invented other terms instead thereof, that were more cautious and mystical. So Diodorus,* speaking to the same purpose, ventured no farther than to say, that "in the mountains of Helicon there grows a certain weed, which bears a flower of so evil a scent as to poison those who offer to smell it." Lucretius gives exactly the same relation:

> "Est etiam in magnis Heliconis montibus arbos,
> Floris odore hominem retro consueta necare." †

But Ctesias, whom we lately quoted, hath been a great deal bolder. He had been used with much severity by the true critics of his own age, and therefore could not forbear to leave behind him at least one deep mark of his vengeance against the whole tribe. His meaning is so near the surface, that I wonder how it possibly came to be overlooked by

---
* Lib.——
† "Near Helicon, and round the learned hill,
   Grow trees whose blossoms with their odour kill."—Lib. vi.

those who deny the antiquity of the true critics. For pretending to make a description of many strange animals about India, he hath set down these remarkable words: "Amongst the rest," says he, "there is a serpent that wants teeth, and consequently cannot bite; but if its vomit, to which it is much addicted, happens to fall upon anything, a certain rottenness or corruption ensues. These serpents are generally found among the mountains where jewels grow, and they frequently emit a poisonous juice, whereof whoever drinks, that person's brains fly out of his nostrils."

There was also among the ancients a sort of critics, not distinguished in specie from the former but in growth or degree, who seem to have been only the tyros, or junior scholars, yet, because of their differing employments, they are frequently mentioned as a sect by themselves. The usual exercise of these younger students was to attend constantly at theatres, and learn to spy out the worst parts of the play, whereof they were obliged carefully to take note, and render a rational account to their tutors. Fleshed at these smaller sports, like young wolves, they grew up in time to be nimble and strong enough for hunting down large game. For it hath been observed, both among ancient and moderns, that a true critic hath one quality in common with a harlot and an alderman, never to change his title or his nature; that a grey critic has been certainly a green one, the perfections and acquirements of his age being only the improved talents of his youth; like hemp, which some naturalists inform us is bad for suffocations, though taken but in the seed. I esteem the invention, or at least the refinement of prologues, to have been owing to these younger proficients, of whom Terence makes frequent and honourable mention, under the name of *malevoli*.

Now, it is certain the institution of the true critics was of absolute necessity to the commonwealth of learning. For all human actions seem to be divided, like Themistocles and his company: one man can fiddle, and another can make a small town a great city; and he that cannot do either one or the other deserves to be kicked out of the creation. The avoiding of which penalty has doubtless given the first birth to the nation of critics, and, withal, an occasion for their secret detractors to report that a true critic is a sort of mechanic, set up with a stock and tools for his trade at as little expense as a tailor, and that there is much analogy between the utensils and abilities of both; that the tailor's hell is the type of a critic's commonplace book, and his wit and learning held forth by the goose; that it requires at least as many of these to the making up of one scholar as of the others to the composition of a man; that the valour of both is equal, and their weapons near of a size. Much may be said in answer to those invidious reflections, and I can positively affirm the first to be a falsehood: for, on the contrary, nothing is more certain than that it requires greater layings-out to be free of the critics' company than of any other you can name. For as to be a true beggar it will cost the richest candidate every groat he is worth, so before one can commence a true critic it will cost a man all the good qualities of his mind, which perhaps for a less purchase would be thought but an indifferent bargain.

Having thus amply proved the antiquity of criticism, and described the primitive state of it, I shall now examine the present condition of this empire, and show how well it agrees with its ancient self. A certain author whose works have many ages since been entirely lost does in his fifth book, and eighth chapter, say of critics, that "their writings are the mirrors of learning."* This I understand in a literal sense, and suppose our author must mean, that whosoever designs to be a perfect writer, must inspect into the books of critics, and correct his invention there, as in a mirror. Now, whoever considers that the mirrors of the ancients were made of brass, and *sine mercurio*, may presently apply the two principal qualifications of a true modern critic, and consequently must needs conclude that these have always been, and must be for ever, the same. For brass is an emblem of duration, and when it is skilfully burnished will cast reflections from its own superficies

---

* A quotation after the manner of a great author. *Vide* Bentley's dissertation, &c.

without any assistance of mercury from behind. All the other talents of a critic will not require a particular mention, being included, or easily reducible to these. However, I shall conclude with three maxims, which may serve both as characteristics to distinguish a true modern critic from a pretender, and will be also of admirable use to those worthy spirits who engage in so useful and honourable an art.

The first is, that criticism, contrary to all other faculties of the intellect, is ever held the truest and best when it is the very first result of the critic's mind; as fowlers reckon the first aim for the surest, and seldom fail of missing the mark if they stay for a second.

Secondly, the true critics are known by their talent of swarming about the noblest writers, to which they are carried merely by instinct, as a rat to the best cheese, or a wasp to the fairest fruit. So when the king is on horseback he is sure to be the dirtiest person of the company, and they that make their court best are such as bespatter him most.

Lastly, a true critic, in the perusal of a book, is like a dog at a feast, whose thoughts and stomach are wholly set upon what the guests fling away, and consequently is apt to snarl most when there are the fewest bones.

Thus much, I think, is sufficient to serve by way of address to my patrons, the true modern critics, and may very well atone for my past silence, as well as that which I am like to observe for the future. I hope I have deserved so well of their whole body as to meet with generous and tender usage from their hands. Supported by which expectation, I go on boldly to pursue those adventures already so happily begun.

SECTION IV.

A TALE OF A TUB.

I HAVE now with much pains and study conducted the reader to a period where he must expect to hear of great revolutions. For no sooner had our learned brother, so often mentioned, got a warm house of his own over his head, than he began to look big, and take mightily upon him; insomuch that, unless the gentle reader, out of his great candour, will please a little to exalt his idea, I am afraid he will henceforth hardly know the hero of the play when he happens to meet him, his part, his dress, and his mien being so much altered.

He told his brothers he would have them to know that he was their elder, and consequently his father's sole heir; nay, a while after he would not allow them to call him brother, but Mr. PETER; and then he must be styled FATHER PETER; and sometimes MY LORD PETER. To support this grandeur, which he soon began to consider could not be maintained without a better *fonde* than what he was born to, after much thought, he cast about at last to turn projector and virtuoso, wherein he so well succeeded, that many famous discoveries, projects, and machines which bear great vogue and practice at present in the world, are owing entirely to Lord PETER'S invention. I will deduce the best account I have been able to collect of the chief amongst them, without considering much the order came they out in, because I think authors are not well agreed as to that point.

I hope, when this treatise of mine shall be translated into foreign languages (as I may without vanity affirm that the labour of collecting, the faithfulness in recounting, and the great usefulness of the matter to the public, will amply deserve that justice), that the worthy members of the several academies abroad, especially those of France and Italy, will favourably accept these humble offers for the advancement of universal knowledge. I do also advertise the most reverend fathers, the eastern missionaries, that I have, purely for their sakes, made use of such words and phrases as will best admit an easy turn into any of the oriental languages, especially the Chinese. And so I proceed, with great content of mind, upon reflecting how much emolument this whole globe of the earth is like to reap by my labours.

The first undertaking of Lord Peter was to purchase a large continent,* lately said to have been

---

* That is, Purgatory.

discovered in *Terra Australis Incognita*. This tract of land he bought at a very great pennyworth from the discoverers themselves (though some pretended to doubt whether they had ever been there), and then retailed it into several cantons to certain dealers, who carried over colonies, but were all shipwrecked in the voyage. Upon which Lord Peter sold the said continent to other customers again, and again, and again, with the same success.

The second project I shall mention was his sovereign remedy for the worms,* especially those in the spleen. The patient was to eat nothing after supper for three nights.† As soon as he went to bed he was carefully to lie on one side; and when he grew weary to turn upon the other. He must also duly confine his two eyes to the same object, and by no means break wind at both ends together, without manifest occasion. These prescriptions diligently observed, the worms would void insensibly, by perspiration ascending through the brain.

A third invention was the erecting of a whispering-office,‡ for the public good and ease of all such as are

---

* Penance and absolution are played upon under the notion of a sovereign remedy for the worms, especially in the spleen : which, by observing Peter's prescription, would void insensibly by perspiration, ascending through the brain, &c.—*W. Wotton.*

† Here the author ridicules the penances of the Church of Rome, which may be made as easy to the sinner as he pleases, provided he will pay for them accordingly.

‡ By his whispering-office for the relief of eavesdroppers, physicians,

hypochondriacal, or troubled with the cholic, as likewise of all eavesdroppers, physicians, midwives, small politicians, friends fallen out, repeating poets, lovers happy or in despair, privy counsellors, pages, parasites, and buffoons; in short, of all such as are in danger of bursting with too much wind. An ass's head was placed so conveniently that the party affected might easily with his mouth accost either of the animal's ears, to which he was to apply close for a certain space, and by a fugitive faculty peculiar to the ears of that animal, receive immediate benefit, either by eructation, or expiration, or evomition.

Another very beneficial project of Lord Peter's was an office of insurance * for tobacco-pipes, martyrs of the modern zeal, volumes of poetry, shadows, ——, and rivers, that these, nor any of these, shall receive damage by fire, from whence our friendly societies may plainly find themselves to be only transcribers from this original, though the one and the other have been of great benefit to the undertakers, as well as of equal to the public.

Lord Peter was also held the original author of puppets and raree-shows, the great usefulness whereof being so generally known I shall not enlarge further upon this particular.

---

and privy counsellors, he ridicules auricular confessions; and the priest who takes it is described by the ass's head.—*W. Wotton.*

* This I take to be the office of indulgences, the gross abuse whereof first gave occasion for the Reformation.

But another discovery, for which he was much renowned, was his famous universal pickle.* For having remarked how your common pickle† in use among housewives was of no further benefit than to preserve dead flesh, and certain kinds of vegetables, Peter, with great cost as well as art, had contrived a pickle proper for houses, gardens, towns, men, women, children, and cattle, wherein he could preserve them as sound as insects in amber. Now this pickle, to the taste, the smell, and the sight, appeared exactly the same with what is in common service for beef and butter and herrings, and has been often that way applied with great success, but for its many sovereign virtues was quite a different thing. For Peter would put in a certain quantity of his powder *pimper-limpimp*,‡ after which it never failed of success. The operation was performed by spargefaction,§ in a proper time of the moon. The patient who was to be pickled, if it were a house, would infallibly be preserved from all spiders, rats, and weazels; if the

---

* Holy water he calls a *universal pickle*, to preserve houses, gardens, towns, men, women, children, and cattle, wherein he could preserve them as sound as insects in amber.—*W. Wotton.*

† This is easily understood to be holy water, composed of the same ingredients with many other pickles.

‡ And because holy water differs only in consecration from common water, as used for a beverage, &c., therefore he tells us that his pickle by the powder of *pimper-limpimp* receives new virtues, though it differs not in sight nor smell from the common pickles which preserve beef and butter and herrings.—*W. Wotton.*

§ Sprinkling.

party affected were a dog, he should be exempt from mange and madness and hunger. It also infallibly took away all scabs and lice and scald-heads from children, never hindering the patient from any duty, either at bed or board.

But of all Peter's rarities he most valued a certain set of bulls,* whose race was by great fortune preserved in a lineal descent from those that guarded the golden fleece, though some, who pretended to observe them curiously, doubted the breed had not been kept entirely chaste, because they had degenerated from their ancestors in some qualities, and had acquired others very extraordinary, but a foreign mixture. The bulls of Colchis are recorded to have brazen feet: but whether it happened by ill pasture and running, by an alloy from intervention of other parents, from stolen intrigues; whether a weakness in their progenitors had impaired the seminal virtue, or by a decline necessary through a long course of time, the originals of nature being depraved in these latter sinful ages of the world—whatever was the cause, it is certain that Lord Peter's bulls were extremely vitiated by the rust of time in the metal of their feet, which was now sunk into common lead.

---

* The papal bulls are ridiculed by name, so that here we are at no loss for the author's meaning.—*W. Wotton.*

Ibid. Here the author has kept the name, and means the Pope's bulls, or rather his fulminations and excommunications of heretical princes, all signed with lead and the seal of fishermen, and therefore said to have leaden feet and fishes' tails.

However, the terrible roaring peculiar to their lineage was preserved, as likewise that faculty of breathing out fire from their nostrils, which, notwithstanding, many of their detractors took to be a feat of art, and to be nothing so terrible as it appeared, proceeding only from their usual course of diet, which was of squibs and crackers.* However, they had two peculiar marks, which extremely distinguished them from the bulls of Jason, and which I have not met together in the description of any other monster beside that in Horace.

"Varias inducere plumas;"

and

"Atrum desinit in piscem."

For these had fishes' tails, yet upon occasion could out-fly any bird in the air. Peter put these bulls upon several employs. Sometimes he would set them a roaring to fright naughty boys† and make them quiet. Sometimes he would send them out upon errands of great importance, where, it is wonderful to recount, and perhaps the cautious reader may think much to believe it, an *appetitus sensibilis*, deriving itself, through the whole family, from their noble ancestors, guardians of the golden fleece, they continued so extremely fond of gold, that if Peter sent them abroad, though it were only upon a compli-

---

* These are the fulminations of the Pope, threatening hell and damnation to those princes who offend him.

† That is, kings who incurred his displeasure.

ment, they would roar, and spit, and belch and snivel out fire, and keep a perpetual coil* till you flung them a bit of gold; but then, *pulveris exigui jactu,* they would grow calm and quiet as lambs. In short, whether by secret connivance or encouragement from their master, or out of their own liquorish affection to gold, or both, it is certain they were no better than a sort of sturdy, swaggering beggars, and where they could not prevail to get an alms, would make women miscarry and children fall into fits, who to this very day usually call spirits and hobgoblins by the name of *bull-beggars.* They grew at last so very troublesome to the neighbourhood, that some gentlemen of the north-west got a parcel of right English bulldogs, and baited them so terribly that they felt it ever after.

I must needs mention one more of Lord Peter's projects, which was very extraordinary, and discovered him to be a master of a high reach and profound invention. Whenever it happened that any rogue of Newgate was condemned to be hanged, Peter would offer him a pardon for a certain sum of money, which when the poor caitiff had made all shifts to scrape up and send, his lordship would return a piece of paper in this form:

"To all mayors, sheriffs, jailors, constables, bailiffs,

---

* Confusion.
† This is a copy of a general pardon signed *Servus Servorum.*
Ibid. Absolution *in articula mortis,* and the tax *camera aposto licæ,* are jested upon in Emperor Peter's letter.—*W. Wotton.*

hangmen, &c. Whereas we are informed that *A. B.* remains in the hands of you, or some of you, under the sentence of death, we will and command you, upon sight hereof, to let the said prisoner depart to his own habitation, whether he stands condemned for murder, sodomy, rape, sacrilege, incest, treason, blasphemy, &c., for which this shall be your sufficient warrant. And if you fail thereof, God punish you and yours to all eternity. And so we bid you heartily farewell.

"Your most humble

"Man's man,

"EMPEROR PETER."

The wretches, trusting to this, lost their lives and money too.

I desire of those whom the learned among posterity will appoint for commentators upon this elaborate treatise, that they will proceed with great caution upon certain dark points, wherein all who are not *vere adepti* may be in danger to form rash and hasty conclusions, especially in some mysterious paragraphs, where certain *arcana* are joined for brevity's sake, which in the operation must be divided. And I am certain that future sons of art will return large thanks to my memory for so grateful, so useful an *inuendo*.

It will be no difficult part to persuade the reader that so many worthy discoveries met with great success in the world, though I may justly assure him that I have related much the smallest number, my design having been only to single out such as will be of most benefit for public imitation, or which best serve to give some idea of the reach and wit of the inventor. And therefore it need not be wondered if by this time Lord Peter was become exceedingly rich. But, alas! he had kept his brain so long and so violently upon the rack, that at last it shook itself, and began to turn round for a little ease. In short, what with pride, projects, and knavery, poor Peter was grown distracted, and conceived the strangest imaginations in the world. In the height of his fits, as it is usual with those who run mad out of pride, he would call himself God Almighty,* and sometimes monarch of the universe. I have seen him (says my author) take three old high-crowned hats,† and clap them all on his head, three-storey high, with a huge bunch of keys at his girdle,‡ and an angling rod in his hand; in which guise, whoever went to take him by the hand in the way of salutation, Peter, with

* The Pope is not only allowed to be the vicar of Christ, but by several divines is called God *upon earth*, and other blasphemous titles are given him.

† The triple crown.

‡ The keys of the Church. The Church is here taken for the gate of heaven; for the keys of heaven are assumed by the Pope in consequence of what our Lord said to Peter, "I will give unto thee the keys of the kingdom of heaven."—*Hawkes.*

Ibid. The Pope's universal monarchy, and his triple crown, and fisher's ring.—*W. Wotton.*

much grace, like a well-educated spaniel, would present them with his foot;* and if they refused his civility, then he would raise it as high as their chops, and give them a kick on the mouth, which hath ever since been called a salute. Whoever walked by without paying him their compliments, having a wonderful strong breath, he would blow their hats off into the dirt.

Meantime his affairs at home went upside down, and his two brothers had a wretched time, where his *boutade* † was to kick both their wives one morning out of doors,‡ and his own too, and, in their stead, gave orders to pick up the first three strollers that could be met with in the streets. Awhile after he nailed up the cellar door, and would not allow his brothers a drop of drink to their victuals.§ Dining one day at an alderman's in the city, Peter observed him expatiating, after the manner of his brethren, in the praises of his sirloin of beef. "Beef," said the said magistrate, "is the king of meat: beef comprehends in it the quintessence of partridge, and quail,

---

* Neither does his arrogant way of requiring men to kiss his slipper escape reflection.—*W. Wotton.*

† This word properly signifies a sudden jerk or lash of a horse, when you do not expect it.

‡ The celibacy of the Romish clergy is struck at in Peter's beating his own and brothers' wives out of doors.—*W. Wotton.*

§ The Pope's refusing the cup to the laity, persuading them that the blood is contained in the bread, and that the bread is the real and entire body of Christ.

and venison, and pheasant, and plum-pudding, and custard." When Peter came home, he would needs take the fancy of cooking up his doctrine into use, and apply the precept, in default of a sirloin, to his brown loaf. "Bread," says he, "dear brothers, is the staff of life: in which bread is contained, inclusive, the quintessence of beef, mutton, veal, venison, partridge, plum-pudding, and custard: and to render all complete, there is intermingled a due quantity of water, whose crudities are also corrected by yeast or barm, through which means it becomes a wholesome fermented liquor, diffused through the mass of the bread." Upon the strength of these conclusions, next day at dinner was the brown loaf served up in all the formality of a city feast. "Come, brothers," said Peter, "fall to, and spare not; here is excellent good mutton:[*] or hold, now my hand is in, I will help you." At which word, in much ceremony, with fork and knife he carves out two good slices of a loaf, and presents each on a plate to his brothers. The elder of the two, not suddenly entering into Lord Peter's conceit, began with very civil language to examine the mystery. "My lord," said he, "I doubt, with great submission, there may be some mistake." "What!" says Peter, "you are pleasant:

---

[*] Transubstantiation. Peter turns his bread into mutton, and, according to the Popish doctrine of concomitants, his wine too, which in his way he calls palming his crusts upon his brothers for mutton.—*W. Wotton.*

come then, let us hear this jest your head is so big with." "None in the world, my lord: but unless I am very much deceived, your lordship was pleased awhile ago to let fall a word about mutton, and I would be glad to see it with all my heart." "How!" said Peter, appearing in great surprise; "I do not comprehend this at all." Upon which, the younger interposing to set the business aright, "My lord," said he, "my brother, I suppose, is hungry, and longs for the mutton your lordship hath promised us for dinner." "Pray," said Peter, "take me along with you. Either you are both mad, or disposed to be merrier than I approve of. If you there do not like your piece, I will carve you another, though I should take that to be the choice bit of the whole shoulder." "What, then, my lord," replied the first, "it seems this is a shoulder of mutton all this while!" "Pray, sir," says Peter, "eat your victuals, and leave off your impertinence, if you please; for I am not disposed to relish it at present." But the other could not forbear, being over-provoked at the affected seriousness of Peter's countenance. "By G—, my lord," said he, "I can only say, that to my eyes, and fingers, and teeth, and nose, it seems to be nothing but a crust of bread." Upon which the second put in his word: "I never saw a piece of mutton in my life so nearly resembling a slice from a twelve-penny loaf." "Look ye, gentlemen," cries Peter in a rage, "to convince you what a couple of blind, positive, ignorant, wilful puppies you are, I will use but this plain argument: I assert it is true, good, natural mutton, as any in Leadenhall Market; and confound you both eternally if you offer to believe otherwise." Such a thundering proof as this left no further room for objection. The two unbelievers began to gather and pocket up their mistakes as hastily as they could. "Why, truly," said the first, "upon more mature consideration"—— "Ay," says the other, interrupting him, "now I have thought better on the thing, your lordship seems to have a great deal of reason." "Very well," said Peter. "Here, boy, fill me a beer glass of claret. Here's to you both with all my heart." The two brethren, much delighted to see him so readily appeased, returned their most humble thanks, and said they would be glad to pledge his lordship. "That you shall," said Peter. "I am not a person to refuse you anything that is reasonable. Wine, moderately taken, is a cordial. Here is a glass a-piece for you; it is true natural juice from the grape, none of your vintner's brewings." Having spoken thus, he presented to each of them another large dry crust, bidding them drink it off, and not to be bashful, for it would do them no hurt. The two brothers, after having performed the usual office in such delicate conjunctures, of staring a sufficient period at Lord Peter and each other, and finding how matters were like to go, resolved not to enter on a new dispute, but let him carry the point as he pleased : for he was now got into one of his mad fits, and to argue or expostulate further would only serve to render him a hundred times more untractable.

I have chosen to relate this worthy matter in all its circumstances, because it gave a principal occasion to that great and famous rupture* which happened about the same time among these brethren, and was never afterwards made up. But of that I shall treat at large in another section.

However, it is certain that Lord Peter, even in his lucid intervals, was very lewdly given in his common conversation, extremely wilful and positive, and would at any time rather argue to the death, than allow himself once to be in an error. Besides, he had an abominable faculty of telling huge palpable lies upon all occasions; and not only swearing to the truth, but cursing the whole company if they pretended to make the least scruple of believing him. One time he swore he had a cow at home which gave as much milk at a meal as would fill three thousand churches ; and what was yet more extraordinary, would never turn sour.† Another time he was telling of an old sign-post ‡ that belonged to his father, with nails and

---

* By this rupture is meant the Reformation.

† The ridiculous multiplying of the Virgin Mary's milk among the Papists, under the allegory of a cow which gave as much milk at a meal as would fill three thousand churches.—*W. Wotton.*

‡ By this sign-post is meant the cross of our blessed Saviour ; and

timber enough in it to build sixteen large men-of-war. Talking one day of Chinese waggons, which were made so light as to sail over mountains, "Zounds," said Peter, "where's the wonder of that? I swear I saw a large house of lime and stone travel over sea and land, granting that it stopped sometimes to bait, above two thousand German leagues." * And that which was the good of it, he would swear desperately all the while that he never told a lie in his life; and every word, "I swear, gentlemen, I tell you nothing but the truth; and may they broil eternally that will not believe me."

In short, Peter grew so scandalous, that all the neighbourhood began in plain words to say he was no better than a knave. And his two brothers, long weary of his ill usage, resolved at last to leave him; but first they humbly desired a copy of their father's will, which had now lain by neglected time out of mind. Instead of granting this request, he called them "rogues, traitors," and the rest of the vile names

---

if all the wood that is shown for parts of it was collected, the quantity would sufficiently justify this sarcasm.—*Hawkes.*

* The chapel of Loretto. He falls here only upon the ridiculous invention of Popery. The Church of Rome intended by these things to gull silly, superstitious people, and rook them out of their money. The world had been too long in slavery, but our ancestors gloriously redeemed us from that yoke. The Church of Rome therefore ought to be exposed, and he deserves well of mankind that does expose it.—*W. Wotton.*

Ibid. The chapel of Loretto, which travelled from the Holy Land to Italy.

he could muster up. However, while he was abroad one day upon his projects, the two youngsters watched their opportunity, made a shift to come at the will, and took a *copia vera*,* by which they presently saw how grossly they had been abused, their father having left them equal heirs, and strictly commanded that whatever they got should lie in common among them all. Pursuant to which, their next enterprise was to break open the cellar door, and get a little good drink to spirit and comfort their hearts.† In copying the will they had met another precept against divorce and separate maintenance, and other evil practices of their brother Peter, upon which their next work was to discard their concubines and send for their wives.‡ Whilst all this was in agitation there enters a solicitor from Newgate, desiring Lord Peter would please to procure pardon for a thief that was to be hanged to-morrow. But the two brothers told him he was a coxcomb to seek pardons from a fellow who deserved to be hanged much better than his client; and discovered all the method of that imposture in the same form I delivered it a while ago, advising the solicitor to put his friend upon obtaining a pardon from the king. In the midst of all this clutter and revolution in comes Peter with a file of dragoons at his heels; and gathering from all hands what was in the wind,

---

* Translated the Scriptures into the vulgar tongue.
† Administered the cup to the laity at the communion.
‡ Allowed the marriages of priests.

he and his gang, after several millions of scurrilities and curses, not very important here to repeat, by main force very fairly kick them both out of doors, and would never let them come under his roof from that day to this.

SECTION V.

---o---

A DIGRESSION IN THE MODERN KIND.

HE, whom the world is pleased to honour with the title of modern authors, should never have been able to compass our great design of an everlasting remembrance, and never-dying fame, if our endeavours had not been so highly serviceable to the general good of mankind. This, O Universe! is the adventurous attempt of me thy secretary;

> Quemvis preferre laborem
> Suadet, et inducit noctes vigilare serenas.

To this end, I have some time since, with a world of pains and art, dissected the carcass of human nature, and read many useful lectures upon the several parts both containing and contained, till at last it smelled so strong I could preserve it no longer. Upon which I have been at a great expense to fit up all the bones with exact contexture, and in due symmetry, so that I am ready to show a very complete anatomy thereof to all curious "gentlemen and others." But not to digress further in the midst of a digression, as I have known some authors enclose digressions in one another, like a nest of boxes, I do affirm, that having carefully cut up human nature, I have found a very strange, new, and important discovery—that the public good of mankind is performed by two ways, instruction and diversion. And I have further proved in my said several readings (which perhaps the world may one day see, if I can prevail on any friend to steal a copy, or on any certain gentlemen of my admirers to be very importunate), that as mankind is now disposed, he receives much greater advantage by being diverted than instructed, his epidemical diseases being fastidiousness, amorphy, and oscitation; whereas in the present universal empire of wit and learning, there seems but little matter left for instruction. However, in compliance with a lesson of great age and authority, I have attempted carrying the point in all its heights, and accordingly, throughout this divine treatise have skilfully kneaded up both together, with a layer of *utile* and a layer of *dulce*.

When I consider how exceedingly our illustrious moderns have eclipsed the weak glimmering lights of the ancients, and turned them out of the road of all fashionable commerce, to a degree that our choice town-wits of most refined accomplishments are in grave dispute whether there have been ever any ancients or no,* in which point we are like to receive wonderful satisfaction from the most useful labours and lucubrations of that worthy modern, Dr. Bentley, —I say, when I consider all this, I cannot but bewail that no famous modern hath ever yet attempted an universal system, in a small portable volume, of all things that are to be known, or believed, or imagined, or practised in life. I am, however, forced to acknowledge that such an enterprise was thought on some time ago by a great philosopher of O. Brazil.† The method he proposed was by a certain curious receipt, a nostrum, which after his untimely death I found among his papers, and do here, out of my great affection for the modern learned, present them with it, not doubting it may one day encourage some worthy undertaker.

"You take fair, correct copies, well-bound in calf-skin, and lettered at the back, of all modern bodies of arts and science whatsoever, and in what language you please. These you distil in balneo Mariæ, infusing quintessence of poppy q. s., together with three pints of lethe, to be had from apothecaries. You cleanse away carefully the sordes and caput mortuum,

---

* The learned person here meant hath been endeavouring to annihilate so many ancient writers, that until he is pleased to stop his hand, it will be dangerous to affirm whether there have been any ancients in the world.

† This is an imaginary island, akin to that which is called *Painter's wives island*, placed in some unknown part of the ocean, merely at the fancy of the map-maker.

letting all that is volatile evaporate. You preserve only the first running, which is again to be distilled seventeen times, till what remains will amount to about two drams. This you keep in a glass vial hermetically sealed for one-and-twenty days; then you begin your catholic treatise, taking every morning fasting, first shaking the vial, three drops of this elixir, snuffing it strongly up your nose. It will dilate itself about the brain (where there is any) in fourteen minutes, and you immediately perceive in your head an infinite number of abstracts, summaries, compendiums, extracts, collections, medullas, excerpta quædams, florilegias, and the like, all disposed into great order, and reducible upon paper."

I must needs own it was by the assistance of this arcanum that I, though otherwise *impar*, have adventured upon so daring an attempt, never achieved or undertaken before but by a certain author called Homer, in whom, though otherwise a person not without some abilities, and, *for an ancient*, of a tolerable genius, I have discovered many gross errors, which are not to be forgiven his very ashes, if by chance any of them are left. For whereas we are assured he designed his work for a complete body [*] of all knowledge, human, divine, political, and mechanic, it is manifest he hath wholly neglected some, and been very imperfect in the rest. For, first

---

[*] Homerus omnes res humanas poematis complexus est.—*Xenophon in conviv.*

of all, as eminent a cabalist as his disciples would represent him, his account of the "opus magnum" is extremely poor and deficient; he seems to have read but very superficially, either Sendivogus, Behmen, or Antophrosophia Theomagica.* He is also quite mistaken about the *sphæra pyroplastica*, a neglect not to be atoned for; and if the reader will admit so severe a censure, *vix crederem autorem hunc unquam audivisse ignis vocem*. His failings are not less prominent in several parts of the mechanics. For having read his writings with the utmost application usual among modern wits, I could never yet discover the least direction about the structure of that useful instrument, a save-all. For want of which, if the moderns had not lent their assistance, we might yet have wandered in the dark. But I have still behind a fault far more notorious to tax this author with; I mean his gross ignorance in the common laws of this realm, and in the doctrine as well as discipline of the Church of England; † a defect indeed for which both he and all the ancients stand most justly censured by my worthy and ingenious friend, Mr. Wotton, Bachelor of Divinity,

---

* A treatise written about fifty years ago by a Welsh gentleman of Cambridge. His name, as I remember, was Vaughan, as appears by the answer written to it by the learned Dr. Henry Moor. It is a piece of the most unintelligible fustian that perhaps was ever published in any language.

† Mr. Wotton (to whom our author never gives any quarter), in his comparison of ancient and modern learning, numbers divinity, law, &c., among those parts of knowledge wherein we excel the ancients.

in his incomparable treatise on ancient and modern learning, a book never to be sufficiently valued, whether we consider the happy turns and flowings of the author's wit, the great usefulness of his sublime discoveries upon the subject of flies and spittle, or the laborious eloquence of his style. And I cannot forbear doing that author the justice of my public acknowledgment for the great helps and liftings I had out of his incomparable piece while I was penning this treatise.

But besides these omissions in Homer already mentioned, the curious reader will also observe several defects in that author's writings for which he is not altogether so accountable. For whereas every branch of knowledge has received such wonderful acquirements since his age, especially within these last three years or thereabouts, it is almost impossible he could be so very perfect in modern discoveries as his advocates pretend. We freely acknowledge him to be the inventor of the compass, of gunpowder, and the circulation of the blood. But I challenge any of his admirers to show me in all his writings a complete account of the spleen. Does he not also leave us wholly to seek in the art of political wagering? What can be more defective and unsatisfactory than his long dissertation upon tea? And as to his method of salivation without mercury, so much celebrated of late, it is, to my own knowledge and experience, a thing very little to be relied on.

It was to supply such momentous defects that I have been prevailed on, after long solicitation, to take pen in hand; and, I dare venture to promise, the judicious reader shall find nothing neglected here that can be of use upon any emergency of life. I am confident to have included and exhausted all that human imagination can rise or fall to. Particularly I recommend to the perusal of the learned certain discoveries that are wholly untouched by others, whereof I shall only mention, among a great many more, my *New Help for Smatterers ; or, the Art of being Deep-learned and Shallow-read. A Curious Invention about Mouse-traps. A universal Rule of Reason: or, every Man his own Carver ;* together with a most useful engine for catching of owls, all which the judicious reader will find largely treated on in the several parts of this discourse.

I hold myself obliged to give as much light as is possible into the beauties and excellences of what I am writing, because it is become the fashion and humour most applauded among the first authors of this polite and learned age, when they would correct the ill-nature of critical, or inform the ignorance of courteous readers. Besides, there have been several famous pieces lately published, both in verse and prose, wherein, if the writers had not been pleased, out of their great humanity and affection to the public, to give us a nice detail of the sublime and the admirable they contain, it is a thousand to one whether we should ever have discovered one grain of either. For my own particular, I cannot deny that whatever I have said upon this occasion had been more proper in a preface, and more agreeable to the mode which usually directs it thither. But I here think fit to lay hold on that great and honourable privilege of being the last writer; I claim an absolute authority in right, as the freshest modern, which gives me a despotic power over all authors before me, in the strength of which title I do utterly disapprove and declare against that pernicious custom of making the preface a bill of fare to the book; for I have always looked upon it as a high point of indiscretion in monster-mongers, and other retailers of strange sights, to hang out a fair large picture over the door, drawn after the life, with a most elegant description underneath. This hath saved me many a threepence; for my curiosity was fully satisfied, and I never offered to go in, though often invited by the urging and attending orator, with his last moving and standing piece of rhetoric, "Sir, upon my word, we are just going to begin." Such is exactly the fate, at this time, of Prefaces, Epistles, Advertisements, Introductions, Prolegomenas, Apparatuses, To the Readers, &c. This expedient was admirable at first. Our great Dryden has long carried it as far as it would go, and with incredible success. He hath often said to me, in confidence, that the world would have never suspected him to be so great a poet if he had not assured them so frequently in his prefaces, that it was impossible they could either doubt or forget it. Perhaps it may be so: however, I much fear his instructions have edified out of their place, and taught men to grow wiser in certain points where he never intended they should; for it is lamentable to behold with what a lazy scorn many of the yawning readers of our age do nowadays twirl over forty or fifty pages of preface and dedication (which is the usual modern stint) as if it were so much Latin. Though it must be also allowed, on the other hand, that a very considerable number is known to proceed critics and wits by reading nothing else. Into which two factions, I think, all present readers may justly be divided. Now, for myself, I profess to be of the former sort : and therefore having the *modern* inclination to expatiate upon the beauty of my own productions, and display the bright parts of my discourse, I thought best to do it in the body of the work ; where, as it now lies, it makes a very considerable addition to the bulk of the volume ; a circumstance by no means to be neglected by a skilful writer.

Having thus paid my due deference and acknowledgment to an established custom of our newest authors, by a long digression unsought for, and a universal censure unprovoked, by forcing into the light, with much pains and dexterity, my own excellences and other men's defaults with great justice to myself and candour to them, I now happily resume my subject, to the infinite satisfaction both of the reader and the author.

SECTION VI.

A TALE OF A TUB.

WE left Lord Peter in open rupture with his two brethren, both for ever discarded from his house, and resigned to the wide world, with little or nothing to trust to, which are circumstances that render them proper subjects for the charity of a writer's pen to work on, scenes of misery ever affording the fairest harvest for great adventures. And in this the world may perceive the difference between the integrity of a generous author and that of a common friend. The latter is observed to adhere close in prosperity, but on the decline of fortune to drop suddenly off: whereas the generous author, just on the contrary, finds his hero on the dunghill, from thence by gradual steps raises him to a throne, and then immediately withdraws, expecting not so much as thanks for his pains. In imitation of which example, I have placed Lord Peter in a noble house, given him a title to wear, and money to spend. There I shall leave him for some time, returning where common charity directs me, to the assistance of his two brothers, at their lowest ebb. However I shall by no means forget my character of a historian, to follow the truth step by step, whatever happens, or wherever it may lead me.

The two exiles, so nearly united in fortune and interest, took a lodging together, where, at their first leisure, they began to reflect on the numberless misfortunes and vexations of their life past, and could not tell, on the sudden, to what failure in their conduct they ought to impute them, when, after some recollection, they called to mind the copy of their father's will which they had so happily recovered. This was immediately produced, and a firm resolution taken between them to alter whatever was already amiss, and reduce all their future measures to the strictest obedience prescribed therein. The main body of the will (as the reader cannot easily have forgot) consisted in certain admirable rules about the wearing of their coats: in the perusal whereof, the two brothers at every period duly comparing the doctrine with the practice, there was never seen a wider difference between two things—horrible, downright transgressions of every point. Upon which they both resolved, without further delay, to fall immediately upon reducing the whole exactly after their father's model.

But here it is good to stop the hasty reader, ever impatient to see the end of an adventure, before we writers can duly prepare him for it. I am to record, that these two brothers began to be distinguished at this time by certain names. One of them desired to be called MARTIN,* and the other took the appellation of JACK.† These two had lived in much friendship and agreement, under the tyranny of their brother Peter, as it is the talent of fellow-sufferers, men in misfortune being like men in the dark, to whom all colours are the same. But when they came forward into the world, and began to display themselves to each other, and to the light, their complexions appeared extremely different, which the present posture of their affairs gave them sudden opportunity to discover.

But here the severe reader may justly tax me (as a writer) of short memory, a deficiency to which a true modern cannot but of necessity be a little subject; because memory, being an employment of the mind upon things past, is a faculty for which the learned in our illustrious age have no manner of occasion, who deal entirely with invention, and strike all things out of themselves, or at least by collision from each other, upon which account we think it highly reasonable to produce our great forgetfulness as an argument unanswerable for our great wit. I ought, in method, to have informed the reader about fifty pages ago of a fancy Lord Peter took, and infused into his brothers, to wear on their coats whatever trimmings came up

* Martin Luther. † John Calvin.

in fashion, never pulling off any as they went out of the mode, but keeping on all together, which amounted in time to a medley the most antic you can possibly conceive ; and this to a degree, that upon the time of their falling out there was hardly a thread of their original coat to be seen, but an infinite quantity of lace and ribbons and fringe and embroidery, and points (I mean only those tagged with silver,* for the rest fell off). Now this material circumstance having been forgot in due place, as good fortune hath ordered, comes in very properly here, when the two brothers are just going to reform their vestures into the primitive state prescribed by their father's will.

They both unanimously entered upon this great work, looking sometimes on their coats and sometimes on the will. Martin laid the first hand; at one twitch he brought off a large handful of points, and with a second pull stripped away ten dozen yards of fringe. But when he had gone thus far he demurred a while. He knew very well there yet remained a great deal more to be done. However, the first heat being over, his violence began to cool, and he resolved to proceed more moderately in the rest of the work, having already very narrowly escaped a swinging rent in pulling off the points, which, being tagged with silver, as we have observed before, the judicious

---

* Points tagged with silver, or those doctrines that promote the greatness and wealth of the Church, which have been therefore woven deepest in the body of Popery.

workman had with much sagacity double sewn, to preserve them from falling. Resolving therefore to rid his coat of a huge quantity of gold lace, he picked up the stitches with much caution, and diligently gleaned out all the loose threads as he went, which proved to be a work of time. Then he fell about the embroidered Indian figures of men, women, and children, against which, as you have heard in its due place, their father's testament was extremely exact and severe : these, with much dexterity and application, were, after a while, quite eradicated, or utterly defaced. For the rest, where he observed the embroidery to be worked so close as not to be got away without damaging the cloth, or where it served to hide or strengthen any flaw in the body of the coat, contracted by the perpetual tampering of workmen upon it, he concluded the wisest course was to let it remain, resolving in no case whatsoever that the substance of the stuff should suffer injury, which he thought the best method for serving the true intent and meaning of his father's will. And this is the nearest account I have been able to collect of Martin's proceedings upon this great revolution.

But his brother Jack, whose adventures will be so extraordinary as to furnish a great part in the remainder of this discourse, entered upon the matter with other thoughts, and a quite different spirit. For the memory of Lord Peter's injuries produced a degree of hatred and spite, which had a much greater share of inciting him than any regards after his father's commands, since these appeared at best only secondary and subservient to the other. However, for this medley of humour he made a shift to find a very plausible name, honouring it with the title of zeal, which is perhaps the most significant word that hath been ever yet produced in any language, as, I think, I have fully proved in my excellent analytical discourse upon that subject, wherein I have deduced a histori-theo-phisi-logical account of zeal, showing how it first proceeded from a notion into a word, and from thence, in a hot summer, ripened into a tangible substance. This work, containing three large volumes in folio, I design very shortly to publish by the modern way of subscription, not doubting but the nobility and gentry of the land will give me all possible encouragement, having had already such a taste of what I am able to perform.

I record, therefore, that brother Jack, brimful of this miraculous compound, reflecting with indignation upon Peter's tyranny, and further provoked by the despondency of Martin, prefaced his resolutions to this purpose. "What," said he, "a rogue that locked up his drink, turned away our wives, cheated us of our fortunes, palmed his crusts upon us for mutton, and at last kicked us out of doors, must we be in his fashions: a rascal, besides, that all the streets cry against?" Having thus kindled and inflamed himself as high as possible, and by consequence in a delicate temper for beginning a reformation, he set about the work immediately, and in three minutes made more despatch than Martin had done in as many hours. For, courteous reader, you are given to understand that zeal is never so highly obliged as when you set it a tearing; and Jack, who doted on that quality in himself, allowed it at this time its full swing. Thus it happened that stripping down a parcel of gold lace a little too hastily, he rent the main body of his coat from top to bottom; and whereas his talent was not of the happiest in taking up a stitch, he knew no better way than to darn it again with pack-thread and a skewer. But the matter was yet infinitely worse (I record it with tears) when he proceeded to the embroidery: for being clumsy by nature, and of temper impatient, withal beholding millions of stitches that required the nicest hand and sedatest constitution to extricate, in a great rage he tore off the whole piece, cloth and all, and flung it into the kennel, and furiously thus continued his career: "Ah, good brother Martin," said he, "do as I do, for the love of God; strip, tear, pull, rend, flay off all, that we may appear as unlike the rogue Peter as it is possible. I would not, for a hundred pounds, carry the least mark about me that might give occasion to the neighbours of suspecting I was related to such a rascal." But Martin, who at this time happened to be extremely phlegmatic and sedate, begged his brother, of all love, not to damage his coat by any means; for he never would get such another; desired him to consider that it was not their business to form their actions by any reflections upon Peter, but by observing the rules prescribed in their father's will: that he should remember Peter was still their brother, whatever faults or injuries he had committed, and therefore they should by all means avoid such a thought as that of taking measures for good and evil from no other rule than of opposition to him: that it was true, the testament of their good father was very exact in what related to the wearing of their coats, yet was it no less penal and strict in prescribing agreement and friendship and affection between them; and therefore, if straining a point were at all dispensable, it would certainly be so rather to the advance of unity than increase of contradiction.

Martin had still proceeded as gravely as he began; and doubtless would have delivered an admirable lecture of morality, which might have exceedingly contributed to my reader's repose, both of body and mind, the true ultimate end of ethics, but Jack was already gone a flight-shot beyond his patience. And as, in scholastic disputes, nothing serves to rouse the spleen of him that opposes so much as a kind of pedantic affected calmness in the respondent, disputants being for the most part like unequal scales, where the gravity of one side advances the lightness of the other, and causes it to fly up and kick the beam, so it happened here, that the weight of Martin's arguments exalted Jack's levity, and made him fly out and spurn against his brother's moderation. In short, Martin's patience put Jack in a rage. But that which most affected him was to observe his brother's coat so well reduced into the state of innocence, while his own was either wholly rent to his shirt, or those places which had escaped his cruel clutches were still in Peter's livery; so that he looked like a drunken beau half rifled by bullies, or like a fresh tenant in Newgate when he has refused the payment of garnish, or like a discovered shoplifter left to the mercy of Exchange women,* or like a bawd in her old velvet petticoat resigned into the secular hands of the *mobile*. Like any, or like all of these—a medley of rags and lace and rents and fringes, unfortunate Jack did now appear. He would have been extremely glad to see his coat in the condition of Martin's, but infinitely gladder to find that of Martin in the same predicament with his. However, since neither of these was likely to come to pass, he thought fit to lend the whole business another turn, and to dress up necessity into a virtue. Therefore, after as many of the fox's

* The galleries over the piazzas in the Royal Exchange were formerly filled with shops, kept chiefly by women. The same use was made of a building called the New Exchange in the Strand. This edifice has been pulled down; the shopkeepers have removed from the Royal Exchange into Cornhill and the adjacent streets, and there are now no remains of Exchange women but in Exeter 'Change,† and they are no longer deemed the first ministers of fashion.—*Hawkes.*

† Pulled down in 1829.—*Ed.*

arguments * as he could muster up for bringing Martin to reason, as he called it, or, as he meant it, into his own ragged, bob-tailed condition, and observing he said all to little purpose, what, alas! was left for the forlorn Jack to do, but, after a million of scurrilities against his brother, to run mad with spleen and spite and contradiction? To be short, here began a mortal breach between these two. Jack went immediately to new lodgings, and in a few days it was for certain reported that he had run out of his wits. In a short time after he appeared abroad, and confirmed the report by falling into the oddest whimsies that ever a sick brain conceived.

And now the little boys in the streets began to salute him with several names. Sometimes they would call him Jack the Bald,† sometimes Jack with the Lantern,‡ sometimes Dutch Jack,§ sometimes French Hugh,|| sometimes Tom the Beggar,¶ and sometimes Knocking Jack of the North;** and it was

---

* The fox in the fable, who, having been caught in a trap, and lost his tail, used many arguments to persuade the rest to cut off theirs, that the singularity of his deformity might not expose him to derision.— *Hawkes.*

† That is, Calvin; from *calvus*, bald.

‡ All those who pretend to inward light.

——— Melleo contingens cuncta lepore.

§ Jack of Leyden, who gave rise to the Anabaptists.

|| The Huguenots.

¶ The Gueuses, by which name some Protestants in Flanders were called.

** John Knox, the Reformer of Scotland.

under one, or some, or of all these appellations, which I leave the learned reader to determine, that he hath given rise to the most illustrious and epidemic sect of Æolists, who, with honourable commemoration, do still acknowledge the renowned JACK for their author and founder. Of whose original, as well as principles, I am now advancing to gratify the world with a very particular account.

SECTION VII.

A DIGRESSION IN PRAISE OF DIGRESSIONS.

I HAVE sometimes heard of an iliad in a nutshell, but it hath been my fortune to have much oftener seen a nut-shell in an iliad. There is no doubt that human life has received most wonderful advantages from both, but to which of the two the world is chiefly indebted I shall leave among the curious, as a problem worthy of their utmost inquiry. For the invention of the latter I think the commonwealth of learning is chiefly employed to the great modern improvement of digressions, the late refinements in knowledge running parallel to those of diet in our nation, which, among men of a judicious taste, are dressed up in various compounds, consisting in soups and olios, fricassees and ragouts.

It is true, there is a sort of morose, detracting, ill-bred people, who pretend utterly to disrelish these polite innovations. And as to the similitude from diet, they allow the parallel, but are so bold to pronounce the example itself a corruption and degeneracy of taste. They tell us that the fashion of jumbling fifty things together in a dish was at first introduced in compliance to a depraved and debauched appetite, as well as to a crazy constitution: and to see a man hunting through an olio after the head and brains of a goose, a widgeon, or a woodcock, is a sign he wants a stomach and digestion for more substantial victuals. Farther, they affirm that digressions in a book are like foreign troops in a state, which argue the nation to want a heart and hands of its own, and either subdue the natives or drive them into the most unfruitful corners.

But after all that can be objected by their supercilious censors, it is manifest the society of writers would quickly be reduced to a very inconsiderable number, if men were put up to making books with the fatal confinement of delivering nothing beyond what is to the purpose. It is acknowledged that were the case the same among us as with the Greeks and Romans, when learning was in its cradle to be reared and fed and clothed by inventors, it would be an easy task to fill up volumes upon particular occasions, without farther expatiating from the subject than by moderate excursions, helping to advance or clear the main design. But with knowledge it has fared as with a numerous army encamped in a fruitful country, which for a few days maintains itself by the product of the soil it is on, till, provisions being spent, they are sent to forage many a mile, among friends or enemies, it matters not. Meanwhile, the neighbouring fields, trampled and beaten down, become barren and dry, affording no sustenance but clouds of dust.

The whole course of things being thus entirely changed between us and the ancients, and the moderns wisely sensible of it, we of this age have discovered a shorter and a more prudent method to become scholars and wits, without the fatigue of reading and thinking. The most accomplished way of using books at present is twofold: either, first, to serve them as some men do lords, learn their titles exactly, and then brag of their acquaintance; or, secondly, which is indeed the choicer, the more profound, and more polite method, to get a thorough insight into the index, by which the whole book is governed and turned, like fishes by the tail. For to enter the palace of learning at the great gate requires an expense of time and forms, therefore men of much haste and little ceremony are content to get in by the back-door. For the arts are all in a flying march, and therefore more easily subdued by attacking them in the rear. Thus physicians discover the state of the whole body by consulting only what comes from behind. Thus men catch knowledge by throwing their wit on the posteriors of a book, as boys do sparrows by flinging salt upon their tails. Thus human life is best understood by the wise man's rule of regarding the end. Thus are the sciences found, like Hercules' oxen, by tracing them backwards. Thus are old sciences unravelled like old stockings, by beginning at the foot.

Besides all this, the army of the sciences hath been of late, with a world of martial discipline, drawn into its close order, so that a view or a muster may be taken of it with abundance of expedition. For this great blessing we are wholly indebted to systems and abstracts, in which the modern fathers of learning, like prudent usurers, spent their sweat for the ease of us their children. For labour is the seed of idleness, and it is the peculiar happiness of our noble age to gather the fruit.

Now, the method of growing wise, learned, and sublime having become so regular an affair, and so established in all its forms, the number of writers must needs have increased accordingly, and to a pitch that has made it of absolute necessity for them to interfere continually with each other. Besides, it is reckoned that there is not at this present a sufficient quantity of new matter left in nature to furnish and adorn any one particular subject to the extent of a volume. This I am told by a very skilful computer, who hath given a full demonstration of it from the rules of arithmetic.

This perhaps may be objected against by those who maintain the infinity of matter, and therefore will not allow that any species of it can be exhausted. For answer to which let us examine the noblest branch of modern wit or invention, planted and cultivated by the present age, and which, of all other, had borne the most and the fairest fruit. For though some remains of it were left us by the ancients, yet have not any of those, as I remember, been translated or compiled into systems for modern use. Therefore, we may affirm, to our own honour, that it hath, in some sort, been both invented and brought to a perfection by the same hands. What I mean is, that highly celebrated talent among the modern wits of deducing similitudes, allusions, and applications, very surprising, agreeable, and apposite, from the *pudenda* of either sex, together with their proper uses. And truly, having observed how little invention bears any vogue besides what is derived into these channels, I have sometimes had a thought that the happy genius of our age and country was prophetically held forth by that ancient typical description of the Indian pigmies, whose statue did not exceed two feet, *sed quorum pudenda crassa, et ad talos usque pertingentia.** Now, I have been very curious to inspect the late productions wherein the beauties of this kind have most prominently appeared. And although this vein hath bled so freely, and all endeavours have been used in the power of human breath to dilate, extend, and keep it open,—like the Scythians, who had a custom and an instrument to blow up the privities of their mares, that they might

---

* Ctesiæ fragmentæ apud Photium.

yield the more milk *—yet I am under an apprehension it is near growing dry, and past all recovery, and that either some new *fonde* of wit should, if possible, be provided, or else that we must e'en be content with repetition here, as well as upon all other occasions.

This will stand as an incontestable argument that our modern wits are not to reckon upon the infinity of matter for a constant supply. What remains, therefore, but that our last recourse must be had to large indexes and little compendiums? Quotations must be plentifully gathered, and booked in alphabet. To this end, though authors need be little consulted, yet critics and commentators and lexicons carefully must. But, above all, those judicious collectors of bright parts and flowers and observandas are to be nicely dwelt on, by some called the sieves and boulters of learning, though it is left undetermined whether they dealt in pearls or meal, and, consequently, whether we are more to value that which passed through or what stayed behind.

By these methods, in a few weeks there starts up many a writer capable of managing the profoundest and most universal subjects. For what though his head be empty, provided his commonplace book be full? And if you will bate him but the circumstances of method and style and grammar and invention, allow him but the common privileges of transcribing

---

* Herodotus l. 4.

from others, and digress from himself as often as he shall see occasion, he will desire no more ingredients towards fitting up a treatise that shall make a very comely figure on a bookseller's shelf, there to be preserved neat and clean for a long eternity, adorned with the heraldry of its title fairly inscribed on a label, never to be thumbed or greased by students, nor bound to everlasting chains of darkness in a library, but when the fulness of time is come, shall happily undergo the trial of purgatory in order to ascend the sky.

Without these allowances, how is it possible we modern wits should ever have an opportunity to introduce our collections, listed under so many thousand heads of a different nature? for want of which the learned world would be deprived of infinite delight, as well as instruction, and we ourselves buried beyond redress in an inglorious and undistinguished oblivion.

From such elements as these I am alive to behold the day wherein the corporation of authors can outvie all its brethren in the guild; a happiness derived to us, with a great many others, from our Scythian ancestors, among whom the number of pens was so infinite, that the Grecian eloquence had no other way of expressing it than by saying that, in the region far to the north, it was hardly possible for a man to travel, the very air was so replete with feathers.[*]

The necessity of this digression will easily excuse

[*] Herodotus l. 4.

the length; and I have chosen for it as proper a place as I could readily find. If the judicious reader can assign a fitter, I do here empower him to remove it into any other corner he pleases. And so I return, with great alacrity, to pursue a more important concern.

SECTION VIII.

A TALE OF A TUB.

THE learned Æolists * maintain the original cause of all things to be wind, from which principle this whole universe was at first produced, and into which it must at last be resolved: that the same breath which had kindled and blown up the flame of nature should one day blow it out:

> Quod procul a nobis flectat fortuna gubernans.

This is what the *adepti* understand by their *anima mundi*: that is to say, the *spirit*, or *breath*, or *wind*, of the world. For examine the whole system by the particulars of nature, and you will find it is not to be disputed. For whether you please to call the *forma informans* of man by the name of *spiritus, animus afflatus*, or *anima*, what are all these but several appellations for wind, which is the ruling element in every compound, and into which they all resolve upon

---

* All pretenders to inspiration whatsoever.

their corruption? Farther, what is life itself but, as as it is commonly called, the breath of our nostrils? Whence it is very justly observed by naturalists, that wind still continues of great emolument in certain mysteries not to be named, giving occasion for those happy epithets of *turgidus* and *inflatus*, applied either to the emittent or recipient organs.

By what I have gathered out of ancient records, I find the compass of their doctrine took in two-and-thirty points, wherein it would be tedious to be very particular. However, a few of their most important precepts, deducible from it, are by no means to be omitted, among which the following maxim was of much weight. That since wind had the master-share as well as operation in every compound, by consequence those beings must be of chief excellence wherein that *primordium* appears most prominently to abound; and therefore man is in highest perfection of all created things, as having, by the great bounty of philosophers, been endued with three distinct *animas* or *winds*, to which the sage Æolists, with much liberality, have added a fourth, of equal necessity, as well as ornament, with the other three, by this *quartum principium* taking in our four corners of the world, which gave occasion for that renowned cabalist, Bumbastus,[*] of placing the body of men in due position to the four cardinal points.

---

[*] This is one of the names of Paracelsus. He was called Christophorus Theophrastus Paracelsus Bumbastus.

In consequence of this, their next principle was that man brings with him into the world a peculiar portion or grain of wind, which may be called a *quinta essentia*, extracted from the other four. The quintessence is of a catholic use upon all emergencies of life, is improvable into all arts and sciences, and may be wonderfully refined, as well as enlarged, by certain methods in education. This, when blown up to its perfection, ought not to be covetously hoarded up, stifled, or hid under a bushel, but freely communicated to mankind. Upon these reasons, and others of equal weight, the wise Æolists affirm the gift of *belching* to be the noblest act of a rational creature. To cultivate which art, and render it more serviceable to mankind, they made use of several methods. At certain seasons of the year you might behold the priests among them in vast numbers, with their mouths gaping wide enough against a storm.* At other times were to be seen several hundreds linked together in a circular chain, with every man a pair of bellows applied to his neighbour's breech, by which they blew up each other to the shape and size of a tun, and for that reason, with great propriety of speech, did usually call their bodies their vessels. When, by these and the like performances, they were grown sufficiently replete, they would immediately depart and disembogue, for the public good, a plenti-

---

* This is meant of those seditious preachers who blow up the seeds of rebellion, &c.

ful share of the acquirements into their disciples chaps. For we must here observe, that all learning was esteemed among them to be compounded from the same principle; because, first, it is generally affirmed or confessed that learning puffeth men up: and, secondly, they proved it by the following syllogism: "Words are but wind, and learning is nothing but words; *ergo*, learning is nothing but wind." For this reason, the philosophers among them did, in their schools, deliver to their pupils all their doctrines and opinions by eructation, wherein they had acquired a wonderful eloquence and of incredible variety. But the great characteristic by which their chief sages were best distinguished was a certain position of countenance, which gave undoubted intelligence to what degree of proportion the spirit agitated the inward mass. For after certain gripings the wind and vapours issuing forth, having first, by their turbulence and convulsions within caused an earthquake in man's little world, distorted the mouth, bloated the cheeks, and given the eyes a terrible kind of *relievo*, at which juncture all their belches were received for sacred, the sourer the better, and swallowed with infinite consolation by their meagre devotees. And to render these yet more complete, because the breath of man's life is in his nostrils, therefore the choicest, most edifying, and most enlivening belches were very wisely conveyed through that vehicle, to give them a tincture as they passed.

Their gods were the four winds, whom they worshipped as the spirits that pervade and enliven the universe, and as those from whom alone all inspiration can properly be said to proceed. However, the chief of these, to whom they performed the adoration of *latria*,* was the almighty North, an ancient deity, whom the inhabitants of Megalopolis, in Greece, had likewise in the highest reverence: *Omnium deorum Boream maxime celebrant*.† This god, though endued with ubiquity, was yet supposed by the profounder Æolists to possess one peculiar habitation, or, to speak in form, a *cœlum empyræum*, wherein he was more intimately present. This was situated in a certain region, well known to the ancient Greeks, by them called Σκοτία, or the land of darkness. And although many controversies have arisen upon that matter, yet so much is undisputed, that from a region of the like denomination the most refined Æolists have borrowed their original; from whence in every age the zealous among their priesthood have brought over their choicest inspiration, fetching it with their own hands from the fountainhead in certain bladders, and disploding it among the sectaries in all nations, who did, and do, and ever will, daily grasp and pant after it.

Now, their mysteries and rites were performed in this manner. It is well known, among the learned,

---

* *Latria* is that worship which is paid only to the Supreme Deity.— *Hawkes.*

† Pausanius i. 8.

that the virtuosos of former ages had a contrivance for carrying and preserving winds in casks or barrels, which was of great assistance upon long sea-voyages; and the loss of so useful an art at present is very much to be lamented, although, I know not how, with great negligence omitted by Pancirollus.* It was an invention ascribed to Æolus himself, from whom this sect is denominated; and who, in honour of their founder's memory, have to this day preserved great numbers of those barrels, whereof they fix one in each of their temples, first beating out the top. Into this barrel, upon solemn days, the priest enters, where, having before duly prepared himself by the methods already described, a secret funnel is also conveyed from his posteriors to the bottom of the barrel, which admits new supplies of inspiration from a northern chink, or cranny. Whereupon you behold him swell immediately to the shape and size of his vessel. In this posture he disembogues whole tempests upon his auditory, as the spirit from beneath gives him utterance, which, issuing *ex adytis et penetralibus*, is not performed without much pain and gripings. And the wind, in breaking forth, deals with his face as it does with that of the sea, first blackening, then wrinkling, and at last bursting it into a foam.† It is in

* An author who wrote *de artibus perditis*, &c., of arts lost, and of arts invented.

† This is an exact description of the changes made in the face by enthusiastic preachers.

this guise the sacred Æolist delivers his oracular belches to his panting disciples, of whom some are greedily gaping after the sanctified breath, others are all the while hymning out the praises of the winds, and gently wafted to and fro by their own humming, do thus represent the soft breezes of their deities appeased.

It is from this custom of the priests that some authors maintain these Æolists to have been very ancient in the world, because the delivery of their mysteries, which I have just now mentioned, appears exactly the same with that of other ancient oracles, whose inspirations were owing to certain subterraneous effluviums of wind delivered with the same pain to the priest, and much about the same influence on the people. It is true, indeed, that these were frequently managed and directed by female officers, whose organs were understood to be better disposed for the admission of those oracular gusts, as entering and passing up through a receptacle of greater capacity, and causing also a pruriency by the way, such as, with due management, hath been refined from carnal into a spiritual ecstasy. And to strengthen this profound conjecture, it is farther insisted that this custom of female priests* is kept up still in certain refined colleges of our modern Æolists, who are agreed to receive their inspiration, derived through the receptacle aforesaid, like their ancestors, the Sibyls.

* Quakers, who suffer their women to preach and pray.

And whereas the mind of man, when he gives the spur and bridle to his thoughts, doth never stop, but naturally sallies out into both extremes of high and low, of good and evil, his first flight of fancy commonly transports him to ideas of what is most perfect, finished, and exalted; till, having soared out of his own reach and sight, not well perceiving how near the frontiers of height and depth border upon each other, with the same course and wing he falls down plumb into the lowest bottom of things, like one who travels from the east into the west, or like a straight line drawn by its own length into a circle. Whether a tincture of malice in our natures makes us fond of furnishing every bright idea with its reverse, or whether reason, reflecting upon the sum of things, can, like the sun, serve only to enlighten one half of the globe, leaving the other half by necessity under shade and darkness; or whether fancy, flying up to the imagination of what is highest and best, becomes over-short and spent and weary, and suddenly falls, like a dead bird of paradise, to the ground; or whether, after all these metaphysical conjectures, I have not entirely missed the true reason, the proposition, however, which hath stood me in so much circumstance is altogether true, that as the most uncivilised parts of mankind have some way or other climbed up into the conception of a god, or supreme power, so they have seldom forgot to provide their fears with certain ghastly notions, which, instead of better, have served them pretty tolerably for a devil. And this proceeding seems to be natural enough; for it is with men, whose imaginations are lifted up very high, after the same rate as with those whose bodies are so, that as they are delighted with the advantage of a nearer contemplation upwards, so they are equally terrified with the dismal prospect of the precipice below. Thus, in the choice of a devil, it hath been the usual method of mankind to single out some being, either in act or in vision, which was in most antipathy to the god they had framed. Thus also the sect of Æolists possessed themselves with a dread and horror and hatred of two malignant natures, betwixt whom and the deities they adored perpetual enmity was established. The first of these was the *Camelion*,* sworn foe to inspiration, who in scorn devoured large influences of their god, without refunding the smallest blast by eructation. The other was a huge terrible monster called *Moulinavent*, who, with four strong arms, waged eternal battle with all their divinities, dexterously turning to avoid their blows, and repay them with interest.

Thus furnished, and set out with gods as well as devils, was the renowned sect of Æolists, which makes at this day so illustrious a figure in the world, and whereof that polite nation of Laplanders are,

---

* I do not well understand what the author aims at here, any more than by the terrible monster mentioned in the following lines, called *Moulinavent*, which is the French name for a windmill.

beyond all doubt, a most authentic branch, of whom I therefore cannot, without injustice, here omit to make honourable mention, since they appeared to be so closely allied, in point of interest as well as inclinations, with their brother Æolists among us, as not only to buy their winds by wholesale from the same merchants, but also to retail them after the same rate and method, and to customers much alike.

Now, whether the system here delivered was wholly compiled by Jack, or, as some writers believe, rather copied from the original at Delphos, with certain additions and emendations suited to the times and circumstances, I shall not absolutely determine. This I may affirm, that Jack gave it at least a new turn, and formed it into the same dress and model as it lies deduced by me.

I have long sought after this opportunity of doing justice to a society of men for whom I have a peculiar honour, and whose opinions, as well as practices, have been extremely misrepresented and traduced by the malice or ignorance of their adversaries. For I think it one of the greatest and best of human actions to remove prejudices, and place things in their truest and fairest light, which I therefore boldly undertake, without any regards of my own, besides the conscience, the honour, and the thanks.

SECTION IX.

A DIGRESSION CONCERNING THE ORIGIN, THE USE, AND IMPROVEMENT OF MADNESS IN A COMMONWEALTH.

NOR shall it anywise detract from the just reputation of this famous sect, that its rise and institution are owing to such an author as I have described Jack to be, a person whose intellectuals were overturned, and his brain shaken out of its natural position, which we commonly suppose to be a distemper, and call by the name of madness, or frenzy. For if we take a survey of the greatest actions that have been performed in the world under the influence of single men, which are, the establishment of new empires by conquest, the advance and progress of new schemes in philosophy, and the contriving, as well as the propagating, of new religions, we shall find the authors of them all to have been persons whose natural reasons had admitted great revolutions from their diet, their education, the prevalency of some certain temper, together with the particular influence of air and climate. Besides, there is something individual in human minds that easily kindles at the accidental approach and collision of certain circumstances, which, though of paltry and mean appearance, do often flame out into the greatest emergencies of life. For the great turns are not always given by strong hands, but by lucky adaption, and at proper seasons. And it is of no import where the fire was kindled, if the vapour has once got up into the brain. For the upper region of man is furnished like the middle region of the air, the materials are formed from causes of the widest difference, yet produce at last the same substance and effect. Mists arise from the earth, steams from dunghills, exhalations from the sea, and smoke from fire, yet all clouds are the same in compositions, as well as consequences, and the fumes issuing from a jakes will furnish as comely and useful a vapour as incense from an altar. Thus far, I suppose, will easily be granted me; and then it will follow, that as the face of nature never produces rain but when it is overcast and disturbed, so human understanding, seated in the brain, must be troubled and overspread by vapours, ascending from the lower faculties, to water the invention and render it fruitful. Now, although these vapours (as it hath been already said) are of as various origins as those of the skies, yet the crops they produce differ both in kind and degree merely according to the soil. I will produce two instances to prove and explain what I am now advancing.

A certain great prince raised a mighty army, filled his coffers with infinite treasures, provided an invincible fleet, and all this without giving the least part of his design to his greatest ministers or his nearest favourites.* Immediately the whole world was alarmed, the neighbouring crowns in trembling expectations towards what point the storm would burst, the small politicians everywhere forming profound conjectures. Some believed he had laid a scheme for universal monarchy; others, after much insight, determined the matter to be a project of pulling down the pope, and setting up the reformed religion, which had once been his own. Some again, of a deeper sagacity, sent him into Asia, to subdue the Turk, and recover Palestine. In the midst of all these projects and preparations, a certain state-surgeon,† gathering the nature of the disease by these symptoms, attempted the cure; at one blow performed the operation, broke the bag, and out flew the vapour. Nor did anything want to render it a complete remedy, only that the prince unfortunately happened to die in the performance. Now is the reader exceeding curious to learn from whence this vapour took its rise, which had so long set the nations at a gaze? what secret wheel, what hidden spring, could put into motion so wonderful an engine? It was afterwards discovered that the movement of

---

* This was Harry the Great of France.
† Ravillac, who stabbed Henry the Great in his coach.

this whole machine had been directed by an absent female, whose eyes had raised a protuberancy, and, before emission, she was removed into an enemy's country. What should an unhappy prince do in such ticklish circumstances as these? He tried in vain the poet's never-failing receipt of *corpora quæque:* For,

> Idque petit corpus mens, unde est saucia amore;
> Unde feritur, eo tendit, gestitque coire.—*Lucretia.*

Having to no purpose used all peaceable endeavours, the collected part of the semen, raised and inflamed, became a dust, converted to choler, turned head upon the spinal duct, and ascended to the brain. The very same principle that influences a bully to break the windows of a woman who has jilted him naturally stirs up a great prince to raise mighty armies, and dream of nothing but sieges, battles, and victories.

> Teterrimi belli
> Causa———

The other instance is, what I have read somewhere, in a very ancient author, of a mighty king,* who for the space of above thirty years amused himself to take and lose towns, beat armies and be beaten, drive princes out of their dominions, fright children from their bread and butter, burn, lay waste, blunder, dragoon, massacre subject and stranger, friend and foe, male and female. It is recorded that the philo-

* This is meant of the French king, Louis XIV.

sophers of each country were in grave dispute upon causes natural, moral, and political, to find out where they should assign an original solution of this phenomenon. At last the vapour or spirit which animated the hero's brain, being in perpetual circulation, seized upon that region of the human body so renowned for furnishing the *zibeta occidentalis*,* and gathering there into a tumour, left the rest of the world for that time in peace. Of such mighty consequence it is where those exhalations fix and of so little from whence they proceed. The same spirits which, in their superior progress, would conquer a kingdom, descending upon the *anus* conclude in a *fistula*.

Let us next examine the great introducers of new schemes in philosophy, and search till we can find from what faculty of the soul the disposition arises in mortal man, of taking it into his head to advance new systems with such an eager zeal, in things agreed on all hands impossible to be known; from what seeds this disposition springs, and to what quality of human nature these grand innovators have been indebted for their number of disciples: because it is plain, that several of the chief among them, both ancient and modern, were usually mistaken by their

---

* Paracelsus, who was so famous for chemistry, tried an experiment upon human excrement, to make a perfume of it, which when he had brought to perfection, he called *zibeta occidentalis*, or *western civet*, the back parts of man (according to his division mentioned by the author p. 361) being the west.

adversaries, and indeed by all except their own followers, to have been persons crazed, or out of their wits, having generally proceeded, in the common course of their words and actions, by a method very different from the vulgar dictates of unrefined reason; agreeing, for the most part, in their several models with their present undoubted successors in the academy of modern Bedlam, whose merits and principles I shall farther examine in due place. Of this kind were Epicurus, Diogenes, Apollonius, Lucretius, Paracelsus, Descartes, and others, who, if they were now in the world, tied fast, and separate from their followers, would, in this our undistinguished age, incur manifest danger of phlebotomy, and whips, and chains, and dark chambers, and straw. For what man, in the natural state or course of thinking, did ever conceive it in his power to reduce the notions of all mankind exactly to the same length and breadth and height of his own? Yet this is the first humble and civil design of all innovators in the empire of reason. Epicurus modestly hoped that, one time or other, a certain fortuitous concourse of all men's opinions, after perpetual jostlings, the sharp with the smooth, the light and the heavy, the round and the square, would, by certain *clinamina*, unite in the notions of atoms and void; as these did in the originals of all things. Cartesius reckoned to see, before he died, the sentiments of all philosophers, like so many lesser stars in his romantic system, wrapped and drawn within his own vortex. Now I would gladly be informed how it is possible to account for such imaginations as these in particular men, without recourse to my phenomenon of vapours ascending from the lower faculties to overshadow the brain, and there distilling into conceptions, for which the narrowness of our mother-tongue has not yet assigned any other name besides that of madness or frenzy. Let us therefore now conjecture how it comes to pass, that none of these great prescribers do ever fail providing themselves and their notions with a number of implicit disciples. And I think the reason is easy to be assigned, for there is a peculiar string in the harmony of human understanding, which in several individuals is exactly of the same tuning. This, if you can dexterously screw up to its right key, and then strike gently upon it, whenever you have the good fortune to light among those of the same pitch, they will, by a secret necessary sympathy, strike exactly at the same time. And in this one circumstance lies all the skill or luck of the matter: for if you chance to jar the string among those who are either above or below your own height, instead of subscribing to your doctrine, they will tie you fast, call you mad, and feed you with bread and water. It is therefore a point of the nicest conduct to distinguish and adapt this noble talent with respect to the difference of persons and of times. Cicero understood this very well when writing to a friend in England, with a caution, among other matters, to beware of being cheated by our hackney-coachmen (who, it seems, in those days, were as arrant rascals as they are now), has these remarkable words: *Est quod gaudeas te in ista loca venisse, ubi aliquid sapere viderere.** For, to speak a bold truth, it is a fatal miscarriage so ill to order affairs as to pass for a fool in one company when in another you might be treated as a philosopher, which I desire some certain gentlemen of my acquaintance to lay up in their hearts, as a very seasonable inuendo.

This, indeed, was the fatal mistake of that worthy gentleman, my most ingenious friend, Mr. Wotton, a person, in appearance, ordained for great designs, as well as performances. Whether you will consider his notions or his looks, surely no man ever advanced into the public with fitter qualifications of body and mind for the propagation of a new religion. Oh, had those happy talents, misapplied to vain philosophy, been turned into their proper channels of dreams and visions, where distortion of mind and countenance are of such sovereign use, the base detracting world would not then have dared to report that something is amiss, that his brain hath undergone an unlucky shake, which even his brother-modernists themselves, like ungrates, do whisper so loud that it reaches up to the very garret I am now writing in.

Lastly, whosoever pleases to look into the fountains

* Epist. ad Fam. Trebat.

of enthusiasm, from whence, in all ages, have eternally proceeded such fattening streams, will find the spring-head to have been as troubled and muddy as the current. Of such great emolument is a tincture of this vapour, which the world calls madness, that without its help the world would not only be deprived of those two great blessings, conquests and systems, but even all mankind would unhappily be reduced to the same belief in things invisible.

Now, the former *postulatum* being held, that it is of no import from what originals this vapour proceeds, but either in what angles it strikes and spreads over the understanding or upon what species of brain it ascends, it will be a very delicate point to cut the feather and divide the several reasons to a nice and curious reader, how this numerical difference in the brain can produce effects of so vast a difference from the same vapour, as to be the sole point of individuation between Alexander the Great, Jack of Leyden, and Monsieur Descartes. The present argument is the most abstracted that ever I engaged in; it strains my faculties to their highest stretch: and I desire the reader to attend with utmost perpensity, for I now proceed to unravel this knotty point.

There is in mankind a certain * . . . .

---

* Here is another defect in the manuscript; but I think the author did wisely, and that the matter which thus strained his faculties was not worth a solution; and it were well if all metaphysical cobweb problems were no otherwise answered.

. . . . *Hic multa*
. . . . *desiderantur*
. . . . And
this I take to be a clear solution of the matter.

Having therefore so narrowly passed through this intricate difficulty, the reader will, I am sure, agree with me in the conclusion, that if the moderns mean by madness only a disturbance or transposition of the brain, by force of certain vapours issuing up from the lower faculties, then has this madness been the parent of all those mighty revolutions that have happened in empire, in philosophy, and in religion. For the brain, in its natural position and state of serenity, disposeth its owner to pass his life in the common forms, without any thoughts of subduing multitudes to his own power, his reasons, or his visions: and the more he shapes his understanding by the pattern of human learning, the less he is inclined to form parties after his particular notions, because that instructs him in his private infirmities, as well as in the stubborn ignorance of the people. But when a man's fancy gets astride on his reason, when imagination is at cuffs with the senses, and common understanding, as well as common sense, is kicked out of doors, the first proselyte he makes is himself; and when that is once compassed the difficulty is not so great in bringing over others, a strong delusion always operating from without as vigorously as from within. For cant and vision are, to the ear and the eye, the same that tickling is to the touch. Those entertainments and pleasures we most value in life are such as dupe and play the wag with the senses. For if we take an examination of what is generally understood by happiness, as it has respect either to the understanding or the senses, we shall find all its properties and adjuncts will herd under this short definition, that it is a perpetual possession of being well deceived. And, first, with relation to the mind or understanding, it is manifest what mighty advantages fiction has over truth: and the reason is just at our elbow, because imagination can build nobler scenes, and produce more wonderful revolutions, than fortune or nature will be at expense to furnish. Nor is mankind so much to blame in his choice thus determining him, if we consider that the debate merely lies between things past and things conceived. And so the question is only this, whether things that have place in the imagination may not as properly be said to exist as those that are seated in the memory? which may be justly held in the affirmative, and very much to the advantage of the former, since this is acknowledged to be the womb of things, and the other allowed to be no more than the grave. Again, if we take this definition of happiness, and examine it with reference to the senses, it will be acknowledged wonderfully adapt. How fading and insipid do all objects accost us that are not conveyed in the vehicle of delusion! How shrunk is everything as it appears in the glass of nature! So that if it were not for the assistance of artificial mediums, false lights, refracted angles, varnish, and tinsel, there would be a mighty level in the felicity and enjoyments of mortal men. If this were seriously considered by the world, as I have a certain reason to suspect it hardly will, men would no longer reckon among their high points of wisdom the art of exposing weak sides and publishing infirmities, an employment, in my opinion, neither better nor worse than that of unmasking, which, I think, has never been allowed fair usage, either in the world or the playhouse.

In the proportion that credulity is a more peaceful possession of the mind than curiosity, so far preferable is that wisdom which converses about the surface to that pretended philosophy which enters into the depth of things, and then comes gravely back with informations and discoveries that in the inside they are good for nothing. The two senses to which all objects first address themselves are the sight and the touch. These never examine farther than the colour, the shape, the size, and whatever other qualities dwell, or are drawn by art upon the outward of bodies; and then comes reason officiously with tools for cutting, and opening, and mangling, and piercing, offering to demonstrate that they are not of the same consistence quite through. Now I take all this to be the last degree of perverting nature, one of whose eternal laws it is to put her best furniture forward. And therefore, in order to save the charges of all such expensive anatomy for the time to come, I do here think fit to inform the reader, that in such conclusions as these reason is certainly in the right; and that in the most corporeal beings which have fallen under my cognisance, the outside hath been infinitely preferable to the inside, whereof I have been farther convinced from some late experiments. Last week I saw a woman flayed, and you will hardly believe how much it altered her person for the worse. Yesterday I ordered the carcass of a beau to be stripped in my presence, when we were all amazed to find so many unsuspected faults under one suit of clothes. Then I laid open his brain, his heart, and his spleen. But I plainly perceived, at every operation, that the farther we proceeded we found the defects increase upon us in number and bulk. From all which I justly formed this conclusion to myself: that whatever philosopher or projector can find out an art to solder and patch up the flaws and imperfections of nature, will deserve much better of mankind, and teach us a more useful science, than that so much in present esteem, of widening and exposing them, like him who held anatomy to be the ultimate end of physic. And he whose fortunes and dispositions have placed him in a convenient station to enjoy the fruits of this noble art, he that can, with Epicurus, content his ideas with the films and images that fly off upon his sense from the superficies of things—such a man, truly wise, creams off nature, leaving the sour and the dregs for philosophy and reason to lap up. This is the sublime and refined point of felicity, called the possession of being well deceived, the serene, peaceful state of being a fool among knaves.

But to return to madness: it is certain that, according to the system I have above deduced, every species thereof proceeds from a redundancy of vapours; therefore, as some kinds of frenzy give double strength to the sinews, so there are of other species which add vigour and life and spirit to the brain. Now, it usually happens that these active spirits, getting possession of the brain, resemble those that haunt other waste and empty dwellings, which, for want of business, either vanish and carry away a piece of the house, or else stay at home and fling it all out of the windows. By which are mystically displayed the two principal branches of madness, and which some philosophers, not considering so well as I, have mistaken to be different in their causes, overhastily assigning the first to deficiency and the other to redundance.

I think it therefore manifest, from what I have here advanced, that the main point of skill and address is to furnish employment for this redundancy of vapour, and prudently to adjust the season of it, by which means it may certainly become of cardinal and catholic emolument in a commonwealth. Thus one man, choosing a proper conjecture, leaps into a gulf, from thence proceeds a hero, and is called the saver of his country: another achieves the same enterprise, but unluckily timing it, has left the brand of madness fixed as a reproach upon his memory. Upon so nice a distinction are we taught to repeat the name of Curtius with reverence and love, that of Empedocles with hatred and contempt. Thus also it is usually conceived that the elder Brutus only personated the fool and madman for the good of the public. But this was nothing else than a redundancy of the same vapour long misapplied, called by the Latins *ingenium par negotiis;* * or, to translate it as nearly as I can, a sort of frenzy never in its right element till you take it up in the business of the state.

Upon all which, and many other reasons of equal weight, though not equally curious, I do here gladly embrace an opportunity I have long sought for, of recommending it as a very noble undertaking to Sir Edward Seymour, Sir Christopher Musgrave, Sir John Bowles, John How, Esq., and other patriots concerned, that they would move for leave to bring in a bill for appointing commissioners to inspect into Bedlam, and the parts adjacent, who shall be empowered to send for persons, papers, and records; to examine into the merits and qualifications of every student and professor; to observe with the utmost exactness their several dispositions and behaviour, by

* Tacitus.

which means, duly distinguishing and adapting their talents, they might produce admirable instruments for the several offices in a state ———,* civil, and military, proceeding in such methods as I shall here humbly propose. And I hope the gentle reader will give some allowance to my great solicitude in this important affair, upon account of the high esteem I have borne that honourable society, whereof I had some time the happiness to be an unworthy member.

Is any student tearing his straw in piecemeal, swearing and blaspheming, biting his grate, foaming at the mouth, and emptying his foul water in the spectators' faces, let the Right Worshipful the Commissioners of Inspection give him a regiment of dragoons, and send him into Flanders among the rest. Is another eternally talking, sputtering, gaping, bawling, in a sound without period or article? What wonderful talents are here mislaid! Let him be furnished immediately with a green bag and papers, and threepence † in his pocket, and away with him to Westminster Hall. You will find a third gravely taking the dimensions of his kennel, a person of foresight and insight, though kept quite in the dark; for why, like Moses, *ecce cornuta erat ejus facies.*‡ He walks duly in pace; entreats your penny

---

* Ecclesiastical.—*Hawkes.*

† A lawyer's coach-hire, when four together, from any of the inns of court to Westminster.

‡ *Cornutus* is either horned or shining; and by this term Moses is described in the vulgar Latin of the Bible.

with due gravity and ceremony; talks much of hard times, and taxes, and the harlot of Babylon; bars up the wooden window of his cell constantly at eight o'clock; dreams of fire and shop-lifters, and court-customers and privileged places. Now, what a figure would all these acquirements amount to, if the owner were sent into the city among his brethren! Behold a fourth, in much and deep conversation with himself, biting his thumbs at proper junctures; his countenance chequered with business and design; sometimes walking very fast, with his eyes nailed to a paper that he holds in his hands; a great saver of time; somewhat thick of hearing: very short of sight, but more of memory; a man ever in haste, a great hatcher and breeder of business, and excellent at the famous art of whispering nothing: a huge idolater of monosyllables and procrastination; so ready to give his word to everybody, that he never *keeps* it; one that has got the common meaning of words, but an admirable retainer of the *sound;* extremely subject to the *looseness,* for his *occasions* are perpetually *calling him away.* If you approach his grate in his familiar intervals, " Sir," says he, " give me a penny, and I'll sing you a song; but give me the penny first." (Hence comes the common saying, and commoner practice, of parting with money for a song.) What a complete system of court-skill is here described in every branch of it, and all utterly lost with wrong application! Accost the hole of another kennel (first stopping your nose), you will behold a surly, gloomy, nasty, slovenly mortal, raking in filth and ordure. His complexion is of a dirty yellow, with a thin scattered beard, exactly agreeable to his filthy occupation; like other insects, who, having their birth and education in an excrement, from thence borrow their colour and their smell. The student of this apartment is very sparing of his words, but somewhat over-liberal of his breath: he holds his hand out ready to receive your penny, and immediately upon receipt withdraws to his former occupations. Now, is it not amazing to think the society of Warwick Lane should have no more concern for the recovery of so useful a member, who, if one may judge from these appearances, would become the greatest ornament to that illustrious body? Another student struts up fiercely to your teeth, puffing with his lips, half squeezing out his eyes, and very graciously holds you out his hand to kiss. The keeper desires you not to be afraid of this professor, for he will do you no hurt. To him alone is allowed the liberty of the antechamber, and the orator of the place gives you to understand that this solemn person is a tailor run mad with pride. This considerable student is adorned with many other qualities, upon which at present I shall not further enlarge———. Hark in your ear ———.* I am strangely mistaken

---

* I cannot conjecture what the author means here, or how this chasm could be filled, though it is capable of more than one interpretation.

if all his address, his motions, and his airs, would not then be very natural, and in their proper element.

I shall not descend so minutely as to insist upon the vast number of beaux, fiddlers, poets, and politicians, that the world might recover by such a reformation. But what is more material, besides the clear gain redounding to the commonwealth, by so large an acquisition of persons to employ, whose talents and acquirements, if I may be so bold to affirm it, are now buried, or at least misapplied, it would be a mighty advantage accruing to the public from this inquiry, that all these would very much excel and arrive at great perfection in their several kinds; which I think is manifest from what I have already shown, and shall enforce by this one plain instance, that even I myself, the author of these momentous truths, am a person whose imaginations are hard-mouthed, and exceedingly disposed to run away with his reason, which I have observed, from long experience, to be a very light rider, and easily shaken off: upon which account my friends will never trust me alone, without a solemn promise to vent my speculations in this or the like manner for the universal benefit of human kind, which perhaps the gentle, courteous, and candid reader, brimful of that *modern* charity and tenderness usually annexed to his office, will be very hardly persuaded to believe.

SECTION X.

A FURTHER DIGRESSION.*

IT is an unanswerable argument of a very refined age, the wonderful civilities that have passed of late years between the nation of authors and that of readers. There can hardly pop out a play, a pamphlet, or a poem, without a preface full of acknowledgment to the world for the general reception and applause they have given it, which the Lord knows where, or when, or how, or from whom it received.† In due deference to so laudable a custom, I do here return my humble thanks to his Majesty, and both Houses of Parliament; to the Lords of the King's Most Honourable Privy Council; to the reverend the judges; to the clergy and gentry and

---

* This section has in former editions been entitled *A Tale of a Tub*; but the tale not being continued till Section XI., and this being only a further digression, no apology can be thought necessary for making the title correspond with the contents.—*Hawkes*.

† This is literally true, as we may observe in the prefaces to most plays, poems, &c.

yeomanry of this land: but in a more especial manner to my worthy brethren and friends at Wills' coffee-house, and Gresham College, and Warwick Lane, and Moorfields, and Scotland Yard, and Westminster Hall, and Guildhall: in short, to all inhabitants and retainers whatsoever, either in court, or church, or camp, or city, or country, for their generous and universal acceptance of this divine treatise. I accept their approbation and good opinion with extreme gratitude, and to the utmost of my poor capacity, shall take hold of all opportunities to return the obligation.

I am also happy that fate has flung me into so blessed an age for the mutual felicity of booksellers and authors, whom I may safely affirm to be at this day the only two satisfied parties in England. Ask an author how his last piece has succeeded? Why, truly, he thanks his stars the world has been very favourable, and he has not the least reason to complain. And yet he swears he writ it in a week, at fits and starts, when he would steal an hour from his urgent affairs; as it is a hundred to one you may see farther in the preface, to which he refers you, and for the rest to the booksellers. There you go as a customer, and make the same question: he blesses his God the thing takes wonderfully; he is just printing the second edition, and has but three left in his shop. You beat down the price; "Sir, we shall not differ:" and in hopes of your custom another time lets you have it as reasonable as you please: "And pray send as many of your acquaintance as you will; I shall, upon your account, furnish them all at the same rate."

Now, it is not well enough considered to what accident and occasions the world is indebted for the greatest part of those noble writings which hourly start up to entertain it. If it were not for a rainy day, a drunken vigil, a fit of the spleen, a course of physic, a sleepy Sunday, an ill run at dice, a long tailor's bill, a beggar's purse, a factious head, a hot sun, costive diet, want of books, and a just contempt of learning—but for these events, I say, and some others too long to recite (especially a prudent neglect of taking brimstone inwardly), I doubt not the number of authors and of writings would dwindle away to a degree most woful to behold. To confirm this opinion, hear the words of the famous Troglodyte philosopher. "It is certain," said he, "some grains of folly are of course annexed as part of the composition of human nature; only, the choice is left us whether we please to wear them inlaid or embossed: and we need not go very far to seek how that is usually determined, when we remember it is with human faculties as with liqours, the lightest will be ever at the top."

There is in this famous island of Britain a certain paltry scribbler, very voluminous, whose character the reader cannot wholly be a stranger to. He deals in a pernicious kind of writings called second parts, and usually passes under the name of the author of the first. I easily foresee that, as soon as I lay down my pen, this nimble operator will have stolen it, and treat me as inhumanly as he hath already done Dr. Blackmore, L'Estrange, and many others who shall be here nameless. I therefore fly for justice and relief into the hands of that great rectifier of saddles* and lover of mankind, Dr. Bentley, begging he will take this enormous grievance into his most modern consideration; and if it should so happen that the furniture of an ass, in the shape of a second part, must for my sins be clapped by a mistake upon my back, that he will immediately please, in the presence of the world, to lighten me of the burden, and take it home to his own house till the true beast thinks fit to call for it.

In the meantime, I do here give this public notice, that my resolutions are to circumscribe within this discourse the whole stock of matter I have been so many years providing. Since my vein is once opened, I am content to exhaust it all at a running, for the peculiar advantage of my dear country, and for the universal benefit of mankind. Therefore, hospitably considering the number of my guests, they shall have my whole entertainment at a meal, and I scorn to set up the leavings in the cupboard. What

---

* Alluding to the trite phrase, "Place the saddle on the right horse." —*Hawkes.*

the guest cannot eat may be given to the poor, and the dogs under the table may gnaw the bones.* This I understand for a more generous proceeding than to turn the company's stomach by inviting them again to-morrow to a scurvy meal of scraps.

If the reader fairly considers the strength of what I have advanced in the foregoing section, I am convinced it will produce a wonderful revolution in his notions and opinions, and he will be abundantly better prepared to receive and to relish the concluding part of this miraculous treatise. Readers may be divided into three classes: the superficial, the ignorant, and the learned; and I have with much felicity fitted my pen to the genius and advantage of each. The superficial reader will be strangely provoked to laughter, which clears the breast and the lungs, is sovereign against the spleen, and the most innocent of all diuretics. The ignorant reader, between whom and the former the distinction is extremely nice, will find himself disposed to stare, which is an admirable remedy for ill eyes, serves to raise and enliven the spirits, and wonderfully helps perspiration. But the reader truly learned, chiefly for whose benefit I wake when others sleep, and sleep when others wake, will here find sufficient matter to employ his speculations for the rest of his life. It were much to be wished, and I do hereby humbly propose for an ex-

---

* By dogs the author means common, injudicious critics, as he explains it himself before, in his *Digression upon Critics*.

periment, that every prince in Christendom will take seven of the deepest scholars in his dominions, and shut them up close for seven years in seven chambers, with a command to write seven ample commentaries on this comprehensive discourse. I shall venture to affirm, that whatever difference may be found in their several conjectures, they will be all, without the least distortion, manifestly deducible from the text. Meantime, it is my earnest request, that so useful an undertaking may be entered upon, if their Majesties please, with all convenient speed; because I have a strong inclination, before I leave the world, to taste a blessing which we mysterious writers can seldom reach till we have gotten into our graves; whether it is that fame, being a fruit grafted on the body, can hardly grow, and much less ripen, till the stock is in the earth; or whether she be a bird of prey, and is lured among the rest to pursue after the scent of a carcass; or whether she conceives her trumpet sounds best and farthest when she stands on a tomb, by the advantage of a rising ground, and the echo of a hollow vault.

It is true, indeed, the republic of dark authors, after they once found out this excellent expedient of dying, have been peculiarly happy in the variety as well as extent of their reputation. For night being the universal mother of things, wise philosophers hold all writings to be fruitful in the proportion they are dark; and therefore the true illuminated * (that is to say, the darkest of all) have met with such numberless commentators, whose scholastic midwifery hath delivered them of meanings that the authors themselves perhaps never conceived, and yet may very justly be allowed the lawful parents of them; the words of such writers being like seed, which, however scattered at random, when they light upon a fruitful ground will multiply far beyond either the hopes or imagination of the sower.

And therefore, in order to promote so useful a work, I will here take leave to glance a few inuendos, that may be of great assistance to those sublime spirits who shall be appointed to labour in a universal comment upon this wonderful discourse. And, first, I have couched a very profound mystery in the number of O's multiplied by seven and divided by nine. Also, if a devout brother of the Rosy Cross will pray fervently for sixty-three mornings, with a lively faith, and then transpose certain letters and syllables according to prescription, in the second and fifth sections, they will certainly reveal into a full receipt of the *opus magnum*. Lastly, whoever will be at the pains to calculate the whole number of each letter in this treatise, and sum up the difference exactly between the several numbers, assigning the

---

* A name of the Rosicrucians. "These were fanatic alchymists, who, in search after the great secret, had invented a means altogether proportioned to their end. It was a kind of theological philosophy, made up of almost equal mixtures of Pagan Platonism, Christian Quietism, and the Jewish Cabala."—*Warburton* on the *Rape of the Lock*.

true natural cause for every such difference, the discoveries in the product will plentifully reward his labour. But then he must beware of *Bythus* and *Sige*,* and be sure not to forget the qualities of *Achamoth; a cujus lacrymis, humecta prodit substantia, a risu lucida, a tristitia, solida, et a timore mobilis;* wherein Eugenius Philalethes † hath committed an unpardonable mistake.

---

* I was told by an eminent divine, whom I consulted on this point, that these two barbarous words, with that of *Achamoth*, and its qualities, as here set down, are quoted from Irenæus. This he discovered by searching that ancient writer for another quotation of our author, which was placed in the title-page, and refers to the book and chapter. The curious were very inquisitive whether those barbarous words, *basyma cacabasa*, &c., are really in Irenæus; and, upon inquiry, it was found they were a sort of cant or jargon of certain heretics, and therefore very properly prefixed to such a book as this of our author.

† *Vide* Anima magica abscondita. To the above-mentioned treatise, called *Anthroposophia Theomagica*, there is another annexed, called *Anima magica abscondita*, written by the same author, Vaughan, under the name of Eugenius Philalethes; but in neither of those treatises is there any mention of *Achamoth* or its qualities: so that this is nothing but amusement, and a ridicule of dark, unintelligible writers; only the words *a cujus lacrymis*, &c., are, as we have said, transcribed from Irenæus, though I know not from what part. I believe one of the author's designs was to set curious men hunting through indexes, and inquiring for books out of the common road.

SECTION XI.

A TALE OF A TUB.

AFTER so wide a compass as I have wandered, I do now gladly overtake and close in with my subject, and shall henceforth hold on with it an even pace to the end of my journey, except some beautiful prospect appears within sight of my way: whereof, though at present I have neither warning nor expectation, yet upon such an accident, come when it will, I shall beg my reader's favour and company, allowing me to conduct him through it along with myself. For in writing it is as in travelling: if a man is in haste to be at home (which I acknowledge to be none of my case, having never so little business as when I am there), if his horse be tired with long riding and ill ways, or be naturally a jade, I advise him clearly to make the straightest and the commonest road, be it ever so dirty. But then surely we must own such a man to be scurvy companion at best: he spatters himself and his fellow-travellers at every step; all their thoughts and wishes and conversation turn entirely upon the subject of their journey's end, and at every splash and plunge and stumble they heartily wish one another at the devil.

On the other side, when a traveller and his horse are in heart and plight, when his purse is full and the day before him, he takes the road only where it is clean and convenient, entertains his company there as agreeably as he can, but upon the first occasion carries them along with him to every delightful scene in view, whether of art, of nature, or of both; and if they chance to refuse, out of stupidity or weariness, lets them jog on by themselves, and he'll overtake them at the next town; at which arriving, he rides furiously through, the men, women, and children run out to gaze, a hundred noisy curs* run barking after him, of which, if he honours the boldest with a lash of his whip, it is rather out of sport than revenge; but should some sourer mongrel dare too near an approach, he receives a salute on the chops by an accidental stroke from the courser's heels (nor is any ground lost by the blow), which sends him yelping and limping home.

I now proceed to sum up the singular adventures of my renowned Jack, the state of whose dispositions and fortunes the careful reader does, no doubt, most exactly remember, as I last parted with them in the conclusion of a former section; therefore his next

---

* By these are meant what the author calls true critics.

care must be, from two of the foregoing to extract a scheme of notions that may best fit his understanding for a true relish of what is to ensue.

Jack had not only calculated the first revolution of his brain so prudently as to give rise to that epidemic sect of Æolists, but succeeding also into a new and strange variety of conceptions, the fruitfulness of his imagination led him into certain notions which, although in appearance very unaccountable, were not without their mysteries and their meanings, nor wanted followers to countenance or improve them. I shall therefore be extremely careful and exact in recounting such material passages of this nature as I have been able to collect, either from undoubted tradition, or indefatigable reading; and shall describe them as graphically as it is possible, and as far as notions of that height and latitude can be brought within the compass of a pen. Nor do I at all question but they will furnish plenty of noble matter for such whose converting imaginations dispose them to reduce all things into types; who can make shadows, no thanks to the sun, and then mould them into substances, no thanks to philosophy; whose peculiar talent lies in fixing tropes and allegories to the letter, and refining what is literal into figure and mystery.

Jack had provided a fair copy of his father's will, engrossed in form upon a large skin of parchment: and resolving to act the part of a most dutiful son, he became the fondest creature of it imaginable. For though, as I have often told the reader, it consisted wholly in certain plain, easy directions about the management and wearing of their coats, with legacies and penalties in case of obedience or neglect, yet he began to entertain a fancy that the matter was deeper and darker, and therefore must needs have a great deal more of mystery at the bottom. "Gentlemen," said he, "I will prove this very skin of parchment to be meat, drink, and cloth; to be the philosopher's stone and the universal medicine."* In consequence of which raptures he resolved to make use of it in the most necessary, as well as the most paltry, occasions of life. He had a way of working it into any shape he pleased, so that it served him for a night-cap when he went to bed, and for an umbrella in rainy weather. He would lap a piece of it about a sore toe; or when he had fits, burn two inches under his nose; or if anything lay heavy on his stomach, scrape off and swallow as much of the powder as would lie on a silver penny: they were all infallible remedies. With analogy to these refinements, his common talk and conversation ran wholly in the phrase of his will,† and he cir-

---

* The author here lashes those pretenders to purity who place so much merit in using Scripture phrases on all occasions.

† The Protestant dissenters use Scripture phrases in their serious discourses and composures more than the Church of England men. Accordingly, Jack is introduced making his common talk and conversation to run wholly in the phrase of his *Will.—W. Wotton.*

cumscribed the utmost of his eloquence within that compass, not daring to let slip a syllable without authority from thence. Once, at a strange house, his dress being by accident much soiled, he chose rather, as the most prudent course, to incur the penalty in such cases usually annexed; neither was it possible for the united rhetoric of mankind to prevail with him to make himself clean again; because, having consulted the will upon this emergency, he met with a passage near the bottom (whether foisted in by the transcribers is not known) which seemed to forbid it.*

He made it a part of his religion never to say grace to his meat,† nor could all the world persuade him, as the common phrase is, to eat his victuals like a Christian.‡

He bore a strange kind of appetite to snap-dragon, and to the livid smuts of a burning candle, which he

---

* I cannot guess the author's meaning here, which I would be very glad to know, because it seems to be of importance.

Ibid. "Incurring the penalty in such cases usually annexed" wants no explanation. "He would not make himself clean, because, having consulted the will [*i.e.*, the New Testament], he met with a passage near the bottom [*i.e.*, in the 11th verse of the last chapter of the Revelation, 'He which is filthy, let him be filthy still,'] which seemed to forbid it." "Whether foisted in by the transcriber" is added, because this paragraph is wanted in the Alexandrian MS., the oldest and most authentic copy of the New Testament.—*Hawkes.*

† The slovenly way of receiving the sacrament among the fanatics.

‡ This is a common phrase to express eating cleanly, and is meant for an invective against that indecent manner among some people in receiving the sacrament; so in the lines before, which is to be understood of the dissenters refusing to kneel at the sacrament.

would catch and swallow with an agility wonderful to conceive, and by this procedure maintained a perpetual flame in his belly, which issued in a glowing steam from both his eyes, as well as his nostrils and his mouth, and made his head appear, in a dark night, like the skull of an ass wherein a roguish boy had conveyed a farthing candle, to the terror of his Majesty's liege subjects. Therefore he made use of no other expedient to light himself home, but was wont to say that a wise man was his own lantern.

He would shut his eyes as he walked along the street, and if he happened to bounce his head against a post, or fall into the kennel, as he seldom missed either to do one or both, he would tell the gibing apprentices who looked on that he submitted, with entire resignation, as to a trip or blow of fate, with whom he found, by long experience, how vain it was either to wrestle or to cuff, and whoever durst undertake to do either would be sure to come off with swinging fall or a bloody nose. "It was ordained," said he, " some few days before the creation, that my nose and this very post should have an encounter; and therefore nature thought fit to send us both into the world in the same age, and to make us countrymen and fellow-citizens. Now, had my eyes been open, it is very likely the business might have been a great deal worse, for how many a confounded slip is daily got by man, with all his foresight about him? Besides, the eyes of the understanding see best when those of the senses are out of the way, and therefore blind men are observed to tread their steps with much more caution and conduct and judgment than those who rely with too much confidence upon the virtue of the visual nerve, which every little accident shakes out of order, and a drop of film can wholly disconcert; like a lamp among a pack of roaring bullies, when they scour the streets, exposing its owner and itself to outward kicks and buffets, which both might have escaped, if the vanity of appearing would have suffered them to walk in the dark.

"But farther, if we examine the conduct of these boasted lights, it will prove yet a great deal worse than their fortune. It is true, I have broke my nose against this post, because fortune either forgot, or did not think it convenient, to twitch me by the elbow and give me notice to avoid it. But let not this encourage either the present age or posterity to trust their noses into the keeping of their eyes, which may prove the fairest way of losing them for good and all. For, O ye eyes! ye blind guides! miserable guardians are ye of our frail noses. Ye, I say, who fasten upon the first precipice in view, and then tow our wretched willing bodies after you to the very brink of destruction: but, alas! that brink is rotten, our feet slip, and we tumble down prone into a gulf, without one hospitable shrub in the way to break the fall to which not any nose of mortal make is equal, except that of the giant* Laurcalco, who was lord of the silver bridge. Most properly, therefore, O eyes! and with great justice, may you be compared to those foolish lights which conduct men through dirt and darkness, till they fall into a deep pit or a noisome bog."

This I have produced as a scantling of Jack's great eloquence, and the force of his reasoning upon such abstruse matters.

He was, besides, a person of great design and improvement in affairs of devotion, having introduced a new deity, who hath since met with a vast number of worshippers—by some called *Babel*, by others *Chaos* —who had an ancient temple of Gothic structure upon Salisbury Plain, famous for its shrine, and celebration by pilgrims.

When he had some roguish trick to play, he would fall down with his knees, up with his eyes, and fall to prayers, though in the midst of the kennel. Then it was that those who understood his pranks would be sure to get far enough out of his way, and whenever curiosity attracted strangers to laugh or to listen, he would of a sudden bespatter them with mud and filth with both hands.

In winter he went always loose and unbuttoned, and clad as thin as possible, to let *in* the ambient heat; and in summer lapped himself close and thick to keep it *out*.

In all revolutions of government he would make

* *Vide* Don Quixote.

his court for the office of hangman-general, and in the exercise of that dignity, wherein he was very dexterous, would make use of no other vizor than a long prayer.

He had a tongue so musculous and subtile that he could twist it up into his nose, and deliver a strange kind of speech from thence. He was also the first in these kingdoms who began to improve the Spanish accomplishment of braying; and having large ears, perpetually exposed and erected, he carried his art to such a perfection that it was a point of great difficulty to distinguish, either by the view or the sound, between the *original* and the *copy*.

He was troubled with a disease reverse to that called the stinging of the *tarantula*, and would run dog-mad at the noise of music, especially a pair of bagpipes;* but he would cure himself again by taking two or three turns in Westminster Hall, or Billingsgate, or in a boarding-school, or the Royal Exchange, or a state coffee-house.

He was a person that feared no colours,† but mortally hated all, and upon that account bore a cruel aversion against painters, insomuch that in his paroxysms, as he walked the streets, he would have his pockets laden with stones to pelt at the signs.

---

* This is to expose our dissenters' aversion against instrumental music in churches.—*W. Wotton.*

† They quarrel at the most innocent decency and ornament, and defaced the statues and paintings on all the churches in England.

Having, from this manner of living, frequent occasion to wash himself, he would often leap over head and ears into water, though it were in the midst of winter, and was always observed to come out again much dirtier, if possible, than he went in.*

He was the first that ever found out the secret of contriving a soporiferous medicine to be conveyed in at the ears. It was a compound of sulphur and balm of Gilead, with a little pilgrim's salve.

He wore a large plaister of artificial caustics on his stomach, with the fervour of which he could set himself a groaning, like the famous board upon application of a red-hot iron.

He would stand in the turning of a street, and calling to those who passed by, would cry to one, "Worthy sir, do me the honour of a good slap in the chaps;" to another, "Honest friend, pray favour me with a handsome kick on the breech;" "Madam, shall I entreat a small box on the ear from your ladyship's fair hand?" "Noble captain, lend a reasonable thwack, for the love of God, with that cane of yours over these poor shoulders." And when he had, by such earnest solicitations, made a shift to procure a basting sufficient to swell up his fancy and his sides, he would return home extremely comforted, and full of terrible accounts of what he had undergone for the public good. "Observe this stroke," said he, showing his bare shoulders; "a plaguy janissary gave it me

---

* Baptism of adults by plunging.—*Hawkes*.

this very morning at seven o'clock, as, with much ado, I was driving off the Great Turk. Neighbours, mind this broken head deserves a plaister. Had poor Jack been tender of his noddle, you would have seen the pope and the French king long before this time of day among your wives and your warehouses. Dear Christians, the Great Mogul was come as far as White-chapel, and you may thank these poor sides that he hath not (God bless us!) already swallowed up man, woman, and child."

It was highly worth observing the singular effects of that aversion or antipathy which Jack and his brother Peter seemed, even to an affectation, to bear against each other.* Peter had lately done some rogueries that forced him to abscond, and he seldom ventured to stir out before night for fear of bailiffs. Their lodgings were at the two most distant parts of the town from each other, and whenever their occasions or humours called them abroad, they would make choice of the oddest, unlikely times, and most uncouth rounds they could invent, that they might be sure to avoid one another. Yet, after all this, it was

---

* The papists and fanatics, though they appear the most averse against each other, bear a near resemblance in many things, as hath been observed by learned men.

Ibid. The agreement of our dissenters and the papists in that which Bishop Stillingfleet called the fanaticism of the Church of Rome, is ludicrously described for several pages together by Jack's likeness to Peter, and their being often mistaken for each other, and their frequent meetings when they least intended it.—*W. Wotton.*

their perpetual fortune to meet. The reason of which is easy enough to apprehend: for the frenzy and the spleen of both having the same foundation, we may look upon them as two pairs of compasses, equally extended, and the fixed foot of each remaining in the same centre, which, though moving contrary ways at first, will be sure to encounter somewhere or other in the circumference. Besides, it was among the great misfortunes of Jack to bear a huge personal resemblance to his brother Peter. Their humour and dispositions were not only the same, but there was a close analogy in their shape and size and their mien, insomuch that nothing was more frequent than for a bailiff to seize Jack on the shoulders, and cry, "Mr. Peter, you are the king's prisoner!" or, at other times, for one of Peter's nearest friends to accost Jack with open arms, "Dear Peter, I am glad to see thee; pray, send me one of your best medicines for the worms." This, we suppose, was a mortifying return of those pains and proceedings Jack had laboured in so long; and finding how directly opposite all his endeavours had answered to the sole end and intention which he had proposed to himself, how could it avoid having terrible effects upon a head and heart so furnished as his? However, the poor remainders of his coat bore all the punishment. The orient sun never entered upon his diurnal progress without missing a piece of it. He hired a tailor to stitch up the collar so close that it was ready to choke him, and squeezed out his eyes at such a rate as one could see nothing but the white. What little was left of the main substance of the coat he rubbed every day, for two hours, against a rough cast wall, in order to grind away the remnants of lace and embroidery; but at the same time went on with so much violence, that he proceeded a heathen philosopher. Yet, after all he could do of this kind, the success continued still to disappoint his expectation. For as it is the nature of rags to bear a kind of mock resemblance to finery, there being a sort of fluttering appearance in both, which is not to be distinguished at a distance in the dark, or by short-sighted eyes, so, in those junctures, it fared with Jack and his tatters, that they offered to the first view a ridiculous flaunting, which, assisting the resemblance in person and air, thwarted all his projects of reparation, and left so near a similitude between them as frequently deceived the very disciples and followers of both.. . . . .

. . . . *Desunt*
. . . . *non nulla.*
. . . .

The old Sclavonian proverb said well, That it is with men as with asses; whoever would keep them fast must find a very good hold at their ears. Yet I think we may affirm that it hath been verified by repeated experience, that

    Effugiet tamen hæc sceleratus vincula Proteus.

It is good, therefore, to read the maxims of our ancestors with great allowances to times and persons. For if we look into primitive records, we shall find that no revolutions have been so great or so frequent as those of human ears. In former days there was a curious invention to catch and keep them, which I think we may justly reckon among the *artes perditæ*. And how can it be otherwise, when in these latter centuries the very species is not only diminished to a very lamentable degree, but the poor remainder is also degenerated so far as to mock our skilfulest tenure. For if the only slitting of one ear in a stag hath been found sufficient to propagate the defect through a whole forest, why should we wonder at the greatest consequences for so many loppings and mutilations to which the ears of our fathers and our own have been of late so much exposed? It is true, indeed, that while this island of ours was under the dominion of grace, many endeavours were made to improve the growth of ears once more among us. The proportion of largeness was not only looked upon as an ornament of the outward man, but as a type of grace in the inward. Besides, it is held by naturalists that if there be a protuberancy of parts in the superior region of the body, as in the ears and nose, there must be a parity also in the inferior. And therefore, in that truly pious age, the males in every assembly, according as they were gifted, appeared very forward in exposing their ears to view, and the regions about them; because Hippocrates tells us that when the vein behind the ear happens to be cut, a man becomes a eunuch.* And the females were nothing backwarder in beholding and edifying by them: whereof those who had already used the means looked about them with great concern, in hopes of conceiving a suitable offspring by such a prospect. Others, who stood candidates for benevolence, found there a plentiful choice, and were sure to fix upon such as discovered the largest ears, that the breed might not dwindle between them. Lastly, the more devout sisters, who look upon all extraordinary dilatations of that member as protrusions of zeal or spiritual excrescences, were sure to honour every head they sat upon as if they had been marks of grace; but especially that of the preacher, whose ears were usually of the prime magnitude, which, upon that account, he was very frequent and exact in exposing with all advantages to the people, in his rhetorical paroxysms turning sometimes to hold forth the one, and sometimes to hold forth the other. From which custom, the whole operation of preaching is to this very day, among their professors, styled by the phrase of holding forth.

Such was the progress of the saints for advancing the size of that member, and it is thought the success would have been every way answerable, if in process of time a cruel king had not arisen, who raised a bloody persecution against all ears above a certain

* Lib. de aere, locis, et aquis.

standard.* Upon which some were glad to hide their flourishing sprouts in a black border, others crept wholly under a periwig, some were slit, others cropped, and a great number sliced off to the stumps. But of this more hereafter in my General History of Ears, which I design very speedily to bestow upon the public.

From this brief survey of the falling state of ears in the last age, and the small care had to advance their ancient growth in the present, it is manifest how little reason we can have to rely upon a hold so short, so weak, and so slippery; and that whoever desires to catch mankind fast must have recourse to some other methods. Now, he that will examine human nature with circumspection enough may discover several handles, whereof the six † senses afford one a-piece, besides a great number that are screwed to the passions, and some few riveted to the intellect. Among these last curiosity is one, and, of all others, affords the firmest grasp: curiosity, that spur in the side, that bridle in the mouth, that ring in the nose, of a lazy and impatient and a grunting reader. By this handle it is that an author should seize upon his readers, which, as soon as he hath once compassed, all resistance and struggling are in vain, and they become his prisoners as close as he pleases, till weariness or dulness forces him to let go his grip.

* This was Charles II., who at his restoration turned out all the dissenting teachers that would not conform.
† Including Scaliger's.

And therefore I, the author of this miraculous treatise, having hitherto, beyond expectation, maintained, by the aforesaid handle, a firm hold upon my gentle readers, it is with great reluctance that I am at length compelled to remit my grasp, leaving them in the perusal of what remains to that natural oscitancy inherent in the tribe. I can only assure thee, courteous reader, for both our comforts, that my concern is altogether equal to thine, for my unhappiness in losing or mislaying among my papers the remaining part of these memoirs, which consisted of accidents, turns, and adventures, both new, agreeable, and surprising, and therefore calculated in all due points to the delicate taste of this our noble age. But, alas! with my utmost endeavours, I have been able only to retain a few of the heads, under which there was a full account how Peter got a protection out of the King's Bench, and of a reconcilement between Jack and him, upon a design they had, in a certain rainy night, to trepan brother Martin into a spunging-house, and there strip him to the skin: how Martin, with much ado, showed them both a fair pair of heels; how a new warrant came out against Peter, upon which how Jack left him in the lurch, stole his protection, and made use of it himself. How Jack's tatters came into fashion in court and city; how he got upon a great horse,*

---

* Sir Humphrey Edwin, a Presbyterian, was some years ago Lord Mayor of London, and had the insolence to go in his formalities to a conventicle, with the ensigns of his office.

and ate custard.* But the particulars of all these, with several others, which have now slid out of my memory, are lost beyond all hopes of recovery. For which misfortune, leaving my readers to condole with each other, as far as they shall find it to agree with their several constitutions, but conjuring them, by all the friendship that hath passed between us from the title-page to this, not to proceed so far as to injure their healths for an accident past remedy, I now go on to the ceremonial part of an accomplished writer, and therefore, by a courtly modern, least of all others to be omitted.

* Custard is a famous dish at a lord mayor's feast.

THE CONCLUSION.

GOING too long is a cause of abortion as effectual, though not so frequent, as going too short, and holds true especially in the labours in the brain. Well fare the heart of that noble Jesuit * who first adventured to confess in print that books must be suited to their several seasons, like dress and diet and diversions: and better fare our noble nation for refining upon this, among other French modes. I am living fast to see the time when a book that misses its tide shall be neglected as the moon by day, or like mackerel a week after the season. No man hath more nicely observed our climate than the bookseller who bought the copy of this work. He knows to a tittle what subjects will best go off in a dry year, and which is proper to expose foremost when the weather-glass is fallen to much rain. When he had seen this treatise, and consulted his almanac upon it, he gave me to understand that he had manifestly considered the

* Père d'Orleans.

two principal things, which were the bulk and the subject, and found it would never take but after a long vacation, and then only in case it should happen to be a hard year for turnips. Upon which I desired to know, considering my urgent necessities, what he thought might be acceptable that month. He looked westward, and said, "I doubt not we shall have a fit of bad weather; however, if you could prepare some pretty little banter, but not in verse, or a small treatise upon the ———, it would run like wild-fire. But if it hold up, I have already hired an author to write something against Dr. Bentley, which I am sure will turn to account."*

At length we agreed upon the expedient, that when a customer comes for one of these, and desires in confidence to know the author, he will tell him very privately, as a friend, naming whichever of the wits shall happen to be that week in vogue; and if Durfey's last play should be in course, I had as lieve he may be the person as Congreve. This I mention because I am wonderfully well acquainted with the present relish of courteous readers, and have often observed, with singular pleasure, that a fly driven from a honey-pot will immediately with very good appetite alight and finish his meal on an excrement.

---

* When Dr. Prideaux brought the copy of his Connection of the Old and New Testament to the bookseller, he told him it was a *dry subject*, and the printing could not safely be ventured unless he could enliven it with a little humour.—*Hawkes.*

I have one word to say upon the subject of profound writers, who are grown very numerous of late; and I know very well the judicious world is resolved to list me in that number. I conceive, therefore, as to the business of being profound, that it is with writers as with wells: a person with good eyes may see to the bottom of the deepest, provided any water be there, and often when there is nothing in the world at the bottom besides dryness and dirt, though it be but a yard and a half under ground, it shall pass however for wondrous *deep*, upon no wiser a reason than because it is wondrous *dark*.

I am now trying an experiment very frequent among modern authors, which is, to write upon nothing: when the subject is utterly exhausted to let the pen still move on, by some called the ghost of wit delighting to walk after the death of its body. And to say the truth, there seems to be no part of knowledge in fewer hands than that of discerning when to have done. By the time that an author hath written out a book, he and his readers are become old acquaintance, and grow very loth to part; so that I have sometimes known it to be in writing as in visiting, where the ceremony of taking leave has employed more time than the whole conversation before. The conclusion of a treatise resembles the conclusion of human life, which hath sometimes been compared to the end of a feast, where few are satisfied to depart *ut plenus vitæ* *conviva:* for men will sit down after the fullest meal, though it be only to dose or to sleep out the rest of the day. But in this latter I differ extremely from other writers, and shall be too proud if by all my labours I can have any ways contributed to the repose of mankind in times so turbulent and unquiet as these.* Neither do I think such an employment so very alien from the office of a wit, as some would suppose. For among a very polite nation in Greece there were the same temples built and consecrated to Sleep and the Muses, between which two deities they believed the strictest friendship was established.†

I have one concluding favour to request of my reader, that he will not expect to be equally diverted and informed by every line or every page of this discourse, but give some allowance to the author's spleen, and short fits or intervals of dulness, as well as his own, and lay it seriously to his conscience whether, if he were walking the streets in dirty weather, or a rainy day, he would allow it fair dealing in folks at their ease from a window to criticise his gait, and ridicule his dress at such a juncture.

In my disposure of employments of the brain, I have thought fit to make invention the master, and to give method and reason the office of his lacqueys.

---

* This was written before the peace of Ryswick, which was signed in September 1697.
† Trezenii, Pausanius l. 2.

The cause of this distribution was, from observing it my peculiar case to be often under a temptation of being witty upon occasions where I could be neither wise nor sound, nor anything to the matter in hand, and I am too much a servant of the modern way to neglect any such opportunities, whatever pains or improprieties I may be at to introduce them. For I have observed, that from a laborious collection of seven hundred and thirty-eight flowers and shining hints of the best modern authors, digested with great reading into my book of commonplaces, I have not been able, after five years, to draw, hook, or force into common conversation any more than a dozen. Of which dozen, the one moiety failed of success by being dropped among unsuitable company, and the other cost me so many strains and traps and *ambages* to introduce, that I at length resolved to give over. Now this disappointment to discover a secret, I must own, gave me the first hint of setting up for an author; and I have since found, among some particular friends, that it is become a very general complaint, and has produced the same effects upon many others. For I have remarked many a towardly word to be wholly neglected or despised in discourse which hath passed very smoothly, with some consideration and esteem, after its preferment and sanction in print. But now, since, by the liberty and encouragement of the press, I am grown absolute master of the occasions and opportunities to expose the talents I have acquired, I already discover that the issues of my *observanda* begin to grow too large for the receipts. Therefore, I shall here pause a while till I find, by feeling the world's pulse and my own, that it will be of absolute necessity for us both to resume my pen.

THE END.

www.ingramcontent.com/pod-product-compliance
Lightning Source LLC
Chambersburg PA
CBHW022115290426
44112CB00008B/680